Formalizing Natural Languages

*For Nadia "Nooj" Malinovich Silberztein,
the Mensch of the family, without whom neither this book,
nor the project named after her,
would have happened.
And for my two children, Avram and Rosa, who remind me
every day of the priorities in my life.*

Series Editor
Patrick Paroubek

Formalizing Natural Languages

The NooJ Approach

Max Silberztein

 WILEY

First published 2016 in Great Britain and the United States by ISTE Ltd and John Wiley & Sons, Inc.

ISTE Ltd
27-37 St George's Road
London SW19 4EU
UK

www.iste.co.uk

John Wiley & Sons, Inc.
111 River Street
Hoboken, NJ 07030
USA

www.wiley.com

Library of Congress Control Number: 2015957115

British Library Cataloguing-in-Publication Data
A CIP record for this book is available from the British Library
ISBN 978-1-84821-902-1

Contents

Acknowledgments

I would like to thank the University of Franche-Comté and my colleagues in the ELLIADD laboratory for believing in the NooJ project and supporting the community of NooJ users unfailingly since its inception.

It would be impossible for me to mention every single one of the colleagues and students who have participated, in one way or another, in the extremely ambitious project described in this book – that of formalizing natural languages! The NooJ software has been in use since 2002 by a community of researchers and students; see www.nooj4nlp.net. NooJ was developed in direct cooperation with all its users who devoted their energy to this or that specific problem, or to one language or another. Spelling in Semitic languages, variation in Asian languages, intonation in Armenian, inflection in Hungarian, phrasal verbs in English, derivation in Slavic languages, composition in Greek and in Germanic languages, etc. pose a wide variety of linguistic problems, and without the high standards of these linguists the NooJ project would never have known the success it is experiencing today. Very often, linguistic questions that seemed "trivial" at the time have had a profound influence on the development of NooJ.

Among its users, there are some "NooJ experts" to whom I would like to give particular thanks, as they participated directly in its design, and had the patience to help me with long debugging sessions. I thank them for their ambition and their patience: Héla Fehri, Kristina Kocijan, Slim Mesfar, Cristina Mota, and Simonetta Vietri.

I would also like to thank Danielle Leeman and François Trouilleux for their detailed review of the original book, and Peter Machonis for his review of the English version, as well as for verifying the relevance of the English examples, which contributed greatly to the quality of this book.

Max SILBERZTEIN
November, 2015.

1

Introduction: the Project

The project described in this book is at the very heart of linguistics; its goal is to describe, exhaustively and with absolute precision, all the sentences of a language likely to appear in written texts[1]. This project fulfills two needs: it provides linguists with tools to help them describe languages exhaustively (*linguistics*), and it aids in the building of software able to automatically process texts written in natural language (*natural language processing*, or NLP).

A linguistic project[2] needs to have a theoretical and methodological framework (how to describe this or that linguistic phenomenon; how to organize the different levels of description); formal tools (how to write each description); development tools to test and manage each description; and engineering tools to be used in sharing, accumulating, and maintaining large quantities of linguistic resources.

There are many potential applications of descriptive linguistics for NLP: spell-checkers, intelligent search engines, information extractors and annotators, automatic summary producers, automatic translators, etc. These applications have the potential for considerable economic usefulness, and it is therefore important for linguists to make use of these technologies and to be able to contribute to them.

---

1 Non-written languages, such as speech or sign language, can be transcribed by using specific alphabets, such as the International Phonetic Alphabet or the American Sign Alphabet. The resulting transcribed text indeed constitutes a written text.
2 [SAU 16, BLO 33] were among the first to attempt to rationalize the description of languages.

For now, we must reduce the overall linguistic project of describing *all* phenomena related to the use of language, to a much more modest project: here, we will confine ourselves to seeking to describe the set of all of the sentences that may be written or read in natural-language texts. The goal, then, is simply to design a system capable of distinguishing between the two sequences below:

a) *Joe is eating an apple*

b) *Joe eating apple is an*

Sequence (a) is a grammatical sentence, while sequence (b) is not.

This project constitutes the mandatory foundation for any more ambitious linguistic projects. Indeed it would be fruitless to attempt to formalize text styles (stylistics), the evolution of a language across the centuries (etymology), variations in a language according to social class (sociolinguistics), cognitive phenomena involved in the learning or understanding of a language (psycholinguistics), etc. without a model, even a rudimentary one, capable of characterizing sentences.

If the number of sentences were finite – that is, if there were a maximum number of sentences in a language – we would be able to list them all and arrange them in a database. To check whether an arbitrary sequence of words is a sentence, all we would have to do is consult this database: it is a sentence if it is in the database, and otherwise it is not. Unfortunately, there are an infinite number of sentences in a natural language. To convince ourselves of this, let us resort to a *redictio ad absurdum*: imagine for a moment that there are n sentences in English.

Based on this finite number n of initial sentences, we can construct a second set of sentences by putting the sequence *Lea thinks that*, for example, before each of the initial sentences:

Joe is sleeping → *Lea thinks that Joe is sleeping*

The party is over → *Lea thinks that the party is over*

Using this simple mechanism, we have just doubled the number of sentences, as shown in the figure below.

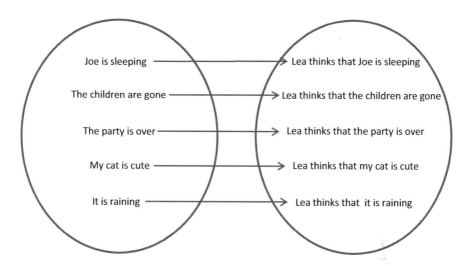

Figure 1.1. *The number of any set of sentences can be doubled*

This mechanism can be generalized by using verbs other than the verb *to think*; for example:

Lea (believes | claims | dreams | knows | realizes | thinks | ...) that Sentence.

There are several hundred verbs that could be used here. Likewise, we could replace *Lea* with several thousand human nouns:

(The CEO | The employee | The neighbor | The teacher | ...) thinks that Sentence.

Whatever the size *n* of an initial set of sentences, we can thus construct $n \times 100 \times 1{,}000$ sentences simply by inserting before each of the initial sentences, sequences such as *Lea thinks that, Their teacher claimed that, My neighbor declared that*, etc.

Language has other mechanisms that can be used to expand a set of sentences exponentially. For example, based on *n* initial sentences, we can construct $n \times n$ sentences by combining all of these sentences in pairs and inserting the word *and* between them. For example:

It is raining + Joe is sleeping → It is raining and Joe is sleeping

This mechanism can also be generalized by using several hundred connectors; for example:

It is raining (but | nevertheless | therefore | where | while |...) Joe is sleeping.

These two mechanisms (linking of sentences and use of connectors) can be used multiple times in a row, as in the following:

Lea claims that Joe hoped that Ida was sleeping.
It was raining while Lea was sleeping, however Ida is now
waiting, but the weather should clear up as soon as night falls.

Thus these mechanisms are said to be *recursive*; the number of sentences that can be constructed with recursive mechanisms is infinite. Therefore it would be impossible to define all of these sentences *in extenso*. Another way must be found to characterize the set of sentences.

1.1. Characterizing a set of infinite size

Mathematicians have known for a long time how to define sets of infinite size. For example, the two rules below can be used to define the set of all natural numbers $\mathbb{N}$:

> (a) Each of the ten elements of set $\{0, 1, 2, 3, 4, 5, 6, 7, 8, 9\}$ is a natural number;
>
> (b) any word that can be written as xy is a natural number if and only if its two constituents x and y are natural numbers.

These two rules constitute a formal definition of all natural numbers. They make it possible to distinguish natural numbers from any other object (decimal numbers or others). For example:

– Is the word "123" a natural number? Thanks to rule (a), we know that "1" and "2" are natural numbers. Rule (b) allows us to deduce from this that "12" is a natural number. Thanks to rule (a) we know that "3" is a natural number; since "12" and "3" are natural numbers, then rule (b) allows us to deduce that "123" is a natural number.

– The word "2.5" is not a natural number. Rule (a) enables us to deduce that "2" is a natural number, but it does not apply to the decimal point ".". Rule (b) can only apply to two natural numbers, therefore it does not apply to the decimal point because it is not a natural number. In this case, "2." is not a natural number; therefore "2.5" is not a natural number either.

There is an interesting similarity between this definition of set ℕ and the problem of characterizing the sentences in a language:

– Rule (a) describes *in extenso* the finite set of numerals that must be used to form valid natural numbers. This rule resembles a dictionary in which we would list all the words that make up the vocabulary of a language.

– Rule (b) explains how numerals can be combined to construct an infinite number of natural numbers. This rule is similar to grammatical rules that specify how to combine words in order to construct an infinite number of sentences.

To describe a natural language, then, we will proceed as follows: firstly we will define *in extenso* the finite number of basic units in a language (its vocabulary); and secondly, we will list the rules used to combine the vocabulary elements in order to construct sentences (its grammar).

1.2. Computers and linguistics

Computers are a vital tool for this linguistic project, for at least four reasons:

– From a theoretical point of view, a computer is a device that can verify automatically that an element is part of a mathematically-defined set. Our goal is then to construct a device that can automatically verify whether a sequence of words is a valid sentence in a language.

– From a methodological point of view, the computer will impose a framework to describe linguistic objects (words, for example) as well as the rules for use of these objects (such as syntactic rules). The way in which linguistic phenomena are described must be consistent with the system: any inconsistency in a description will inevitably produce an error (or "bug").

– When linguistic descriptions have been entered into a computer, a computer can apply them to very large texts in order to extract from these texts examples or counterexamples that validate (or not) these descriptions. Thus a computer can be used as a scientific instrument (this is the *corpus linguistics* approach), as the telescope is in astronomy or the microscope in biology.

– Describing a language requires a great deal of descriptive work; software is used to help with the development of databases containing numerous linguistic objects as well as numerous grammar rules, much like engineers use computer-aided design (CAD) software to design cars, electronic circuits, etc. from libraries of components.

Finally, the description of certain linguistic phenomena makes it possible to construct NLP software applications. For example, if we have a complete list of the words in a language, we can build a spell-checker; if we have a list of rules of conjugation we can build an automatic conjugator. A list of morphological and phonological rules also makes it possible to suggest spelling corrections when the computer has detected errors, while a list of simple and compound terms can be used to build an automatic indexer. If we have bilingual dictionaries and grammars we can build an automatic translator, and so forth. Thus the computer has become an essential tool in linguistics, so much so that opposing "computational linguists" with "pure linguists" no longer makes sense.

1.3. Levels of formalization

When we characterize a phenomenon using mathematical rules, we *formalize* it. The formalization of a linguistic phenomenon consists of describing it, by storing both linguistic objects and rules in a computer. Languages are complicated to describe, partly because interactions between their phonological and writing systems have multiplied the number of objects to process, as well as the number of levels of combination rules. We can distinguish five fundamental levels of linguistic phenomena; each of these levels corresponds to a level of formalization.

> To analyze a written text, we access letters of the alphabet rather than words; thus it is necessary to describe the link between the alphabet and the orthographic forms we wish to process (*spelling*). Next, we must establish a link between the

orthographic forms and the corresponding vocabulary elements (*morphology*). Vocabulary elements are generally listed and described in a lexicon that must also show all potential ambiguities (*lexicography*). Vocabulary elements combine to build larger units such as phrases which then combine to form sentences; therefore rules of combination must be established (*syntax*). Finally, links between elements of meaning which form a predicate transcribed into an elementary sentence, as well as links between predicates in a complex sentence, must be established (semantics).

1.4. Not applicable

We do not always use language to represent and communicate information directly and simply; sometimes we play with language to create sonorous effects (for example in poetry). Sometimes we play with words, or leave some "obvious" information implicit because it stems from the culture shared by the speakers (anaphora). Sometimes we express one idea in order to suggest another (metaphor). Sometimes we use language to communicate statements about the real world or in scientific spheres, and sometimes we even say the opposite of what we really mean (irony).

It is important to clearly distinguish problems that can be solved within a strictly linguistic analytical framework from those that require access to information from other spheres in order to be solved.

1.4.1. *Poetry and plays on words*

Writers, poets, and authors of word games often take the liberty of constructing texts that violate the syntactic or semantic constraints of language. For example, consider the following text[3]:

> *For her this rhyme is penned, whose luminous eyes*
>
> *Brightly expressive as the twins of Leda,*
>
> *Shall find her own sweet name, that nesting lies,*
>
> *Upon the page, enwrapped from every reader.*

---

3 From the poem *A Valentine* by Edgar Allan Poe.

This poem is an acrostic, meaning that it contains a puzzle which readers are invited to solve. We cannot rely on linguistic analysis to solve this puzzle. But, to even understand that the poem is a puzzle, the reader must figure out that *this rhyme* refers to the poem itself. Linguistic analysis is not intended to figure out what in the world *this rhyme* might be referring to; much less to decide among the possible candidates.

> … *luminous eyes brightly expressive as the twins of Leda* …

The association between the adjective *luminous* and *eyes* is not a standard semantic relationship; unless the eyes belong to a robot, eyes are not luminous. This association is, of course, metaphorical: we have to understand that *luminous eyes* means that the owner of the eyes has a luminous intelligence, and that we are perceiving this luminous intelligence by looking at her eyes.

The *twins of Leda* are probably the mythological heroes Castor and Pollux (the twin sons of Leda, the wife of the king of Sparta), but they are not particularly known for being *expressive*. These two heroes gave their names to the constellation *Gemini*, but I confess that I do not understand what *an expressive constellation* might be. I suspect the author rather meant to write:

> … *expressive eyes brightly luminous as the twins of Leda* …

The associations between the noun *name* and the verbal forms *lies*, *nestling*, and *enwrapped* are no more direct; we need to understand that it is the written form of the name which is present on the physical page where the poem is written, and that it is hidden from the reader.

If we wish to make a poetic analysis of this text, the first thing to do is thus to note these non-standard associations, so we will know where to run each poetic interpretive analysis. But if we do not even know that *eyes* are not supposed to be *luminous*, we will not be able to even figure out that there is a metaphor, therefore we will not be able to solve it (i.e. to compute that the woman in question is intelligent), and so we will have missed an important piece of information in the poem. More generally, in order to understand a poem's meaning, we must first note the semantic violations it contains. To do this, we need a linguistic model capable of distinguishing "standard" associations such as *an intelligent woman, a bright constellation, a name written on a page*, etc. from associations requiring poetic analysis, such as *luminous eyes, an expressive constellation, a name lying upon a page*.

Analyzing poems can pose other difficulties, particularly at the lexical and syntactic levels. In standard English, word order is less flexible than in poems. To understand the meaning of this poem, a modern reader has to start by rewriting (in his or her mind) the text in standard English, for example as follows:

> *This rhyme is written for her, whose luminous eyes (as brightly expressive as the twins of Leda) will find her own sweet name, which lies on the page, nestling, enwrapped from every reader.*

> The objective of the project described in this book is to formalize standard language without solving poetic puzzles, or figuring out possible referents, or analyzing semantically non-standard associations.

1.4.2. *Stylistics and rhetoric*

Stylistics studies ways of formulating sentences in speech. For example, in a text we study the use of understatements, metaphors, and metonymy ("figures of style"), the order of the components of a sentence and that of the sentences in a speech, and the use of anaphora. Here are a few examples of stylistic phenomena that cannot be processed in a strictly linguistic context:

Understatement: *Joe was not the fastest runner in the race*

Metaphor: *The CEO is a real elephant*

Metonymy: *The entire table burst into laughter*

In reality, the sentence *Joe was not the fastest runner in the race* could mean here that Joe came in last; so, in a way, this sentence is not saying what it is expressing! Unless we know the result of the race, or have access to information about the real Joe, we cannot expect a purely linguistic analysis system to detect understatements, irony or lies.

To understand the meaning of the sentence *The CEO is a real elephant*, we need to know firstly that a CEO cannot really be an elephant, and therefore that this is a metaphor. Next we need to figure out which "characteristic property" of elephants is being used in the metaphor. Elephants are known for several things: they are big, strong, and clumsy; they have long memories; they are afraid of mice; they are an endangered species; they have big ears; they love to take mud-baths; they live in Africa or India, etc. Is the CEO clumsy? Is he/she afraid of mice? Does he/she love mud-baths? Does he/she have a good memory? To understand this statement, we would have to know the context in which the sentence was said, and we might also need to know more about the CEO in question.

To understand the meaning of the sentence *The entire table burst into laughter*, it is necessary first to know that a table is not really capable of bursting into laughter, and then to infer that there are people gathered around a table (during a meal or a work meeting) and that it is these people who burst out laughing. The noun *table* is neither a collective human noun (such as *group* or *colony*), nor a place that typically contains humans (such as *meeting room* or *restaurant*), nor an organization (such as *association* or *bank*); therefore using only the basic lexical properties associated with the noun *table* will not be enough to comprehend the sentence.

It is quite reasonable to expect a linguistic system to detect that the sentences *The CEO is a real elephant* and *The entire table burst into laugther* are not standard sentences; for example, by describing *CEO* as a human noun, describing *table* as a concrete noun, and requiring *to burst into laughter* to have a human subject, we can learn from a linguistic analysis that these sentences are not "standard", and that it is therefore necessary to initiate an extra-linguistic computation such as metaphor or metonymy calculations in order to interpret them.

> The linguistic project described in this book is not intended to solve understatements, metaphors, or metonymy, but it must be able to detect sentences that are deviant in comparison to the standard language.

1.4.3. *Anaphora, coreference resolution, and semantic disambiguation*

Coreference*: Lea invited Ida for dinner. She brought a bottle of wine.*

Anaphora: *Phelps returned. The champion brought back 6 medals with him.*

Semantic ambiguity: *The round table is in room B17.*

In order to understand that in the sentence *She brought a bottle of wine*, *she* refers to *Ida* and not *Lea*, we need to know that it is usually the guest who travels and brings a bottle of wine. This social convention is commonplace throughout the modern Western world, but we would need to be sure that this story does not take place in a society where it is the person who invites who brings beverages.

In order to understand that *The champion* is a reference to Phelps, we have to know that Phelps is a champion. Note that dozens of other nouns could have been used in this anaphora: *the American, the medal-winner, the record-holder, the swimming superstar, the young man, the swimmer, the former University of Florida student, the breakaway, the philanthropist*, etc.

In order to eliminate the ambiguity of the sequence *round table* (between "a table with a round shape" and "a meeting"), we would need to have access to a wider context than the sentence alone.

> The linguistic project described in this book is not intended to resolve anaphora or semantic ambiguities.

NOTE. – I am not saying that it is impossible to process poetry, word games, understatements, metaphors, metonymy, coreference, anaphora, and semantic ambiguities; I am only saying that these phenomena lie outside the narrow context of the project presented in this book. There are certainly "lucky" cases in which linguistic software can automatically solve some of these phenomena. For example, in the following sequence:

Joe invited Lea for dinner. She brought a bottle of wine

a simple verification of the pronoun's gender would enable us to connect *She* to *Lea*. Conversely, it is easy to build software which, based on the two sentences *Joe invited Lea to dinner* and *Lea brought a bottle of wine*, would produce the sentence *She brought a bottle of wine*. Likewise, in the sentence:

The round table is taking place in room B17

a linguistic parser could automatically figure out that the noun *round table* refers to a meeting, provided that it has access to a dictionary in which the noun *round table* is described as being an abstract noun (synonymous with *meeting*), and the verb *to take place* is described as calling for an abstract subject.

1.4.4. *Extralinguistic calculations*

Consider the following statements:

a) *Two dollars plus three dollars make four dollars.*

b) *Clinton was already president in 1536.*

c) *The word God has four letters.*

d) *This sentence is false.*

These statements are expressed using sentences that are well-formed because they comply with the spelling, morphological, syntactic, and semantic rules of the English language. However, they express statements that are incorrect in terms of mathematics (a), history (b), spelling (c), or logic (d). To detect these errors we would need to access knowledge that is not part of our strictly linguistic project[4].

> The project described in this book is confined to the formalization of language, without taking into account speakers' knowledge about the real world.

1.5. NLP applications

Of course, there are fantastic software applications capable of processing extralinguistic problems! For example, the IBM computer Watson won on the game show *Jeopardy!* in spectacular fashion in 2011; I have a lot of fun

---

4 Some linguists have put forward meta-linguistics examples of type (c) to demonstrate the necessity of using unrestricted grammar to describe languages. In addition, many NLP researchers use phenomena such as metaphors, resolution of anaphora, detection of understatement, etc. to demonstrate the inadequacy of linguistic techniques to handle... what I consider extralinguistic phenomena.

asking my smart watch questions. In the car, I regularly ask Google Maps to guide me verbally to my destination; my language-professor colleagues have trouble keeping their students from using Google Translate; and the subtitles added automatically to YouTube videos are a precious resource for people who are hard of hearing [GRE 11], etc.

All of these software platforms have a NLP part, which analyzes or produces a written or verbal statement, often accompanied by a specialized module, for example a search engine or GPS navigation software. It is important to distinguish between these components: just because we are impressed by the fact that Google Maps gives us reliable directions, it does not mean it speaks perfect English. It is very possible that IBM Watson can answer a question correctly without having really "understood" the question. Likewise, a software platform might automatically summarize a text using simple techniques to filter out words, phrases or sentences it judges to be unimportant [MAN 01][5]. Word-recognition systems use signal processing techniques to produce a sequence of phonemes and then determine the most "probable" corresponding sequence of words by comparing it to a reference database [JUR 00][6], etc.

Most pieces of NLP software actually produce spectacular, almost magical results, with a very low degree of linguistic competence. To produce these results, the software uses "tricks", often based on statistical methods [MAN 99].

Unfortunately, the success of these software platforms is often used in order to show that statistical techniques have made linguistics unnecessary[7]. It is important, then, to understand their limitations. In the next two sections I will take a closer look at the performances of the two "flagship" statistical NLP software platforms: automatic translation and part-of-speech tagging.

---

5 [MAN 01] introduces the field of automatic summarizing and its issues, in particular how to detect the "important" information that should be included in a summary.

6 For the exception that proves the rule, see [RAY 06].

7 For an amusing read about the ravages of statistics in fields other than linguistics, see [SMI 14].

It understands what you say. It knows what you mean.

Talk to Siri as you would to a person. Say something like "Tell my wife I'm running late" or "Remind me to call the vet." Siri not only understands what you say, it's smart enough to know what you mean. So when you ask "Any good burger joints around here?" Siri will reply "I found a number of burger restaurants near you." Then you can say "Hmm. How about tacos?" Siri remembers that you just asked about restaurants, so it will look for Mexican restaurants in the neighborhood. And Siri is proactive, so it will question you until it finds what you're looking for.

Figure 1.2. *Really?*

1.5.1. *Automatic translation*

Today, the best-known translation software platforms use statistical techniques to suggest a translation of texts. These software platforms are regularly cited as examples of the success of statistical techniques, and everyone has seen a "magical" translation demo[8]. It is not surprising, therefore, that most people think the problem of translation has already been solved. I do not agree.

---

8 For example, here is a demonstration of the instantaneous translation used by Google Glasses: www.youtube.com/watch?v=pZKWW3rzT2Q.

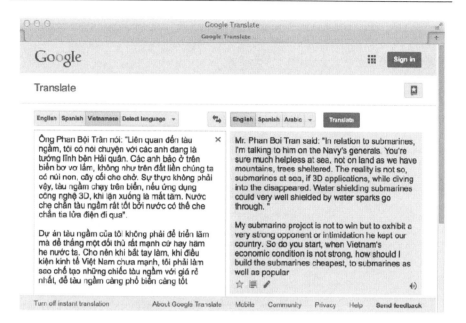

Figure 1.3. *Vietnamese–English translation*
with Google Translate

For example, Figure 1.3 shows how Google Translate has translated part of an article in Vietnamese (www.thanhnieunnews.com, October 2014). The text produced does not make very much sense; what does "I'm talking to him on the Navy's generals" mean? The translated text even contains incorrect constructions ("could very well shielded", for example).

Figure 1.4 allows us to compare Google Translate's results with those obtained using a simple Arabic–English dictionary and a very basic translation grammar; see [BAN 15]. For example, the first sentence was wrongly translated by Google Translate as *The man who went down to work* instead of *The man who fell went to work*. Google Translate was also wrong about the second sentence, which means *The man that you knew went to work* and not *I knew a man who went to work*.

ذهب الرجل الذي سقط إلى العمل	The man who went down to work
ذهب الرجل الذي عرفته إلى العمل	I knew a man who went to work
يروي الطفل القصة التي حفظها عن جده	Tells the story of the child who saved his grandfathe
التقيت صديقاتي اللاتي نجحن	I met my friends who have succeeded
وجدت القط الذي أضعته	I found a cat who lost it
كسرت الطاولة التي بجانبي	Which broke the table next to me
يحتوي البيت الذي أعجبه على حديقة	Contains a house that likes to garden
غادرت الفتيات اللاتي فزن	I left the girls who won
أطعمت القطط التي أحتفظ بها	Fed the cats that keep them
سأربح الجائزة التي حلمت بها	Will win the prize, which dreamed of
قطع الطفل الحبل الذي يربط الكلب	Child cut the cord that connects the dog

ذهب الرجل الذي سقط إلى العمل/The man who fell went to work

ذهب الرجل الذي عرفته إلى العمل/The man that you knew went to work

يروي الطفل القصة التي حفظها عن جده/The child tells the story that he learned from his grandfather

يروي الطفل القصة التي حفظها عن جده/The child tells the story that he learnt from his grandfather

التقيت صديقاتي اللاتي نجحن/I met my friends who succeeded

وجدت القط الذي أضعته/I found the cat that I lost

كسرت الطاولة التي بجانبي/I broke the table that is beside me

يحتوي البيت الذي أعجبه على حديقة/The house that he liked contains a garden

غادرت الفتيات اللاتي فزن/the girls who won left

أطعمت القطط التي أحتفظ بها/I feed the cats that I keep

أطعمت القطط التي أحتفظ بها/I fed the cats that I keep

سأربح الجائزة التي حلمت بها/I will win the award that I dreamed of

سأربح الجائزة التي حلمت بها/I will win the award that I dreamt of

قطع الطفل الحبل الذي يربط الكلب/the child cut the rope that hangs the dog

Figure 1.4. *Translation with Google Translate vs. with NooJ*

When translating languages that are more similar, such as French into English, the results produced by Google Translate are helpful, but still could not be used in a professional context or to translate a novel, a technical report, or even a simple letter, and especially not when submitting a resumé.

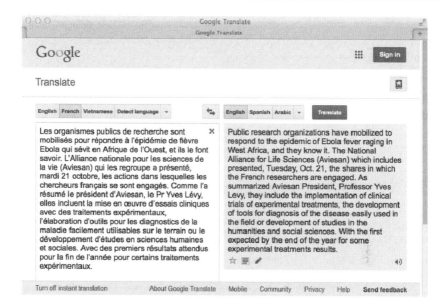

Figure 1.5. *Article from the newspaper Le Monde (October 2014) translated with Google Translate*

Let us look in detail at the result produced by Google Translate. None of the English sentences produced is correct:

– The first sentence has an opposite meaning; the expression *ils le font savoir* has been translated as *they know it* instead of *they make it known*.

– The second sentence has an ungrammatical sequence ...*which includes presented...* The term *action* has been wrongly translated as *share* instead of *action*.

– In the third sentence, the verb *summarized* is placed incorrectly; *essais cliniques avec des traitements experimentaux* should be translated as *clinical trials* with *experimental treatments*; and *utilizable* should be translated as *useable* or *useful* and not as *used*.

– The term *results* is placed incorrectly in the last sentence.

To be fair, it should be noted that every attempt to construct good-quality automatic translation software has failed, including those based on linguistic techniques, such as the European program Eurotra (1978–1992). It is my belief that the reasons for Eurotra's failure have to do with certain scientific and technical choices (as well as real problems with management), and not with a theoretical impossibility of using linguistics to do translations.

I will turn now to another flagship application, which is less "public-at-large" than machine translation, but just as spectacular for NLP specialists: part-of-speech tagging.

1.5.2. *Part-of-speech (POS) tagging*

Part-of-speech (POS) tagging is often presented as the basic application of any piece of NLP software, and has historically justified the sidelining of linguistic methods in favor of stochastic ones. The authors of tagging software frequently speak of 95% precision; these results seem "magical" too, since POS taggers use neither dictionaries nor grammars to analyze the words of any text with such a great precision. Linguists have difficulty justifying their painstaking descriptive work when shown what a computer can do by itself and without linguistic data! It is also commonplace to hear that taggers' results prove that statistical techniques have bypassed linguistic ones; for example:

> *Automatic part of speech tagging is an area of natural language processing where statistical techniques have been more successful than rule-based methods. [BRI 92]*

In their course on NLP (available on YouTube as of December 2015), Dan Jurafsky and Chris Manning consider the problem of the construction of POS taggers as "mostly solved"; more generally, NLP researchers use the spectacular results produced by statistical taggers to validate the massive use of statistical techniques in all NLP applications, always to the detriment of the linguistic approach.

A POS tagger is an automatic program that links each word in a text with a "tag", in practice its POS category: noun, verb, adjective, etc. To do this, taggers use reference corpora which have been manually tagged[9]. To analyze a

---

9 Some people use terms such as "training data" or "machine learning" to indicate that the tagger "learns" something when it "trains" on data. This fancy terminology is impressive, but in fact what POS taggers do is nothing more than copying and pasting codes from a reference text to the text they analyze.

text, the tagger examines the context of each word in the text and compares it with the contexts of the occurrences of this same word in the reference corpus in order to deduce which tag should be linked with the word.

Figure 1.6 shows, for example, an extract from Penn Treebank, which is one of the reference corpora[10] used by English POS taggers.

```
Battle-tested/SingularProperName Japanese/SingularProperName
industrial/Adjective managers/PluralNoun here/Adverb always/Adverb
buck/Verb up/Preposition nervous/Adjective newcomers/PluralNoun
with/Preposition the/Determiner tale/SingularNoun of/Preposition
the/Determiner first/Adjective of/Preposition their/PossessivePronoun
countrymen/PluralNoun to/TO visit/Verb Mexico/SingularProperName ,/,
a/Determiner boatload/SingularNoun of/Preposition samurai/PluralNoun
warriors/PluralNoun blown/PastParticiple ashore/Adverb 375/Number
years/PluralNoun ago/Adverb ./.
From/Preposition the/Determiner beginning/SingularNoun ,/,
it/PersonalPronoun took/PreteritVerb a/Determiner man/SingularNoun
with/Preposition extraordinary/Adjective qualities/PluralNoun to/TO
succeed/Verb in/Preposition Mexico/SingularProperName ,/, "/"
says/Present3rdSingularVerb Kimihide/SingularProperName
Takimura/SingularProperName ,/, president/SingularNoun of/Preposition
Mitsui/PluralNoun group/SingularNoun 's/Possessive
Kensetsu/SingularProperName Engineering/SingularProperName
Inc./SingularProperName unit/SingularNoun ./.
```

Figure 1.6. *Extract from Penn Treebank*

I do not believe that taggers should be considered as successes, and here are my reasons why.

1.5.2.1. *The results of statistical methods are not actually so spectacular*

The number of unambiguous words is so large compared to the very small number of tags used by taggers that a simple software application that

---

10 This extract is described in [MAR 93]. I have replaced the original codes (for example "JJ") with clearer codes ("Adjective").

would tag words just by copying the most frequent tag in the reference corpus would already have a degree of precision greater than 90% [CHA 97].

For example, in English the words *my, his, the* (always determiners), *at, from, of, with* (always prepositions), *him, himself, it, me, she, them, you* (always pronouns), *and, or* (always conjunctions), *again, always, not, rather, too* (always adverbs), *am, be, do, have* (always verbs), and *day, life, moment, thing* (always nouns) are extremely frequent but have only a single possible tag, and thus are always tagged correctly.

The vast majority of ambiguous words are actually favored in terms of analysis; for example, in most of their occurrences, the forms *age, band, card, detail, eye*, etc. represent nouns and not the verbs *to age, to band, to card, to detail, to eye*, etc. A software platform systematically disregarding the rare verbal hypothesis for these words will therefore almost never be wrong.

In these conditions, obtaining a 95% correct result when a simple copy already yields 90% precision is not really spectacular; on average we get one correct result out of two for difficult cases, which is more like a coin-toss than a feat of "learning".

> The degree of precision claimed by taggers is, in reality, not that impressive.

1.5.2.2. *POS taggers disregard the existence of multiword units*

Taggers do not take into account multiword units or expressions, though these frequently occur in texts[11]. In the Penn Treebank extract shown in Figure 1.6, the compound noun *industrial managers*, the phrasal verb *to buck up*, the compound determiner *a boatload of*, the compound noun *samurai warrior*, the expression *to blow N ashore*, the adverb *from the beginning*, and the expression *it takes N to V-inf* have all simply been disregarded.

However, processing *industrial manager* as a sequence of two linguistic units does not make any sense: an *industrial manager* is not a *manager* who

---

11 [SIL 95] shows that up to one-third of the forms present in the texts of the newspaper *Le Monde* are in fact composed of multiword units or expressions.

has been bred or made with industrial methods. Yet this analysis is the general analysis for the adjective *industrial*, for example as in *industrial diamond, industrial food, industrial soap, industrial chicken*, etc. Likewise, the phrasal verb *to buck up* (which means *to encourage*) should not be analyzed word-for-word as *to buck* (which means *to oppose*) followed by the locative preposition *up*. The head word of the noun phrase *a boatload of samurai warriors* is *warriors*, therefore *a boatload of* should be treated as a determiner, and above all *boatload* should not be treated as the head word of the noun phrase.

More generally, systematically tagging texts without taking into account multiword units, phrasal verbs and expressions eliminates any possibility of conducting meaningful linguistic analyses on the resulting tagged text. For example, tagging the sequence `blue`/Adjective `collar`/Noun even when it means *manual laborer* would block the analysis of sentences such as *The blue collars finally accepted their offer*, since the verb *to accept* expects a human subject, and not a part of a shirt. Likewise, disregarding the adverb *all of a sudden* by tagging it as `all`/Pronoun `of`/Preposition `a`/Determiner `sudden`/Adjective would make a syntactic parser crash, since this sequence of categories does not exist in English grammar.

The same is true for expressions, which are extremely numerous in vocabulary and texts: taggers simply disregard them. It is typical to see texts labeled as follows:

> **The**/Determiner **CEO**/Noun **took**/Verb **our**/Determiner
> **request**/Noun **into**/Preposition **account**/Noun

in which the expression *to take ... into account* has not been represented. It is hard to imagine how this tagged text will be processed, or even translated, if the computer really thinks that it is dealing with the verb *to take* (as in *Joe took his pen*) and the noun *account* (as in *an email account*).

I argue in this book that systematically disregarding multiword units and expressions inevitably leads to the production of incorrect analyses that are useless for most NLP applications, including search engines and automatic translation; imagine the quality of a translation in which the French multiword units *tout de suite* [right now] or *carte bleue* [visa card] were translated word for word:

> *Je cherche ma carte bleue tout de suite* → * *I look for my blue card all of rest*

In practice, if multiword units and expressions were taken into account in order to assess the precision of POS taggers, that precision would fall below 70%, meaning that it would be inferior to the precision of a simple program that would access a dictionary that contains all of the multiword units and expressions in a language.

> By not processing frequent multiword units and expressions even though they constitute a non-negligible subset of vocabulary, taggers produce useless results.

1.5.2.3. *Statistical methods are costly*

We often hear that linguistic methods are costly to implement because they require the construction of dictionaries and grammars. However, statistical methods also require a great deal of work to manually construct their reference corpora. In the end, tagging a corpus is necessarily much more labor-intensive than constructing the equivalent dictionary, since a given word occurs multiple times in a corpus but only once in a dictionary, and it would be necessary to manually tag an extremely large corpus if we wished to cover only the standard vocabulary of a language (i.e. to construct a reference corpus in which each use of each standard word occurred at least once).

> The construction of the reference corpus required by taggers is an expensive operation.

1.5.2.4. *Reference corpora are not reliable*

One answer to the argument above is that the people who manually tag a reference corpus do not possess a level of qualification comparable to those who construct dictionaries and grammars, and can therefore be hired at a lower cost. In practice, the consequence of this cynical attitude is that most so-called "reference" corpora contain a high number of errors. For example, note the mistakes in the Penn Treebank extract shown in Figure 1.6: *Battle-tested* and *Japanese* should have been tagged as adjectives (and not proper nouns); *up* is a particle (and not a preposition), *Mitsui* is a proper name (not a plural common noun); *Engineering* is a common noun; and *Inc.* is an adjective. A corpus considered as the "reference" by just about the entire NLP community in fact contains a large number of errors.

The fact that "reference corpora" contain errors is well known to NLP researchers, to the extent that the study of errors in reference corpora has become a sub-field of NLP research[12]. If reference corpora contain so many errors, we cannot expect the programs that use them to provide usable results.

| The reference corpora used by taggers are not reliable.

1.5.2.5. *Statistical taggers are not generalizable*

A text in which word tags are to be figured out must be similar enough to the reference corpus used to train the tagger, otherwise the quality of the results will be significantly impacted. As soon as a new word occurs in the text to be tagged, or a word occurs in the text to be tagged with a context different from those present in the reference corpus, the tagger will produce an error. To construct a tagger capable of producing correct results for any sentence in any type of text, it would be necessary to construct a reference corpus that contains all possible uses of each word in a language, which does not exist.

| Statistical POS taggers produce non-generalizable results.

The only reasonable alternative is to describe the whole vocabulary in a dictionary; this description would be solid, and if it contained errors or gaps these could be easily corrected, which would allow for the accumulation of data on the language.

1.5.2.6. *POS taggers use poor linguistic resources without admitting it*

It is wrong to claim that statistical taggers (as opposed to linguistic ones) do not use dictionaries or grammars: a tagger consults the reference corpus in search of potential tags for each word being tagged, and thus there is indeed an implicit dictionary in the reference corpus. This dictionary can easily be made explicit, by extracting the tagged words from the reference corpus and sorting them in alphabetical order. However, the resulting

---

12 See for example [DIC 05, GRE 10, VOL 11].

dictionary is of much lower quality than a "real" dictionary constructed by professional linguists [KUP 08].

We will see in Chapter 4 that dictionaries constructed by linguists distinguish, at the very minimum, the various uses of words; for example *reader* (+Hum) in *an avid reader* versus *reader* (-Hum) in *a magnetic reader; to give* (+ditransitive) in *Joe gave his pen to Lea* versus *to give* (+intransitive) in *The door finally gave*, etc. This basic level of precision bears no resemblance to the set of tags used by POS taggers.

> Taggers use very low-quality implicit dictionaries and produce very low-quality results.

1.5.2.7. *Rules of disambiguation are fundamentally incorrect*

The same is true for grammar: taggers do use a grammar, made up of the list of contexts of the words that occur in the reference corpus. For example, based on examples such as *I think that art is a worthwhile endeavor*, a tagger will typically decide that the word *that* should be tagged as "Conjunction" since it is preceded by the word *think* and followed by the word *art*, which is equivalent to the grammar rule below:

```
think that art  →  that/CONJUNCTION
```

The grammars used by taggers are automatically computed, based on sequences of successive words taken from the manually tagged reference corpus. These grammars are incorrect, and it is easy to produce counterexamples for each of their "rules". For example, in the sentence *I think that art is hung too low*, the word *that* is a determiner, not a conjunction, even though it appears between the words *think* and *art*.

In fact, the very principle of tagging – disambiguating each word, taking only its immediate context into account – is naïve in the extreme. The ten rules of disambiguation (called "patches") computed automatically by the tagger introduced in [BRI 92] are all incorrect: any linguist would consider it ridiculous to claim that in English, a capitalized word must be followed by a conjugated verb in the preterite tense, or that a verbal form is necessarily in the past participle if the word *had* appears near it in a three-word context; for example in *I had to come, come* is not a past participle.

Taggers overlook the fundamental linguistic principle that sentences are structured objects, and that virtually any category of word can be inserted anywhere in a sentence without changing its structure. For example, after the verbal form *sees*, we might find an adjective (e.g. *Joe sees red apples*), an adverb (e.g. *Joe sees very well*), a determiner (e.g. *Joe sees that apple*), a coordinating conjunction (*Joe sees but says nothing*), a subordinating conjunction (*Joe sees that Lea is happy*), a noun (*Joe sees flowers*), a preposition (*Joe sees behind himself*), a pronoun (*Joe sees that*), a relative pronoun (*Joe sees where Lea is going*), or a verbal form (*Joe sees destroyed buildings*). In these conditions, disambiguating the word form *sees* (or any verbal form) on the basis of its contexts in a reference corpus – which necessarily possesses only a limited sample of all potential contexts – will produce a large number of errors.

Rules computed automatically by taggers are incorrect, and the grammars in which these rules are collected have neither the precision, nor the degree of generality, let alone any scientific value comparable to the grammars designed by linguists[13].

> Sentences are structured objects; any category of words can be inserted anywhere in a sentence without changing its structure. A grammar is not a collection of limited contexts of words and category.

1.5.2.8. *You cannot add apples to oranges*

This is a basic principle: you cannot add together (or calculate averages of) number of objects of different types. Yet this is what is done by most statistical taggers or automatic learning programs. For example, when a statistical program parses the two sentences below:

```
Joe/ProperName writes/Verb. He/Pronoun writes/Verb
a/Determiner novel/Noun.
```

it will deduce that the verb *to write* occurs sometimes without a complement (here: one time out of two), and sometimes with a direct object complement (here: one time out of two). Now if the same program parses the following text:

---

13 For an example of a real French grammar painstakingly created for the construction of an automatic software translation platform, see [SAL 99].

```
Joe/ProperName is/Aux running/Verb a/Determiner
test/Noun. Lea/ProperName is/Aux running/Verb
in/Preposition the/Determiner woods/Noun.
```

it will deduce, in the same way, that the verb *to run* sometimes occurs with a direct object complement, and sometimes with a prepositional complement... But this has nothing to do with it! In the first case, we can say that the verb *to write* has an optional direct object complement, but in the second case, it must be said that there are two homographic verbs *to run*[14]: the first is transitive, while the second is intransitive. We cannot simply add up the number of occurrences of the two verbs *to run* simply because they are spelled in the same way, just as we cannot say that the two forms *steel* and *steal* constitute the same linguistic unit just because they are pronounced in the same way.

> We cannot add up the number of occurrences of word forms that represent distinct elements of the vocabulary.

1.5.2.9. *Tagging does not allow for addressing syntactic or semantic ambiguities*

It is easy to construct examples of superficially identical word sequences that can be tagged correctly only after an overall syntactic analysis of the sentence, or even after a semantic analysis. A well known example, the form *like*, must be tagged "Verb" in the sentence *These horse flies like his arrow* and "Preposition" in the sentence *This horse flies like his arrow*. A simple examination of the immediate context of the word *like*, in other words, is not sufficient to determine whether it is a verb or a preposition. Taggers produce necessarily unreliable results in every case of ambiguity which only a syntactic or semantic analysis could solve.

> In the general case, word ambiguity cannot be resolved until a syntactic or semantic analysis has been carried out.

---

14 Statistical analysis programs are based on an absolute belief in the reliability of spelling. However, if one day a spelling reform were to decide that the noun *a bass* (in the sense of *a deep voice*) should be spelled *a basse* to distinguish it from the noun *a bass* (*the fish*), it would change nothing about the structure or meaning of texts, but it would change the "grammar rules" produced by statistical taggers.

1.5.2.10. *The scientific approach*

Even if the rules automatically produced by a tagger were correct, they would not have much scientific value; it is a bit like noting that in the work of Edgar Allan Poe, nouns containing an "a" and an "n" are all followed by a phrasal verb using particle "in": this remark has no generality, teaches us nothing about American literature, the English language, or Edgar Allan Poe himself, and is quite simply of no scientific interest.

Linguistics seek to understand how a language functions. Therefore even a "magical" statistical tool that could be used to build spectacular NLP applications but did not explain anything about the language is of little interest to us.

1.5.3. *Linguistic rather than stochastic analysis*

I am wary of the results produced by current stochastic methods in the field of NLP, especially when they are compared, on a *truly* level playing field, to those of linguistic methods.

I find it unfortunate that decision-makers in the NLP domain tend to favor stochastic methods that do not cause our understanding of language to advance a single step, to the detriment of projects aimed at building linguistic resources. Formalizing the lexical, morphological, syntactic, and distributional properties of the standard English vocabulary would require the work of a dedicated team, much smaller than the gigantic groups assigned to the construction of tagged corpora for statistical NLP applications (statistical tagging or translation). A project like this would be beneficial for the whole linguistic community and would enable the development of NLP software with unequalled precision. I hope this book will show that such a project is not just useful, but feasible as well.

1.6. Linguistic formalisms: NooJ

To formalize a language, we use mathematical models (referred to as *formalisms*). The vital question, posed by [CHO 57], is therefore: "Which mathematical model do we need in order to describe languages?" Chomsky introduces a hierarchy of increasingly powerful grammars capable of describing increasingly complex linguistic phenomena[15], and hypothesizes that there is a "universal" formal model that can be used to describe any human language.

Paradoxically, this original issue has given rise to the creation of numerous incompatible linguistic formalisms. Today, linguists wishing to formalize linguistic phenomena can choose from among more than a dozen formalisms[16], including CCG, GPSG, HG, HFST, HPSG, LFG, LIG, OpenFst, RG, SFG, SFST, TAG, XFST, etc.

Each of these formalisms and their variants has individual strong and weak points. XFST (or HFST, or SFST) will be of more interest to morphologists, while GPSG, TAG or LFG are better suited to syntacticians, and semanticians will often use RG or SFG, while HPSG, as the most powerful formalism of the group, is typically used by theoreticians and linguists seeking to describe phenomena at the limit of linguistics, such as anaphora. Unfortunately, none of these tools makes it possible to describe in a simple manner the wide variety of linguistic phenomena (often quite trivial) that come into play when "real" texts are to be analyzed (such as journalistic texts or novels), and it is not possible to combine them since their formalisms, their development environments, and IT tools are largely incompatible[17].

The search for a single formalism capable of addressing all types of linguistic phenomena in all languages does not fall within the parameters of the project described in this book; our goal is rather to describe the largest number of linguistic phenomena in their diversity, using the best-suited tools in order to construct simple descriptions, i.e. those that are the simplest to develop, understand, accumulate, share, and manage.

---

15 We will look in detail at the Chomsky-Schützenberger hierarchy in Chapter 5.
16 See the Internet links at the end of this chapter.
17 An exception that proves the rule is the Urdu parser in the ParGram project (based on LFG) which used XFST as a preprocessing tool to transliterate Urdo or Devanagari characters and recognize repetitions; see [BÖG 07]. However, the XFST descriptions did not interact with those of LFG.

Figure 1.7. *A single tool for formalization: NooJ*

It was by abandoning the idea of a universal formalism that I designed the linguistic platform NooJ[18]. With NooJ, orthographic variation in Chinese is not described with the same tools as morphological derivation in Arabic. Neither is agglutination described with the same tools as inflection, which is not described in the same way as syntax, etc. NooJ guarantees high integration of all levels of description thanks to compatible notations and a unified representation for all linguistic analysis results (the text annotated structure or TAS, see Chapter 10), enabling different analyzers at different linguistic levels to communicate with one another. For example, the following transformation:

Lea donates her blood → Lea is a blood donor

brings various levels of linguistic phenomena into play: it is necessary to verify that the verb *to donate* will admit a nominalization (thanks to a lexical property); we must describe the inflectional rule that produces *to donate* from *donates*, the derivational rule that produces *donor* from *donate*, a distributional constraint to verify that *Lea* is a human subject and that *blood* falls under the category of parts of the body (a person donates his/her heart, a kidney, etc.), a syntactic rule to verify that *Lea* is the subject of *donates*, and then a restructuration rule to move the noun *blood* from the role of direct object complement to the role of complement of the noun *donor*. No single formalism could make it possible to describe all these linguistic phenomena in a simple way.

---

18 See [SIL 03a]. NooJ is a linguistic development environment that operates on Windows, Mac OSX, LINUX and Unix, available at no cost at the website www. noo4nlp.net. An open source environment, it is supported by the European project METANET-CESAR.

Thanks to the suitability (and thus simplicity) of each individual tool used to describe each level of linguistic phenomenon, it is now possible to construct, test, accumulate and combine linguistic resources of diverse types, and this for many languages. Through the integration of all levels of analysis in the TAS (see Chapter 10), we will see that it becomes possible to carry out complex analyses of a text by performing a series of different analyses, each of them quite simple[19].

In this book, we will use the NooJ notation to describe linguistic phenomena in their diversity. Using only one notation will simplify their understanding, as the reader does not need to master half a dozen different formalisms to understand how to formalize all types of linguistic phenomena. NooJ also has the advantage of being very easy to use; one can learn NooJ in just a few hours, and even become an "expert" after a week of training[20].

It goes without saying that each of the linguistic phenomena mentioned in this book can be described with one of the formalisms traditionally used in linguistics; for example, XFST could be used to construct the morphological parser introduced in Chapter 11, GPSG to construct syntax trees, LFG to describe agreement constraints such as those shown in Chapter 12, and HPSG to formalize the transformations discussed in Chapter 13.

1.7. Conclusion and structure of this book

The goal of the project depicted in this chapter is to describe natural languages very precisely and mathematically, or more specifically, to formalize the set of sentences that may appear in written texts.

---

19 NooJ shares several characteristics with other integrated toolboxes such as the General Architecture for Text Engineering (GATE) and the Stanford Core NLP. It consists of independent modules applied in cascade (or pipeline) in a bottom-up approach that communicate via a text annotation structure (the TAS, see Chapter 10). The main differences between NooJ and these NLP toolboxes are that NooJ is a pure linguistic tool (for instance, there is no statistical tagger in NooJ) and that all its modules are formalized via descriptive grammars rather than implemented via software programs. In other words, Nooj follows a purely descriptive, rather than algorithmic approach.

20 A growing number of NooJ users are not linguists, but rather historians, scholars of literature, psychologists, and sociologists, who typically use NooJ to extract "interesting" information from their corpora.

Although the number of sentences in a language is infinite, it is nevertheless possible to describe it, starting by using a finite number of basic linguistic elements (letters, morphemes, or words), which I will do in Part 1 of this book. Chapter 2 shows how to formalize the alphabet of a language; Chapter 3 discusses how to delineate its vocabulary; and Chapter 4 shows how to formalize a vocabulary using electronic dictionaries.

Next we must equip ourselves with mechanisms for describing how those basic linguistic elements combine to construct higher-level elements (word forms, phrases or sentences). Part 2 of this book introduces the concepts of *formal language*, *generative grammar*, and *machines*. I will introduce these concepts as well as the Chomsky-Schützenberger hierarchy in Chapter 5, while Chapters 6 to 9 present the four types of languages/grammars/machines.

Part 3 of this book (Chapters 10 to 13) is dedicated to the automatic linguistic analysis of texts. In Chapter 10, I will introduce the TAS used to represent, in a unified manner, the results produced by all linguistic analyses. Chapter 11 is devoted to automatic lexical analysis. Chapter 12 introduces two types of syntactic analysis: local analysis and structural analysis. Chapter 13 presents an automatic transformational analyzer, which can be seen as a linguistic semantic analyzer (that is, providing an analysis of meaning based solely on language, without real-world knowledge or inference).

1.8. Exercises

1) Based on the model of the definition of $\mathbb{N}$ seen in section 1.1, characterize the set $\mathbb{D}$ that contains all the decimal numbers.

2) Take the sentence: *His great uncle was let go on the spot*. Describe the linguistic analyses of this sentence in informal lexical, morphological, syntactic, and semantic terms.

3) Consider the text: *Lea invited Ida for dinner. The graduate student brought a bottle of wine*. How can we figure out to whom the noun *graduate student* is referring? Can this calculation be made using linguistic analyses?

4) How can we improve the translation of the first sentence in Figure 1.5, using only a bilingual dictionary, and without any grammar?

5) Construct the dictionary implicitly given in the reference corpus of Figure 1.6. Compare the content of this dictionary with the content of an editorial dictionary.

1.9. Internet links

The Wikipedia page for the field of linguistics: en.wikipedia.org/wiki/Linguistics

The Wikipedia page for Natural Language Processing: en.wikipedia.org/wiki/Natural_language_processing

An NLP course taught by Dan Jurafsky and Chris Manning, Stanford University, is available on YouTube atwww.youtube.com/watch?v=nfoudtpBV68.

The *Jeopardy!* program of April 11, 2001, which the computer IBM Watson won in spectacular fashion, has been the subject of numerous documentaries, for example: www.youtube.com/watch?v=5Gpaf6NaUEw.

To test a few pieces of machine translation software, such astranslate.google.com, www.systranet.com/translate, www.reverso.net, www.freetranslation.com, etc. you can enter a short paragraph in English, translate it into another language, copy and paste the result, and retranslate that into English.

There are many automatic text-tagging software platforms; see en.wikipedia.org/wiki/Part-of-speech_tagging. Tagging software requires a reference corpus, such as Penn Treebank which can be found at www.cis.upenn.edu/~treebank. Many annotated text corpora can be obtained from the Linguistic Data Consortium at www.ldc.upenn.edu.

Two integrated toolboxes used for building NLP software applications (mostly taggers and annotators) are the General Architecture for Text Engineering (Gate) (gate.ac.uk) and the Stanford CoreNLP: nlp.stanford.edu/software/corenlp.shtml.

The formalisms traditionally used by linguists are:

– CCG (Combinatory Categorial Grammar): groups.inf.ed.ac.uk/ccg/

– HFST (Helsinki Finite-State Transducer): www.ling.helsinki.fi/kielite
knologia/ tutkimus/hfst

– HG (Head Grammar): en.wikipedia.org/wiki/Head_grammar

– HPSG (Head-Driven Phrase Structure Grammar): hpsg.stanford.edu

– LFG (Lexical Functional Grammar): www.essex.ac.uk/linguistics/
external/LFG

– LIG (Linear Indexed Grammar): www.inf.ed.ac.uk/teaching/courses/
inf2a/slides/2011_inf2a_L21_slides.pdf

– OpenFST: www.openfst.org

– RG (Relational Grammar): en.wikipedia.org/wiki/Relational_grammar

– SFST (Stuttgart Finite-State Transducer): code.google.com/p/
cistern/wiki/SFST

– TAG (Tree-adjoining grammar): www.cis.upenn.edu/~xtag/tech-
report/node6.html

– XFST (Xerox Finite-State Tool): www.cis.upenn.edu/~cis639/docs/
xfst.html

The linguistic development environment that will be used to describe all
the linguistic phenomena in this book is NooJ, a free and open-source
software platform made available under GPL license by the European
Community program META-SHARE; see www.nooj4nlp.net.

PART 1

Linguistic Units

In this part I will demonstrate how to define, characterize, and formalize the basic linguistic units that comprise the alphabet (Chapter 2) and vocabulary (Chapter 3) of a language. The description of vocabulary, which has a long linguistic tradition, is generally achieved through the construction of dictionaries. I show in Chapter 4 that traditional linguistic descriptions are not suitable for our project: to formalize languages, we will need to construct dictionaries of a new kind: *electronic dictionaries*.

Formalizing the Alphabet

Before addressing the problems inherent in the formalization of various linguistic phenomena and their computer implementation, we must understand how a computer represents and processes information, and linguistic information more specifically.

2.1. Bits and bytes

To begin with, we consider the two states of a light bulb connected to an electric circuit: either it is turned off, or it is turned on.

Figure 2.1. *Two electrical states: a light bulb turned on or off*

The state of the light bulb can be used to represent all sorts of binary information, meaning any information that can have one of two values. For example, in logic, there are two possible values for a proposition: TRUE or FALSE. We can imagine that the turned-on bulb represents TRUE while the turned-off bulb represents FALSE. There are numerous types of useful binary information: a door can be opened or shut; an elevator can be stopped or moving; a train switch can be toggled to the right or the left, etc.

> Pieces of binary information are called *bits*, and programmers usually represent their values by 0 or 1.

To represent information that is more complex than binary information, multiple bits are combined. For example, if we want to formalize the functioning of a traffic light, we can use two bits in the following way:

– when the first bit is 1 and the second bit is 0, the light will be green;

– when the first bit is 1 and the second bit is 1, the light will be red;

– when the first bit is 0 and the second bit is 1, the light will be flashing yellow[1].

A fundamental question when processing information is therefore: "How many bits are needed to represent a piece of information?". If we can count the possible values the information could take, this question becomes: "How many bits are needed to code the n values that a piece of information might take?". To answer this question, just notice that each time a bit is added, the number of possible values for the information is doubled:

– with 1 bit, we have 2 possible configurations: 0 and 1;

– with 2 bits, we have 4 possible configurations: 00, 01, 10, and 11;

– with 3 bits, we have 8 possible configurations: 000, 001, 010, 011, 100, 101, 110, and 111;

– with 4 bits, we have 16 possible configurations: 0000, 0001, 0010, 0011, 0100, 0101, 0110 0111, 1000, 1001, 1010, 1011, 1100, 1101, 1110, and 1111.

More generally, with n bits, we can represent 2^n values. Earlier computers were built using 8-wire ribbon cables and were thus able to represent information on 8 bits; a sequence of 8 bits is called a *byte*. A piece of information represented by a byte can have $2^8 = 256$ possible values. A piece of information represented by two bytes (16 bits): 2^{16} values, or 65,536 possible values, and a piece of information represented by 4 bytes (32 bits): 2^{32}, or more than 4 billion values. Today, micro-computers and the latest smart phones typically process 64-bit data.

---

1 There is a fourth configuration not used here: both bits are 0. This configuration can be used to make all three bulbs flash, indicating to drivers and pedestrians that the traffic light is not working.

2.2. Digitizing information

Whatever the type of information we wish to file using a computer, we have to find a way of representing its values by sequences of bits. Rich information like sound, images or videos is also represented by sequences of bits. For example, some digital cameras represent each pixel – the smallest picture element, i.e. a single dot – by three series of 14 bits, one for each of the three component colors: red, green, and blue. These devices can thus record 2^{14}, or 16,384 levels of luminance for each of the three primary colors, between absolute black and the highest luminance. That corresponds to a total of $2^{14} \times 2^{14} \times 2^{14} = 4.4 \times 10^{12}$, or more than four thousand billion different colors[2].

Sequences of bits are used to represent any information in a computer; they can themselves be made to correspond with natural numbers. This translation is called *digitization of information*. Let us look now at how to represent natural numbers in a computer.

2.3. Representing natural numbers

Sequences of bits can be used to represent natural numbers very naturally: basically, what we have to do is write the numbers in base 2.

2.3.1. *Decimal notation*

Remember that when we use decimal notation (base 10), we use the ten Arabic numerals: 0, 1, 2, 3, 4, 5, 6, 7, 8, and 9. To write a number larger than 9, we concatenate the numerals (that is, we join them together, one after another). The position of each numeral in the number represents its weight, which is a power of 10, ascending from right to left. For example, in the decimal number 7243, the numeral 3 has a weight of 1, while the numeral 7 has a weight of 1,000. The number 7243 thus represents the following value:

$$7 \times 10^3 + 2 \times 10^2 + 4 \times 10^1 + 3 \times 10^0$$

---

2 This figure seems high, but all of these colors correspond to a small number of levels of luminance: compare the 2^{14} levels of luminance processed by a camera with the typical dynamic of the human eye (2^{26}), which can distinguish the texture of a black object in the shade of a tree under a bright sun, much more easily than current consumer cameras.

In other words, the position furthest to the right represents units ($\times 10^0$), the next position represents tens ($\times 10^1$), the next position hundreds ($\times 10^2$), and the position furthest to the left represents thousands ($\times 10^3$).

2.3.2. *Binary notation*

If we use binary notation, we have only two numerals (0 and 1) instead of ten. In a binary number, the furthest numeral to the right always represents units, and the weight of the other numerals also ascends from left to right, but this time corresponding to a power of 2 rather than 10. Thus, the numeral furthest to the right in a number written in binary notation represents units ($2^0 = 1$), the next numeral represents twos ($2^1 = 2$), the next numeral represents fours ($2^2 = 4$), the next numeral represents eights ($2^3 = 8$), the next numeral represents sixteens ($2^4 = 16$), etc. For example, the binary number 10110 represents the value:

$$1 \times 2^4 + 0 \times 2^3 + 1 \times 2^2 + 1 \times 2^1 + 0 \times 2^0$$

that is, the value:

$$16 + 0 + 4 + 2 + 0 = 22$$

Binary notation makes sequences of bits represent numerical values.

Bits	Value	Bits	Value
0000	0	1000	8
0001	1	1001	9
0010	2	1010	10
0011	3	1011	11
0100	4	1100	12
0101	5	1101	13
0110	6	1110	14
0111	7	1111	15

Figure 2.2. *Representation of numbers in binary notation*

With 4 bits we can represent $2^4 = 16$ values, i.e. all the natural numbers between 0 (which is thus written as "0000") and 15 (which is written as "1111"). Likewise, with a byte (8 bits), we can represent $2^8 = 256$ values, or all the natural numbers between 0 (written as "00000000") and 255 (written as "11111111").

2.3.3. *Hexadecimal notation*

Binary notation, though it closely represents the state of electronic circuits in computers, is rarely used by programmers because it quickly becomes unreadable. Who can instantly work out the value of the binary number 10010111010001011? In practice, programmers often use hexadecimal notation, i.e. notation in base 16. In hexadecimal notation we have 16 symbols: 0, 1, 2, 3, 4, 5, 6, 7, 8, 9, A, B, C, D, E and F. The symbol A corresponds to the decimal value 10; B corresponds to the decimal value 11; C corresponds to the decimal value 12; D corresponds to the decimal value 13; E corresponds to the decimal value 14, and F corresponds to the decimal value 15.

The advantage of hexadecimal notation is that it can be easily translated into binary notation (and vice versa) because 16 is a power of 2 ($16 = 2^4$): in a sense, the two notations are indeed variants of one another. To translate a hexadecimal number into binary, all we have to do is to perform a "symbol by symbol" translation, each hexadecimal symbol corresponding to a sequence of four bits. For example, to translate the hexadecimal number 1A2B into binary, we translate "1" (0001), then "A" (1010), then"2" (0010), then "B" (1011), and then we concatenate the four results, thus obtaining:

$$1A2B_{(16)} = 0001\ 1010\ 0010\ 1011_{(2)}$$

Computer codes are often given in hexadecimal notation.

2.4. Encoding characters

To represent the alphabet of a language in a computer, it must be digitized, that is, each letter must be associated with a sequence of bits. As we have just seen, sequences of bits also correspond to natural numbers. Therefore, we can make each letter of the alphabet correspond to one natural number and only one, this number between 1 and the size of the alphabet. Conversely, we can make each number lower or equal to the size of the alphabet correspond to one and only one letter. This biunivocal correspondence is called an *encoding*; each number is thus a *code*, and we say that the corresponding letter is *encoded* by this number. Computer codes are often expressed in hexadecimal notation.

In Figure 2.3 below, we can see, for example, that the accented letter "à" is represented by the code (expressed in hexadecimal notation) "00E0". In the same table, we can see that the letter "Â" has the code "00C2".

	008	009	00A	00B	00C	00D	00E	00F
0	XXX 0080	DCS 0090	NB SP 00A0	○ 00B0	À 00C0	Đ 00D0	à 00E0	ð 00F0
1	XXX 0081	PU1 0091	¡ 00A1	± 00B1	Á 00C1	Ñ 00D1	á 00E1	ñ 00F1
2	BPH 0082	PU2 0092	¢ 00A2	2 00B2	Â 00C2	Ò 00D2	â 00E2	ò 00F2

Figure 2.3. *Extract from the Unicode table*

To represent the 26 letters of the Latin alphabet in a computer, we could encode each letter from 1 to 26, and then associate each code with its corresponding sequence of bits, see Figure 2.4.

Notice that bits are not enough to encode the Latin alphabet, since with bits we can only represent $2^4 = 16$ values. To encode the Latin alphabet we must therefore use at least 5 bits, which will allow us to represent $2^5 = 32$ values, slightly more than the 26 required. So, we can encode the Latin alphabet using the table shown below.

Code	Bits	Letter	Code	Bits	Letter	Code	Bits	Letter	Code	Bits	Letter
0	00000	*not used*	8	01000	H	16	10000	P	24	11000	X
1	00001	A	9	01001	I	17	10001	Q	25	11001	Y
2	00010	B	10	01010	J	18	10010	R	26	11010	Z
3	00011	C	11	01011	K	19	10011	S	27	11011	*not used*
4	00100	D	12	01100	L	20	10100	T	28	11100	*not used*
5	00101	E	13	01101	M	21	10101	U	29	11101	*not used*
6	00110	F	14	01110	N	22	10110	V	30	11110	*not used*
7	00111	G	15	01111	O	23	10111	W	31	11111	*not used*

Figure 2.4. *One possible encoding of the Latin alphabet*

This table represents the biunivocal matching of the 26 letters and 26 numbers, and thus defines an encoding. For example, the table shows that the letter S is coded 27 and is represented by the 5-bit sequence 10011.

This encoding is arbitrary: if I decide to represent the letter A with the code 1 on my computer, but my counterpart uses code 1 to represent the letter B on his/her computer, all the "A"s in the messages I send will show up as "B"s on his/her screen. Therefore it is important for software platforms to agree on the establishment of a single encoding; in other words, an *encoding standard*.

2.4.1. *Standardization of encodings*

One of the first "standard" computer encodings, Baudot encoding (after Emile Baudot), was developed in 1874 to encode texts sent via telegraph or radio[3]. Very similar to the encoding shown in Figure 2.4, it used 5 bits, and could therefore represent 32 different characters[4]. After some modifications, this encoding became the telegraphic coding ITA2 (International Telegraph Alphabet no. 2) used by all telex and radio teletype machines.

ITA2 encoding was inadequate for the needs of emerging information technology, however; so much so that various computer manufacturers developed their own encoding systems. The need for standardization first made itself felt in the 1960s [BER 60], and the American Standards Association developed ASCII encoding[5], based on ITA2 encoding but using 7 bits instead of 5, thus allowing it to represent 128 characters.

In ASCII, the first 32 codes (0–31), as well as the last code (127), represent computer control characters; for example, code 8 represents character deletion (BS for the *Backspace* key); code 9 represents the tabulation (HT for *Horizontal Tabulation*); code 10 represents the line change (LF or *Line Feed*), etc. Code 32 represents a space, while codes 33 to 47 represent punctuation symbols, and codes 48 to 57 represent the ten

---

3 For the history of the Baudot, Murray, ITA2 and RTTY codes, see [HOB 99].

4 Alongside the 32-letter table similar to the one in Figure 2.4, Baudot encoding also used another 32-code table to encode numerals as well as some punctuation symbols. The user shifted from one encoding to the other using a special code that acted as a switch, somewhat similar to the functioning of the "Caps Lock" key.

5 ASCII = American Standard Code for Information Interchange. The American Standards Association later became the American National Standards Institute (ANSI).

Arabic numerals. Codes 65 to 90 represent the Latin capital letters, while codes 97 to 122 represent the lower-case letters; notice that letter "A" has a different ASCII code depending on whether it is written capitalized as "*A*" or in lower-case as "*a*".

Code	Character	Code	Character	Code	Character	Code	Character
0	NUL	32	SP	64	@	96	`
1	SOH	33	!	65	A	97	a
2	STX	34	"	66	B	98	b
3	ETX	35	#	67	C	99	c
4	EOT	36	$	68	D	100	d
5	ENQ	37	%	69	E	101	e
6	ACK	38	&	70	F	102	f
7	BEL	39	'	71	G	103	g
8	BS	40	(	72	H	104	h
9	HT	41	)	73	I	105	i
10	LF	42	*	74	J	106	j
11	VT	43	+	75	K	107	k
12	FF	44	,	76	L	108	l
13	CR	45	-	77	M	109	m
14	SO	46	.	78	N	110	n
15	SI	47	/	79	O	111	o
16	DLE	48	0	80	P	112	p
17	DC1	49	1	81	Q	113	q
18	DC2	50	2	82	R	114	r
19	DC3	51	3	83	S	115	s
20	DC4	52	4	84	T	116	t
21	NAK	53	5	85	U	117	u
22	SYN	54	6	86	V	118	v
23	ETB	55	7	87	W	119	w
24	CAN	56	8	88	X	120	x
25	EM	57	9	89	Y	121	y
26	SUB	58	:	90	Z	122	z
27	ESC	59	;	91	[	123	{
28	FS	60	<	92	\	124	|
29	GS	61	=	93	]	125	}
30	RS	62	>	94	^	126	~
31	US	63	?	95	_	127	DEL

Figure 2.5. *ASCII encoding*

2.4.2. *Accented tin letters, diacritical marks, and ligatures*

Languages based on the Latin alphabet use numerous combinations of letters and diacritics; for example the "ç" in French, the "ń" in Polish, the "ò" in Italian, the "ş" in Turkish, the "ü" in German, the "ŷ" in Welsh, the double acute accent in Hungarian, the caron (inverted circumflex accent) in Czech, the breve in Romanian (e.g. "ă"), the over dot in Polish (e.g. "ż")[6], etc. ASCII is therefore not sufficient to represent texts written in languages other than English, and requires at least the addition of the accented letters of the Latin alphabet.

Figure 2.6. *Accented Latin letters*

The character "w" (*double u* in English, *double v* in French) was originally a ligature but is now treated as an independent letter. The ampersand (&) was originally a ligature representing the Latin word *et*. In publications of good typographical quality, other ligatures are found as well, in particular the ones shown below:

> *æ (curriculum vitæ), œ (œcumenical), fi (file), fl (flower), ffi (difficult), ffl (effluent), st (stork)*

---

6 The dot on the letters "i" and "j" was originally a diacritical mark; in Turkish, both the letters "ı" (without a dot) and "i" (with a dot) are used.

The ligatures "æ" and "œ" are used in approximately 20 words of Latin origin:

> *cæsium, curriculum vitæ, ex æquo, dramatis personæ, lapsus linguæ, præsidium, fœtus, mœurs, œcumenical, œdema, Œdipus, œnology, œnologist, œuvre*

These two ligatures can only be used in the above words; for example, they are prohibited in the words *maestro, paella, coefficient*, etc. However, the other ligatures serve a strictly graphical purpose, and are used systematically to replace the corresponding sequences of letters, regardless of the word in which they appear.

Other ligatures or digraphs also exist in languages other than English, e.g. the German *esszett* "ß", as well as in other alphabets: the double v av "וו" in Hebrew; contracted characters in Chinese, e.g."云" (for "日之"); ligatures are extremely frequent in the Devanagari alphabet.

2.4.3. *Extended ASCII encodings*

For as long as personal computers and text processing applications have been widely accessible, it has become crucial to exceed the 128-character limit of the ASCII encoding for languages other than English. To represent non-ASCII characters in a computer, some software platforms compounded codes. For example, in the text-processing software Latex[7], the character "é" was initially represented by the three-character sequence "\'e". This type of representation had the advantage of being accessible using English keyboards, and made it possible to enter, process and print texts with all sorts of characters, using simple ASCII files.

Computer manufacturers quickly began building keyboards adapted to each language, and extended ASCII encoding to 8 bits, which allowed them to process 256 different characters, and thus to directly process most other alphabets[8]: Greek, Cyrillic, Arabic, Hebrew, etc. However, computer manufacturers did not work together this time, and so the extended ASCII

---

7 Current versions of Latex use more modern encodings, for example Unicode.
8 Computer manufacturers have used other ASCII extensions to process Asian languages, but this time extended to 16 bits, such as the Guo Biao encoding (for mainland Chinese), Big 5 encoding (to represent traditional Chinese characters), JIS X encoding (for Japanese), etc. Remember that 16 bits make it possible to represent 65,536 characters.

encodings used on IBM-compatible computers, for example, are different from the ASCII encodings used on Apple computers[9]. Because 8 bits allow for the representation of only 256 characters, each language must have its own extended 8-bit ASCII encoding; thus there are extended ASCII for Arabic, others for Russian, others for Greek, etc. The list in Figure 2.8 mentions more than 100 possible encodings for text files: there are, for example, four competing extended ASCII encodings to represent Turkish characters: DOS-IBM857, ISO-8859-9, Mac, and Windows-1254. The two ASCII encodings most frequently used for English are:

– *ISO 8859-1* coding (also called "ISO-LATIN-1"), widely used on the Internet and chosen by Linux;

– *Windows-1252* coding is used by the Microsoft Windows operating system for Western European languages.

Having different extended ASCII encodings does not help communication between systems, and it is common to see texts in which certain characters are displayed incorrectly.

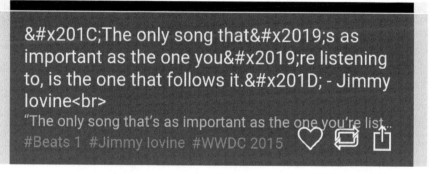

Figure 2.7. *Character encoding is still problematic as of late 2015*

2.4.4. *Unicode*

The Unicode Consortium was created in 1991 to design a single encoding system capable of representing texts in all writing systems. In its version

---

9 IBM also used the EBCDIC encoding for its mini and mainframe computers, and extended it to 8-bit to process languages other than English.

5.1, Unicode contains more than 100,000 characters, organized in code charts, and is compatible with most computer systems, including Microsoft Windows, Mac OSX, Unix and Linux. All the code charts are displayed at www.unicode.org/charts. Selecting a particular script system on this page (for example "Basic Latin") will bring up tables listing all of the characters in this script, along with their corresponding codes (written in hexadecimal notation), an example of which was shown in Figure 2.3.

2.4.4.1. *Implementations*

Unicode encoding only sets correspondences between alphabetical characters and natural numbers. There are several ways of representing natural numbers in the form of sequences of bits in a computer, therefore there are several Unicode implementations. The most natural implementation is called UTF32, in which each code is represented by a binary number written with 32 bits (4 bytes), following the exact method discussed in the previous chapter: just write the code in binary, and add 0s to the left of the bit sequence so that its length is 32 bits long. With 32 bits it is possible to represent more than 4 billion codes, easily covering all the world's languages!

This implementation has the advantage of being very simple, both for human users and computer programs, as, in order to read each character in a text file, one has simply to split the text file into sequences of 4 bytes. However, this is quite an inefficient method: if each character is encoded on 4 bytes instead of a single one as was usual for extended ASCII encodings, the amount of memory needed to store a text file must be multiplied by four, and this reduces the processing speed of computer programs that read or copy texts by four as well.

The Unicode implementation used most frequently today is UTF8, in which Unicode codes are represented by bit sequences of varying length, depending on each character. For the 128 characters already described by ASCII (the most-used characters), UTF is identical to ASCII, and so only 1 byte is needed to represent them. For other characters, UTF8 uses either 1 byte (for example for certain letters in Western languages), 2 bytes (for Arabic, Armenian, Cyrillic, Hebrew, etc.), 3 bytes (for some Chinese, Japanese, and Korean characters), or even 4 bytes (for transcribing other Chinese characters, as well as ancient languages such as Phoenician). The advantage of UTF8 is that it is compact, since the most frequent characters are represented by a single byte.

There are other implementations for Unicode: UTF7 (in which 7 bits or more are used) and UTF16 (16 bits or more)[10].

Figure 2.8 shows the correspondence between the character "é" and its Unicode code (233), as well as the UTF32BE representation of this code in hexadecimal (000000E9).

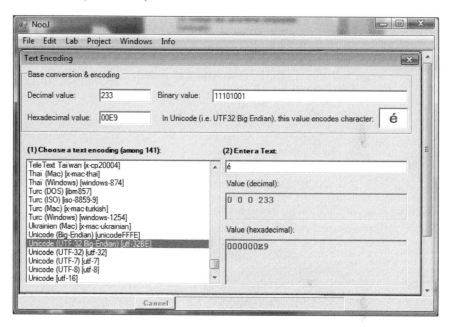

Figure 2.8. *Unicode representation of the character "é"*

Unfortunately, Unicode encoding poses a number of problems, mentioned for example by [TOP 01] and [HAR 02]. I will look now at the two most serious problems for NLP applications.

2.4.4.2. Encoding composite characters

Composite characters, for example, accented letters, can be encoded in several ways with Unicode: either globally (that is, when a composite

---

10 The programming language Java uses UTF16 internally to represent characters. UTF16 and UTF32 each have two variants depending on whether the bits are written from left to right (the most significant bits first: Big-endian) or from right to left (the least significant bits first: Low-endian).

character is associated with a single Unicode code), or by separating the diacritics from the letter (an accented character therefore is represented by a sequence of several Unicode codes). For example, the letter "é" can be represented either by the code E9, or by the sequence composed of code 65 (the code of letter "e") followed by code 0301 (the code of the acute accent).

When there is more than one diacritical character, total confusion occurs. For example, Vietnamese uses a Latin alphabet with doubly accented characters, and the encoding of these often follows the user's typing order. For example, the doubly accented letter "ế" can be encoded in three different ways, depending on the software used to enter the texts, the Vietnamese keyboard management tool, or even the habits of each user.

– the single code: 1EBF;

– the code for "e", then the code for the circumflex accent, then the code for the acute accent: 65 0302 0301;

– the code for "e", then the code for the acute accent, then the code for the circumflex accent: 65 0301 0302.

The problem is systematic with non-Latin alphabets. For example, in Hebrew, if we add to the letter shin "ש" a dot on the upper right (to select the sound "sh") and also a gemination dagesh (a center dot), we get the compound character "שּׁ", which can be encoded in two different ways:

– shin, dagesh, dot: 05E9 05BC 05C1;

– shin, dot, dagesh: 05E9 05C1 05BC.

Unfortunately, texts generated by Microsoft Windows, Mac OS X, and Linux, as well as texts stored on websites, do not use the same conventions.

All NLP applications, including search engines, should take these equivalences into account or they risk missing numerous occurrences: if a user enters a query on his/her keyboard in a certain way, but the corresponding term is encoded in another way on a webpage, the search engine must make sure the term will be found anyway.

2.4.4.3. Incompleteness

Unicode encoding is not suited to Asian languages that use Chinese characters; that is, the five CJKV writing systems: simplified Chinese, traditional Chinese, Japanese, Korean, and Vietnamese.

It is estimated that there are more than 100,000 Chinese characters[11]. Many characters, and especially many variants of characters, are simply missing in Unicode[12]. For example, the composite character shown in the figure below still had no Unicode code as of late 2014.

Figure 2.9. *A Chinese character that has no Unicode code*

If we wish to publish an ancient text or write a proper name containing a non-referenced character, we must either use another encoding system (there are a dozen of them), or use *ad hoc* character fonts; indeed, there are hundreds of character fonts available on the Japanese market alone, and everyone can purchase and use his or her preferred font.

2.4.4.4. Unification

To reduce the number of codes, the Unicode consortium decided to unify certain characters of Chinese origin (Han characters), variants of which are currently used in the five CJKV writing systems. This unified coding is called UniHan encoding and includes around 20,000 characters. Sometimes, a Han character that has different graphical variants in these languages has different Unicode codes, for example the Han character meaning *air* has three UniHan codes (see Figure 2.10).

---

11 One reference dictionary alone, the *Kangxi Dictionary*, first published in 1716, contained more than 47,000 different characters, and its 1831 edition contained more than 49,000 characters.
12 Incompleteness is not just a concern with Chinese; some ancient-language alphabets, such as Sumerian, still do not have a complete Unicode representation.

Traditional Chinese	Simplified Chinese	Japanese
氣(6C23)	气(6C14)	気(6C17)

Figure 2.10. *One Chinese character has three Unicode codes*

However, most of the time, UniHan reserves only a single code to represent all the variants of a given Han character. In these cases, it is necessary to use different character fonts in order to display the characters correctly. For example, the four characters shown in Figure 2.11 all have the same Unicode code 6F22.

Simplified Chinese	Traditional Chinese	Japanese	Korean
漢	漢	漢	漢

Figure 2.11. *Four graphical variants for a single Unicode code*

This unification is problematic when we wish to manage (publish, send, print) ancient texts which are not properly displayed by modern fonts or, on an everyday basis, to write proper names: a Japanese person, for example, will not be happy if his or her name is mangled, which happens every time readers have not installed the right character font on their computer. This problem is a very real one: each time the name of a Korean person or business is written in a Chinese newspaper, it is the Chinese graphical variant of their character that is used, instead of the original one.

The principle of UniHan is questionable: it is as if one had decided to represent the Greek letter "β" and the Latin letter "b" with the same code, on the pretext that they have a common origin, and then counted on the character font (Latin or Greek) to display them correctly. Of course, Unicode suggests two different codes for these two letters, even when they are capitalized and therefore visually identical: the Latin "B" (code 42) does not have the same Unicode code as the Greek "B" (beta) (code 0392).

Designers did not make the same choice for Asian languages due to the intimidating number of characters to be managed: more than 100,000. At the time they hoped to limit Unicode encoding to 2 bytes, or a maximum of 65,536 characters for all the languages together. With the expansion of Unicode to 32 bits (4 billion possible characters) and the increase in computer power, the UniHan initiative is no longer tenable, and Unicode still does not offer a solution to represent all of the characters used for the five CJKV language systems. There are several initiatives underway to complete Unicode, however, notably on the part of the Chinese government. This lacuna explains why users of these languages have not yet adopted Unicode, and continue to use encoding systems and character fonts that are largely incompatible with one another.

Finally, note that there are some alternatives to Unicode, including the encoding system used by the TRON operating systems[13], that have the benefit of not unifying the characters of Asian languages while still remaining quite compact (most Chinese characters can be encoded with only 2 bytes, as opposed to 3 or 4 by Unicode).

2.5. Alphabetical order

Alphabetical order is a convention used to order and locate words in various glossaries, lists, and databases; for example, telephone books and lists of movie showings. In most languages, alphabetical order is used to compare words, taking into account the position of each letter in the words, e.g. $A < B < ... < Z$ in the Latin alphabet.

Languages have traditions of more or less complex alphabetical orders. For example, in a telephone book the name *McKinley* is listed *before* the name *Macintosh*, as "Mc" must be replaced with "Mac" before making comparisons. Here are some other examples of rules specific to languages based on the extended Latin alphabet:

– in German alphabetical order, the letter "ß" and letters with an *umlaut* ("ä", "ö", "ü") are replaced with the digraphs "ss", "ae", "oe", and "ue", respectively, before comparing words;

13 See Internet links at the end of chapter.

– in Swedish, the letter "ä" is treated as a separate letter, listed after "z" in alphabetical order;

– in Spanish "ñ" is considered a separate letter and listed between "n" and "o"; therefore the word *señor* comes after *sensa*. In traditional dictionaries (published before the 1994 reform), the digraphs "ch" and "ll" were also considered separate letters for the purposes of alphabetical order (the word *llanos* therefore came after the word *los*), but that is no longer the case today;

– in Danish, the letters "æ", "ø", and "å" are separate letters that come after "z" in the alphabet;

– in Dutch, the digraph "ij" is often considered an independent letter, listed between "y" and "z".

Languages not based on the Latin alphabet also have relatively complex rules for alphabetical order; for example, in Russian the letters "e" and "ё" are grouped together, while the letters "ъ" and "ь" must be disregarded during lexicographical comparison. Putting two Thai words in alphabetical order involves a complex seven-stage computation in which the first consonant of the words is taken into account first, then unvoiced vowels, double consonants, other values, and finally tonal marks [SLA 07]. Traditional Arabic dictionaries such as the *Lisan al-`Arab* (13th century) and *al-Qamus al-Muhit* (14th century) sorted words by their root, usually three consonants. Thus, all words whose root is "KTB" were grouped together: *katab, niktab, hiktib, kattab, ketiba*, etc.

The Chinese alphabet is much too large for alphabetical order to be useful. It would actually be impossible to learn by heart the order of thousands of characters! Two types of methods are therefore used to order Chinese words: the phonetic method and the graphical method:

– in the phonetic method, to put two Chinese words in order, their pronunciation in Mandarin Chinese is transcribed into Latin characters (*pinyin* transcription [BIN 90][14]); the two transcriptions are then arranged in Latin alphabetical order;

---

14 On the subject of *pinyin* transcription. There are other methods of phonetic transcription into Latin letters for Chinese, including Wade transcription, EFEO transcription, and Bopomofo transcription.

– with the graphical method [HO 78][15], the *radical* and the *number of strokes* of each character are counted in order to compute its position. The radical is a graphical element in Chinese characters; modern dictionaries usually contain 214 radicals, with each section of the dictionary corresponding to one radical. The 214 sections are themselves arranged according to the number of brush strokes used to draw each radical. For example, the radical "匕" ("spoon") is drawn with two strokes, so its section is at the beginning of the dictionary, while the radical "面" ("face") has nine strokes; its section is thus toward the end of the dictionary.

Each of the 214 sections of the dictionary contains all the words whose first character contains the corresponding radical; thus, all the words beginning with a character whose radical is "匕" will be listed in the same section. Next, to arrange words inside a same section, the number of strokes in the following letters is compared. For example, the character "北" ("north") contains the radical "匕" and must therefore be stored in the corresponding section of the dictionary. In addition to the radical, three strokes are required to draw it. The character "阜" ("to surpass") has the same radical (which appears at the top of the character this time) and thus belongs in the same section, but it takes six more strokes to draw it. Consequently, character "阜" is listed with all the words that have six strokes, and therefore after character "北".

The Unicode consortium suggests a generic method for the collation of words according to languages: the "Unicode Collation Algorithm" (UCA). This method uses up to three stages (for example to address accented letters, then capital letters, then delimiters), which makes it possible to produce results similar to those achieved with European languages, but not to respect the lexicographical traditions of non-European languages[16].

The ISO-639 committee of the International Organization for Standardization (ISO) proposes a standard for the identification and addressing of certain formatting properties specific to languages, as

---

15 The graphical method based on 214 radicals is still used today and was first introduced in the Zihui dictionary by Mei Yingzuo, published in 1615.
16 UCA gives each user the ability to design a more complex ordering method in order to meet his or her own needs, but this takes us out of a standardized framework.

well as alphabetical order[17]. Here, a two- or three-letter code is used to identify each language; for example "EN" represents English, and "FR" French.

In modern operating systems, it is possible to specify the ISO-639 code that must be used to format a text. The operating system, and therefore word processing applications, Internet browsers, and database managers can then arrange texts, lists, indices, and dictionaries according to each language, and also format dates correctly (for example 31/1/2011 in French *versus* 1/31/2011 in English); numbers (1 234,50 in French *versus* 1,234.50 in English), monetary symbols (before or after numbers), etc.

2.6. Classification of characters

From now on, I will group the characters of a language into four categories:

– the *letters* of the language, including ligatures and letters with diacritical marks,

– the ten Arabic numerals;

– the *spaces*, including the non-breaking space, en-space, em-space, new-line, line-feed, and carriage-return characters;

– all other characters, including the hyphen (in multiword units such as *well-being*), en-dash (to indicate a range such as 10–12), em-dash as shown here —, apostrophe, punctuation marks, and abbreviation symbols (e.g. $) will be categorized as *delimiters*.

2.7. Conclusion

The first stage of the formalization of a written language involves the management of its system of writing. Currently, Unicode is the indispensable solution for managing and analyzing written texts in natural language, as it is used by nearly all computer systems and is relatively complete. However, NLP applications must address Unicode's two

---

17 The 639-1 standard is managed by the International Information Centre for Terminology (Infoterm); 639-2 is managed by the American Library of Congress. 639-3 is the most complete, with more than 7,000 languages inventoried.

significant weaknesses: composite characters that are represented with potentially more than one code, and miscoded Han characters in the five CJKV writing systems.

The problem of alphabetical order must be solved. The set of ISO-639 standards provides the framework to develop methods that respect the lexicographical traditions of each language.

2.8. Exercises

1) Convert the binary number 10101011 into decimal. Convert the decimal number 233 into binary.

2) Give the Windows extended ASCII code, Mac extended ASCII code, and two ways of encoding the compound character "é" with Unicode.

2.9. Internet links

Tutorials:

– on Binary system: www.mathsisfun.com/binary-number-system.html;

– on Baudot code: en.wikipedia.org/wiki/Baudot_code;

– on ligatures: en.wikipedia.org/wiki/Typographic_ligature;

– on Chinese Han characters: unicode.org/charts/unihan.html.

ASCII encoding is described in the document: tools.ietf.org/pdf/rfc20.pdf.

The Unicode website: unicode.org.

Composite characters: en.wikipedia.org/wiki/Precomposed_character.

TRON encoding: en.wikipedia.org/wiki/TRON_(encoding).

3

Defining Vocabulary

In Chapter 2, we saw how to formalize the alphabets of languages. We will now formalize their vocabularies. At this level, the linguistic units to be digitized are no longer simple characters, but the elements of vocabulary of each language. Like that of alphabets, the formalization of vocabularies is done by identifying and categorizing all of their elements. However, unlike the letters of the alphabet, it is no small task to create an exhaustive enumeration of vocabulary, or even to define what a vocabulary element is.

Before embarking on this project, we must therefore be sure that it is achievable: is it really possible to describe the vocabulary of a language *in extenso*? In other words, is the vocabulary of a natural language finite in size? In concrete terms, does it even make sense to say how many words there are in a modern language? Remember that the linguistic project relies on the fact that it is possible to describe the infinite number of sentences in a language, provided that two sets are described *in extenso:* the set of base units (its vocabulary) and the set of rules for combining these units (its grammar). But if vocabulary itself is infinite in size, or if it is impossible to make a list of its elements, then our project is doomed. Consequently, the constraint of "finiteness" imposes restrictions on what we mean by "vocabulary".

3.1. Multiple vocabularies and the evolution of vocabulary

It is theoretically possible – though not necessarily feasible in practice – to describe technical and scientific vocabularies in their totality: in architecture (e.g. *sheathing*), chemistry (*colloid*), geology (*accretion*), computers (*datagram*), medicine (*prolapse*), etc. Not only the technical and scientific spheres have their own vocabulary: every human activity art – games, leisure, sports – involves terminology: for example cookery (*coddler*), gardening (*cuttage*), chess (*zugzwang*), music (*cavatina*), golf (*bogey*), stamp-collecting (*bisect*), etc. However, to date, no one has compiled a complete description of all the diverse vocabularies of a language.

In the context of the construction of a NLP application, we can describe the vocabulary of a specific business, technical or scientific domain. The description of these vocabularies is indispensable for helping users navigate a scientific or technical documentary database (also called "domain knowledge"). For example, the EuroTermBank terminology dictionaries contain more than 2 million terms covering over 30 languages, while the Unified Medical Lexicon System (UMLS) contains more than 11 million English medical terms. Terminology databases are typically used to aid translators in their work with technical documents; see [KÜB 02].

Most of the texts we encounter (newspapers, for example) contain a large number of proper names. Any NLP application must therefore be able to access dictionaries that identify and describe the names of political figures, places (cities, counties, regions, countries), organizations (e.g. ABCD = Access to Baby and Child Dentistry), corporations (IBM), and products (Gear S2), etc.

There are many varieties of "non-technical" languages as well: Americans, Australians, British, Canadians, Indians, Scots, and South Africans use different vocabularies from one another. Even within the United States, certain terms and expressions are used in Louisiana (*lagniappe*) that would not necessarily be known in New York. There is no dictionary describing the vocabularies of *all* the varieties of modern English[1].

Specialized vocabularies, regional vocabularies, and lists of proper names constitute sets that could be covered in a reasonable manner, but as of yet, there is no academic or private structure capable of undertaking such a project. Initially, then, we must limit ourselves to describing the "standard" language, to put it simply, the language common to all Anglophones, whether they are

---

1 The digital version of the *Dictionary of American Regional English* is available at: dare.wisc.edu.

British or Australians, live in New York or New Orleans, work as cooks or bus drivers, play chess or collect stamps, enjoy sports or prefer music, etc.

One vital characteristic of modern natural languages is that they are constantly evolving; the most visible aspect of this evolution is, of course, vocabulary. New terms are constantly entering the vocabulary as others disappear. For example, the novel *The Portrait of a Lady* [HEN 81] contains around twenty words that are considered obsolete today:

> *applausive, auditress, bedroomy, bestown, consideringly, condonement, custode, disagreeables, flouncey, irreflective, luridity, modicity, outweather, overdarkened, overdrooped, properest, rightest, servanted, smokingly, unlightedly, unthumbed, ofterner*

Vocabulary has naturally evolved in 120 years, though the work of Henry James can still be read in its original edition.

Likewise, new words are also created every day, as can be seen in Figure 3.1.

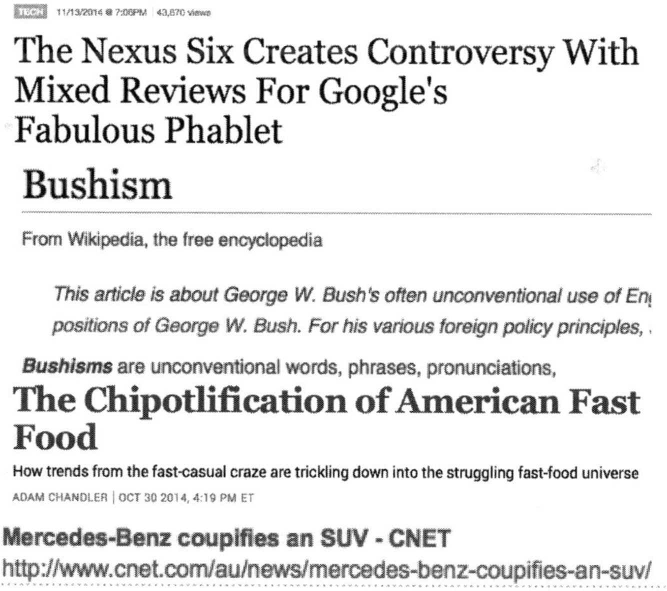

TECH   11/13/2014 @ 7:06PM   43,870 views

The Nexus Six Creates Controversy With Mixed Reviews For Google's Fabulous Phablet

Bushism

From Wikipedia, the free encyclopedia

This article is about George W. Bush's often unconventional use of En[positions of George W. Bush. For his various foreign policy principles, .

Bushisms are unconventional words, phrases, pronunciations,

The Chipotlification of American Fast Food

How trends from the fast-casual craze are trickling down into the struggling fast-food universe

ADAM CHANDLER | OCT 30 2014, 4:19 PM ET

Mercedes-Benz coupifies an SUV - CNET

http://www.cnet.com/au/news/mercedes-benz-coupifies-an-suv/

Figure 3.1. *Phablet, Bushism, Chipotlification, to coupify*

The mechanisms used to construct new words can be grouped into three types of operations: common-word derivation, proper-name or acronym derivation, and borrowing from other languages:

1) Construction of a new word through the prefixing or suffixing of a common word: for example, the verb *to coupify* used in the car industry has been constructed from the noun *coupe* (itself borrowed from the French technical term *coupé*).

This mechanism is very similar to the one used to derive words; both cases involve adding a limited number of prefixes or suffixes (around 50). For example, starting with the noun *nation*, we can construct the adjective *national*, and the verb *to nationalize*; all verbs derived using *-ize* have common syntactic and semantic properties. Thus we can legitimately ask ourselves if it is really necessary to make an exhaustive inventory of the forms derived from words that are already listed in the vocabulary, rather than just use the same productive rules to analyze any derived form, including potential word forms that might become new vocabulary elements (neologisms).

Derivation also involves blends, i.e., a combination of two words, generally the beginning of one and the ending of the other. For example, the term *phablet* is a combination of *phone* and *tablet*.

2) Construction of a new word through the prefixing or suffixing of a proper name or acronym. For example, the terms *Bushism* and *chipotlification* stem from the proper names *Bush* and *Chipotle*. Likewise, the term *GPSing* (using a GPS device) stems from the acronym of *global positioning system*. Furthermore, some acronyms may be ambiguous: the term FPS may refer to a type of video game ("first person shooter") or a measurement unit ("frames per second").

We cannot identify all of the proper names (person, place, product, commercial brand, organization, etc.) and acronyms (of organizations, products and technologies, laws, diseases, etc.) that may be used one day to construct new terms, and even if we were able to make these lists, there are no linguistic criteria we could use to distinguish terms that might actually become vocabulary elements from those that will never been used.

3) Borrowing from another language: for example German (*bunker*), Greek (*theater*), Hebrew (*abbey*), Nahuatl (*tomato*), etc.

Here again, it is impossible to know which of the foreign-language words, terms, pairs of terms, proper names and abbreviations might enrich English vocabulary in the future.

3.2. Derivation

Prefixing and suffixing operations do not apply to *word forms*, but rather to *vocabulary elements* that must be described in a dictionary.

3.2.1. *Derivation applies to vocabulary elements*

For example, we cannot answer the simple question: "Does the verb *to mount* take the prefix *dis-* or not?". An accurate answer depends on each particular use of this verb. For the two uses below:

Joe mounted the exhibition. Joe mounted his horse.

we can indeed construct the corresponding verb *to dismount:*

Joe dismounted the exhibition. Joe dismounted his horse.

However, for the two uses below:

Joe mounted the steps. The bull mounted the cow.

we cannot construct the corresponding verb *to dismount*:

* Joe dismounted the steps. * The bull dismounted the cow.

With the suffix *-able* we can also see differences depending on each use. For example we have the error message on Apple computers: "No Mountable File Systems", and we can say "This pony is easily mountable", but we cannot say:

* This play is mountable in two months. * These steps are easily mountable. * This cow was mountable yesterday.

Though there are rules permitting the addition of prefixes or suffixes to words, these rules do not apply to word forms, but rather to precisely defined vocabulary elements.

To reframe the original question: can we formalize the derivation of words using a set of rules, or must we explicitly list each derived form in a dictionary? Two arguments in favor of the exhaustive listing of derived forms are given below.

3.2.2. *Derivations are unpredictable*

[GRO 75] has shown that each syntactico-semantic use of a verb must be described on an *ad hoc* basis; in other words, one cannot predict all of the linguistic properties of each use of a verb. For example, the uses of *to concern* and *to regard* in the two sentences below are very similar:

> *This event concerns Joe. This event regards Joe.*

These two uses are synonymous; the two sentences have the same syntactic structure, with the same arguments (abstract or sentential subject; human direct object complement). However, only the first use can be made passive:

> *Joe is concerned by this event. * Joe is regarded by this event.*

Likewise, [LEE 90] shows that derivation is not predictable either; for example, the verbs *to laugh* and *to smile* are very similar, with the same syntactic structures, and very similar meanings. However, if we examine the following sentences:

> *One can laugh at Joe. One can smile at Joe*

We can attach the suffix *-able* to the verb of the first sentence, but not the second:

> *Joe is laughable. * Joe is smileable*

In other words: even if we could describe the rules governing various cases of derivation, these rules would contain numerous exceptions that are impossible to predict. For these rules to be applied correctly, we must therefore define their domain of application, i.e.:

– either list the derived forms explicitly; or

– use derivation rules, but then list their exceptions systematically.

Both of these solutions require us to make lists of words, that is to say, dictionaries. I would rather have a dictionary that contains correct derived forms such as "laughable", rather than a list of verbs like "smile" that do not accept the derivation in *-able*. I believe it is more natural and useful to list correct derived forms rather than to list the vocabulary elements that are exceptions to each derivation rule.

3.2.3. *Atomicity of derived words*

Derived forms that are not currently vocabulary elements are potential neologisms. After all, who knows whether the adjective *smileable* might one day be an element of the standard English vocabulary? Therefore, it is legitimate to describe the formation of these forms using rules. And, if we must use these rules to describe them, why not simply use those same rules to process derived words that are already vocabulary elements? It looks like it would be pointless, then, to describe the word *laughable* in a dictionary, since its properties can be automatically computed from the derivation of the verb *to laugh*, exactly like the properties of the potential word *smileable*.

In fact, derivational rules are not enough to describe the properties of derived forms. Consider, for example, the following derived forms:

> *sandification, globalization*

These forms have a very specific meaning, as can be seen in the dictionary en.wiktionary.org/wiki:

> *sandification: 1. An environmental change whereby an environment becomes sandy.*

> *globalization: 1. The process of going to a more interconnected world. 2. The process of making world economy dominated by capitalist models. (World System Theory by I. Wallerstein)*

Even though these words are derived from the dictionary entries *sand* and *global*, their meaning is much richer and more specific than the one we might deduce from the original word and the prefixes or suffixes used. For example, the meaning of the term *sandification* brings into play the concept of *environment*, which is not contained in the noun *sand*. The same is true for the term *globalization*: *global* is not an adjective specific to finance or politics, while *globalization* is. Even though these terms are derived forms, they have acquired a certain semantic independence that makes them fully autonomous vocabulary elements, and they must therefore be described in the same way as any other vocabulary element.

Now consider the following invented forms:

lemonism, demodization, diswebment

These terms might one day become vocabulary elements, but right now we can only use our imaginations to figure out what they possibly mean. And because these forms are constructed from the terms *lemon, mode* (or *demo?*), and *web*, which have several meanings themselves, we can entertain ourselves by making up numerous interpretations. For example, for *demodization*:

– From the term *musical demo*: *trend in the musical industry of requiring artists to record a demo before every concert.* Or from the term *software demo*: *systematic sale of free but limited "demo" versions of software in app-stores.*

– From the term *musical mode*: *freeing of contemporary music from the constraints related to the two musical modes (major and minor).* Or: *progression that leads a melody to change mode several times throughout a musical piece.*

– From the term *operating mode*: *unification for the purpose of simplification of the different operating modes of a mechanical or electrical tool.* Or: *automation of the change of operating mode of a software platform which then becomes capable of adapting to material limitations in real time (usable memory, network bandwidth, processor temperature, etc.).*

– From the term *software mod*: *process consisting of blocking or removing the extensions from a software platform (its "mods").*

Each of these potential meanings might be "activated" if used by a celebrity or a journalist, and if enough people start using it. For example, imagine the following text:

By 2025, crimes by hackers systematically using mods to infect video games had become such a problem that distributors forced studios to protect their software against any mod.

This statement allows us to assign a precise meaning to the word *demodization*, and, who knows, if enough people read this page, perhaps this term will become an element of the standard English vocabulary in the future! In the meantime, the word forms *lemonism, demodization*, and *diswebment* do not have the same status as *sandification* and *globalization*: the meaning of potential word forms can only be guessed by using generic crude rules (we can go no further than breaking them down into prefix + root + suffix), while actual terms that belong fully to the vocabulary and have acquired a precise independent meaning must be explicitly described in a dictionary.

> Formalizing the vocabulary of a natural language consists of describing all its actual elements (including derived words such as *laughable* and *sandification*), while excluding neologisms or potential forms (such as *smileable* and *demodization*).

3.3. Atomic linguistic units (ALUs)

Starting now, I will avoid using the somewhat fuzzy term "word" in favor of the term *atomic linguistic unit* (ALU), which designates the elements of vocabulary of a language:

– ALUs constitute the vocabulary of a language, and are necessarily finite in number; they can and must be exhaustively inventoried.

– ALUs cannot be analyzed even if they seem to be constructed from smaller elements through derivation or compounding.

> ALUs are the elements of vocabulary of a language. They are finite in number, they can and must be explicitly described in dictionaries, and cannot and must not be analyzed.

3.3.1. Classification of ALUs

Based on the definitions of *letter* and *delimiter* seen in Chapter 2, ALUs are grouped into four categories:

> *Simple words* are ALUs that occur in texts as sequences made up exclusively of letters, between two separators.

For example, the text:

She eats an apple

contains 4 simple words.

> *Affixes* (*prefixes* and *suffixes*) are ALUs containing letters, not necessarily between delimiters.

For example, the word form *redenationalization* contains the simple word[2] *nation* and 4 affixes: *re-*, *de-*, *-iz*, and *-ation*.

> *Multiword units* are ALUs containing letters and delimiters.

For example, the text:

He eats more and more sweet potatoes

contains two multiword units: the compound determiner *more and more* and the compound noun *sweet potatoes*.

> *Expressions* are ALUs that can occur in texts in the form of discontinuous sequences of word forms.

For example, the text:

Lea turned the light off.

Contains the discontinuous expression *to turn off*. Expressions can be idiomatic (for example in *Joe takes the bull by the horns*) [NUN 94] or formulaic (for example *Ladies and Gentlemen*), but the vast majority of them are common vocabulary elements:

Nathan gave him up. She took it seriously. They took their jackets off.

---

2 When a simple word is combined with one or more affixes, the term *root* is traditionally used to designate the orthographic form it then takes; for example, the simple word *structure* is spelled *structur* inside the word form *structurable*.

Some expressions are frozen: for example none of the words in the idiomatic expression *to take the bull by the horns* can be modified:

* Joe has caught the bull by the horns

* Joe has taken the cow by the horns

* Joe has taken their bull by its left horn

* Joe has taken the black bull by the horns

Likewise, most phrasal verbs are fixed; for example, it is impossible to replace *to give* with *to offer*, or to replace the particle *in* with the word *inside* in the sentence meaning *Joe surrendered*:

Joe gave in. ** Joe offered in.* ** Joe gave inside.*

In addition, there are several thousand Light Verb/Predicative Noun associations, in which the verb has no function other than to support the noun, which acts semantically as a predicate; for example:

to be in touch, to do someone a favor, to give someone a hand,
to have some courage, to make a deal, to take a walk, etc.

Light Verb/Predicative Noun associations cannot be treated like multiword units or even frozen expressions, since their verbs accept systematic variants. For example, the ALU *to have some courage* must be recognized in the following sentences even though the light verb *to have* is not present explicitly in any of these sentences: *This gave us the courage to come back. They lost their courage. She found the courage to fight back. Her courage inspired me.*

To describe the vocabulary of a language, we will thus formalize the four categories of ALUs. This categorization is largely arbitrary, being based only on orthographical considerations, and knowing that orthography is not always very consistent[3]. However, it is of interest for our project for two reasons:

---

3 Because spaces do not exist in spoken language, the distinction between multiword units and simple words on one hand, and between simple words and affixes on the other, is solely orthographic. Other languages have other orthographic traditions; for example German does not use a space inside most multiword units, while some sequences of clitics in French (such as *dis-le-lui*) correspond to morphemes in Spanish (ex. *digaselo*).

– *generality*: the four categories of ALU defined above can be used to describe any vocabulary element, in all written languages;

– *reproducibility*: anyone who understands this categorization will be able to reliably categorize any ALU of any language into one of the four categories, meaning that data accumulations can be undertaken by independent teams of linguists.

In this section we have introduced the categorization of the ALUs which constitute the basic elements of vocabulary and are classified according to orthographic criteria. It now remains to distinguish multiword units and expressions from analyzable sequences of simple words.

3.4. Multiword units versus analyzable sequences of simple words

No orthographic criterion allows us to distinguish multiword units from sequences of simple words[4]. Most compound nouns have a productive structure such as *Adjective Noun* (*white wine*), *Noun Noun* (*flight simulator*), *Verb Noun* (*washing-machine*) or *Preposition Noun* (*in-law*).

Though most linguists would agree to consider a sequence such as *blue collar* as constituting a vocabulary element when it means *manual laborer* and the sequence *blue table* as fully analyzable, the situation becomes much less clear-cut for hundreds of thousands of word combinations that fall between these 2 simple cases.

Depending on whether we are speaking to a logician, an etymologist, a morphologist, a psycholinguist, a language teacher, a writer, a lexicographer, or a spelling specialist, etc., the definition of *multiword unit* differs widely, and there is still no universally-accepted definition today. I will give a definition of *multiword units* here which is based on three criteria[5] and brings two benefits to our project:

---

4 The hyphen is present in only 7% of multiword units listed in the English DELAC dictionary, for example *ding-a-ling* or *butter-head lettuce*.

5 This set of criteria, introduced in [SIL 93b] was updated based on a study of the electronic dictionary DELAC, which I had constructed at the Laboratoire d'Automatique Documentaire et Linguistique (Université Paris 7-CNRS), conducted by Maurice Gross, as part of my doctoral work on the automatic lexical analysis of texts in natural language.

– These criteria are operational and reproducible. In particular, we oppose the idea put forth by [McC 03] that a continuum exists between analyzable sequences and fixed sequences, because it is not operational. For our linguistic project, either a sequence of words is fully analyzable by means of an explicit set of rules, or it has at least one property that cannot be computed by applying this set of rules. In the latter case, it is not fully analyzable and must therefore be inventoried in order to be described explicitly.

– These criteria fulfill the requirements of most NLP computer applications. As a matter of fact, most of the errors produced by current NLP applications would be prevented if these applications processed ALUs rather than "words" defined using naive orthographical criteria.

NLP software – spell-checkers, search engines, taggers, automatic translators, etc. – do not all necessarily need to compute all the syntactic or semantic properties of a given sequence of words, but seek rather to compute some of these properties, for example to correct possible agreement errors, to normalize a query in order to link all the variants of a term to a single index key, or to compute the distributional class of a noun phrase to disambiguate a verb and work out its translation, etc.

Software uses general rules; for example, a spell-checker will consider that the headword of a noun phrase with the structure *Det Noun of Noun* is the first noun; an automatic translator will attempt to translate an English *Adjective Noun* sequence with the corresponding French *Noun Adjective* sequence, etc. However, there are many exceptions to these general rules. For example, the headword of the noun phrase *a number of people* is not *number*, but *people*. The sequence *blue cheese* cannot be translated into French as *fromage bleu*.

To avoid producing errors, software must have access to a list of exceptions; that is, of word sequences for which the general rules do not apply[6]: it is precisely this list of exceptions that the following criteria will allow us to construct.

Some NLP specialists use statistical criteria to decide whether a sequence of words constitutes an element of vocabulary or not, with the idea being that

---

6 For more on multiword units and their applications for NLP, see [SAG 02].

if two words often appear together (referred to as "co-occurrences" or "colocations"), they are a "repeated sequence of interest" and therefore constitute vocabulary elements. I do not believe that frequency has anything to do with the linguistic status of vocabulary elements: there are words that are frequent (e.g. *house*) and there are words that occur rarely (e.g. *organ*), but no one would ever consider that *organ* is "less" of a word than *house*. Moreover, it is not because certain words often appear together (e.g. *to be in*) that they are more likely to constitute a term than others that appear together less often (e.g. *red tape*).

[SIL 95] showed that only a third of the multiword units inventoried in the French dictionary occurred at least once in the articles of the newspaper *Le Monde* over a five-year period. Knowing that statistical software can detect co-occurrences only if they appear more than once, this type of corpus (though enormous at more than 100 million words) would be far from covering our needs. Therefore I will not use statistical criteria to define multiword units.

3.4.1. *Semantics*

The basic idea of this criterion is well known: if we cannot interpret the meaning of a sequence of words, though we understand each of the words making up the sequence, i.e. if the meaning of the sequence cannot be worked out, then it is necessary to process the sequence as a whole. This means that the sequence constitutes an ALU, and must therefore be processed as an autonomous vocabulary element. For example, the meaning of the word sequence *blue collar* cannot be deduced from the meaning of its components; a *blue collar* is not a collar that is blue. Thus, *blue collar* is a vocabulary element.

Note that it is not a matter of claiming that there is no relationship between the concept of "blue collar" and the two concepts "blue" and "collar". However, though the concepts "blue" and "collar" are part of understanding the meaning of the term *blue collar*, they are far from being the only ones in play: it would also be necessary to bring in the concepts of "uniform", "manual labor", and maybe even to oppose *blue collar* to *white collar*.

So, the criterion of semantic atomicity has two sides: for a sequence of words to be considered semantically analyzable, it is necessary not only for its meaning to be computed from the meaning of its components, but also to not require other concepts to be brought into play. Now consider the six sequences below:

> *a business card, a credit card, an identity card, a memory card,*
> *a penalty card, a post card*

An initial analysis seems to indicate that these five sequences are semantically analyzable: a *business card* is indeed a *card* that has something to do with *business*; a *credit card* is a *card* used in relation to *credit*; an *identity card* is a *card* used in relation to *identity*; a *memory card* is indeed a *card* used in relation to some *memory*; and a *penalty card* is a *card* that has a certain relationship with a *penalty*. However, these analyses are much too rough to give us an idea, even a vague one, of the shape or purpose of these objects and their differences. A more precise analysis would then be to the following effect:

– *a business card is a card containing professional contact information*;

– *a credit card is a card used as a means of payment*;

– *an identity card is a card used to prove one's identity*;

– *a memory card is a card that contains electronic memory used by certain electronic devices*;

– *a penalty card is a card held up to indicate a penalty in certain sports*;

– *a postcard (or post card) is a card on which messages can be written and which is sent by post.*

These analyses, indispensable to grasping the meaning of each of these word sequences, could not be computed from the components of these word sequences. The proof of this is that the analyses cannot be switched around:

– *a business card* is not a card used as a means of payment (for example, one that is accepted at certain business centers); neither is it a card used to prove that you own a business, or an electronic card used during certain business transactions, or a card you receive if you behave badly in a business, or a type of business correspondence;

– *a credit card* does not contain the contact information of some credit company; it is not used as an ID card to prove that you have credit. It does not actually contain any credit, and you do not get one if you have played poorly in a game; nor is it some type of correspondence sent by your credit company.

– *a memory card* does not necessarily contain any memorized contact information; it is not necessarily a means of payment; it is not used as an ID to prove that you have good memory, we do not get one when we play badly in a memory game, and we do not use them to send memorized messages (e.g. reminders);

– *a penalty card* does not contain contact information related to any penalty; it is not used as a means of payment nor to check one's bank penalties, or as an ID to prove whether you have received penalties or not; it is not used as a correspondence to send penalties;

– *a postcard* does not contain your postal contact information, or a means of payment related to the post (such as a money order); it is not used as an ID to prove your postal address, and no referee holds it up when you have behaved badly.

The meaning of each of the sequences *business card, credit card, identity card, memory card, penalty card*, and *postcard* therefore brings explanations into play that must be used on an *ad hoc* basis. This is not the same situation as with the following sequences:

an old card, a brown card, a pretty card, an interesting card

In these examples there is nothing to help us rule out any analysis: *an old card* could be an old business card, an old credit card, an old ID card, an old memory card, an old penalty card, or an old postcard. The fact that these latter sequences are ambiguous (or undefined) proves that they can be analyzed, while the former ones, which are each associated with one interpretation and only one, constitute fully independent elements of vocabulary (ALUs).

It could be argued that the former sequences could actually be analyzed semantically, and that the idiosyncrasy of each analysis can be explained by the combination of some lexical properties, which to some extent allows only the "correct" analysis to be activated while cancelling out the other analyses. Just as its complements make it possible to clear up the ambiguity of the verb *to look* in *Lea looks good* vs *Lea looks for her pen* vs *Lea looks at Joe*, could the context of *identity* be used to clear up the ambiguity of the noun *card*? According to this argument, the term *card* would have around 30 "free" interpretations, but the modifier *identity* would contain certain conceptual properties – such as "administration", "proof", "citizenship" – which would activate the right meaning of (*identity*) *card* and do away with any other interpretation of the word *card*.

Of course, this argument is only valid if *identity* is itself unambiguous. Consider the following sequences:

> *identity element, mistaken identity, religious identity, self identity*

An *identity element* is a mathematical element which, combined with another element with respect to a mathematical operation, leaves it unchanged. *Mistaken identity* is a defense in criminal law pertaining to the actual innocence of a defendant. *Religious identity* implies membership in a religious group. *Self identity* is an awareness of one's personal history and attributes. All these uses of the word *identity* also have their own specific individual interpretations: for example, *self identity* is not a mathematical or a legal concept, and *mistaken identity* is neither a mathematical concept nor a psychological one, while *identity element* is neither a legal nor a psychological concept.

If we consider the fact that the word *identity* has around ten meanings and the word *card* has around thirty, the combination *identity card* should have 10×30 potential meanings: for example, an *identity card* could be a card used by community organizations (with the "community membership" meaning of *identity*), or a flash card used to help remember the mathematical properties of the identity element, or a card used by psychologists to work out the self identity problems of a patient, etc.

How does it happen that, of the 300 potential meanings of *identity card*, a single one is activated by all speakers, while none of the others are even considered? The answer is simple: this is a vocabulary element that speakers "know" and do not analyze. In other words, *identity card* is an ALU.

> Some combinations of words are associated with a specific meaning, while many other potential meanings are blocked. These combinations are therefore not fully analyzable, and thus constitute elements of the vocabulary of the language; these are ALUs that must be inventoried.

3.4.2. *Usage*

In this section, I will not be using any semantic criterion; word sequences exist whose meaning may be perfectly computable, but which must still be inventoried and treated as independent vocabulary elements because they constitute terms used by everyone. For example, consider the term *a washing machine*. Even though its meaning is rather transparent (everyone can imagine what a washing machine does), it is also true that this term is used as a fixed formula, almost like a name of an object. In theory, vocabulary and grammar should allow us to name this object using numerous periphrases. For example, the following phrases could be possible:

> *a linen-washer, a clothes-cleaning device, a personal cleaner, a soap-and-rinse automatic system, a towel centrifuge, a deterging automaton, etc.*

however, the truth is that no one uses these phrases, while everyone uses the term *washing machine*. Compare the following terms (which are vocabulary elements) to the associated "non-terms":

> *a professional musician* versus *a business musician*
>
> *a shopping center* versus *a purchasing building, a commerce mall*
>
> *a hurricane lamp* versus *a tempest torch, a portative electric light*
>
> *a word processor* versus *a piece of writing software, a book processor*
>
> *etc.*

As we have just seen, certain objects around us are lucky enough to be named. But there are many objects which are not so lucky; for example, to mention a shirt on which trains are printed, we cannot use sentences such as *Joe is wearing his train shirt today*. The terms *flowery shirt*, *sport shirt* and *tee-shirt* exist though. Compare the actual terms and the weird sequences below:

> *a wall poster versus a door poster*
>
> *a coffee-table book versus a kitchen-table book*
>
> *a bus pass versus a ship pass, a plane pass*
>
> *etc.*

Many terms exist in one language but not in others[7]: for example, there is no French term for *a coffee table book* (**un livre de table basse, ? un livre de luxe grand format*) and there is no direct English equivalent term for the French term *un roman de gare* (** a railway station novel, ? a dime novel*).

It seems to me that any attempt to describe a language must distinguish real terms – which are elements of its vocabulary – from sequences of words that have no lexical status. Linguistic applications (language teaching, translation) must imperatively distinguish real terms from periphrases, even if only to propose the "right" translation.

3.4.3. *Transformational analysis*

We will see in Chapter 13 that an essential component of the formalization of a language is its transformational grammar: we must be able to describe the relationships linking the various structures that convey a particular meaning[8]. Traditionally, linguists have been more interested in full sentence transformations, but some transformations can be described locally. I now present a series of transformational rules that could be used to analyze certain *Noun Noun* sequences[9]. Terms that have another structure, such as

---

7 [RHE 88] takes a humorous look at many terms that do not exist in English but are present in other languages.

8 We will see how to implement transformations in Chapter 13.

9 [MON 93] has studied the *Noun Adjective* compound nouns in the French DELAC dictionary from a transformational perspective.

Adjective Noun (e.g. *zoological garden*), *Noun of Noun* (e.g. *chamber of commerce*), *Verb Noun* (e.g. *driving force*), etc., should also be associated with transformations.

For example, we link *Noun Noun* terms to periphrases with the structure *Noun Preposition Determiner Noun* as follows:

> *a border dispute* → *a dispute about a border*

> *a hospital stay* → *a stay at a hospital*

> *the media coverage* → *the coverage by the media*

> *an acquisition agreement* → *an agreement on an acquisition*

> *a budget amendment* → *an amendment to the budget*

So, we need to implement several dozen possible transformations, since there are half a dozen productive prepositions (*at, by, on, to*) and half a dozen productive second-noun determiners (*empty, definite, generic, or indefinite determiners*).

However, to these regular transformations we must add thousands of *ad hoc* transformations which involve prepositions that can only be applied to a very few structures:

> *shock therapy* → *therapy consisting of (electric) shocks*

> *an election campaign* → *a campaign during the election*

> *tax fraud* → *fraud against the tax (law)*

> *computer fraud* → *fraud using a computer*

When, in a *Noun Noun* structure, the second noun is derived from a verb, we must link the structure to the corresponding sentence; for example:

> *society expectation* → *society expects something*

> *a heart transplant* → *one transplants a heart*

> *a food collection* → *one collects food*
>
> *a magazine subscription* → *one subscribes to a magazine*

Here again, there are a several transformations to formalize in order to take into account the function of the noun in relation to the verb (subject, direct or indirect object complement). However, it is also necessary to take into account thousands of transformations in which the first noun corresponds to an adverb:

> *a diplomatic confrontation* → *countries confront each other diplomatically*
>
> *a religious education* → *one educates people religiously*
>
> *an accidental death* → *one dies (accidentally | because of an accident)*

The second noun may have a predicative value without being morphologically derived from a verb. For example:

> *consumer fraud* → *consumers are victims of a fraud*
>
> *a strategic error* → *one makes an error in strategy*

For other combinations, it is the first noun that represents the predicate, and the second noun its argument:

> *a compensatory amount* → *an amount (of money) compensates (for something)*

Sometimes one of the nouns acts as a locative complement:

> *a university town* → *there is a university in the town*
>
> *a brain injury* → *there is an injury in the brain*

Finally, note that the transformations shown above are largely independent and may thus be combined; many terms accept more than one transformation, for example:

a student protest → *a protest of students* → *the students protest* →
the students organize a protest

> To analyze phrases with the structure *Determiner Noun Noun*,
> we must not only identify a dozen productive transformations,
> but also the thousands of exceptional transformations that apply
> to one or more specific phrases, as well as the tens of thousands
> of phrases to which regular transformations are not applicable.
> These "exceptions" must therefore be identified and listed: I
> suggest we consider them as ALUs and list them in the general
> dictionary.

3.5. Conclusion

In order to formalize a language, we need to describe its vocabulary
exhaustively. To do this, we must limit ourselves to a synchronic description
of its standard vocabulary, and then define its elements: ALUs, which are
grouped into four orthographically-defined categories: affixes (e.g. the prefix
re-), simple words (e.g. *table*), multiword units (e.g. *sweet potatoes*), and
expressions (e.g. *take ... into account*). Treating affixes as independent
ALUs allows us to analyze prefixed or suffixed forms; conversely, treating
multiword units and expressions as independent ALUs allows us to process
them as a whole and thus block an incorrect word for word analysis.

Although distinguishing multiword units and expressions from simple
word sequences is not always clear-cut, we saw three criteria to establish
these distinctions:

1) the meaning of an ALU is not fully analyzable in a predictable manner;

2) the use of an ALU is formulaic;

3) the ALU constitutes an exception to a productive transformational rule.

These three criteria are reproducible, which allows for the accumulation
of linguistic descriptions and thus makes our linguistic project feasible.
Moreover, these three criteria are of crucial interest for NLP applications
such as search engines or automatic translation, because they allow these
applications to process ALUs rather than word forms.

3.6. Exercises

1) Identify and categorize the ALUs in the following sentence: *The Lieutenant Commander was relieved of duty from the nuclear submarine.*

2) List 15 prefixes (for example *over-*, *re-*) and 5 suffixes (for example *-ize*, *-ation*), that could be used to invent new forms from actual vocabulary elements. Group them according to whether they apply to nouns, verbs, or adjectives.

3) Pick out the multiword units and expressions in the following text (Serge Schmemann, *International Herald Tribune*, November 29, 2014):

> *The experts we corralled for our "Conversation" on aging, as you are about to discover, agree that we are pushing death farther and farther back, so that many of us may now expect to live a century or more. I find this most heartening, sharing as I do the common fear of the Reaper. But I am also aware that I and my fellow centenarians will pose some difficult new problems for our 80-year-old kids and 60-something grandkids, problems memorably identified by the Beatles back in the day: Will you still need me, will you still feed me, when I'm one-oh-four?*

3.7. Internet links

This site lists fifty terminology databases: termcoord.eu/useful-links/terminology-databases

UMLS medical terminology database: www.nlm.nih.gov/research/umls

The DELAC dictionary of multiword units, developed using the criteria discussed in this chapter, is part of the NooJ software platform: www.nooj4nlp.net

The online dictionaries www.urbandictionary.com and www.wordnik.com contain a large number of neologisms.

4

Electronic Dictionaries

The last chapter showed that the project of describing the vocabulary of a language *in extenso* is feasible if the language's evolution is not taken into account (synchronic description) and if its vocabulary is controlled, for example by limiting the description to a "standard" non-technical and non-regional vocabulary.

We must, therefore, construct a database to store the vocabulary of a language, which will resemble editorial dictionaries but with important differences.

4.1. Could editorial dictionaries be reused?

I estimate the size of the standard English vocabulary at around 350,000 elements[1]. Reference dictionaries, for example the *American Heritage Dictionary*, the *Oxford English Dictionary*, and the *Merriam-Webster Unabridged Dictionary*, contain around 500,000 entries and uses, as does the collaborative Wiktionary project. However, these dictionaries contain a large number of obsolete, scientific, and technical terms, as well as proper names (of people, organizations, and places).

---

1 Or fifty affixes, 100,000 simple words, 200,000 multiword units (mostly compound nouns), and around 50,000 expressions (including 30,000 frozen expressions, 20,000 support verb/predicate noun combinations and several thousand phrasal verbs). There is no complete electronic dictionary for the English language; this estimate is based on the size of the standard French vocabulary, described by Maurice Gross' team which worked in the Laboratoire d'Automatique Documentaire et Linguistique (LADL) in the 1990s.

Because these dictionaries do exist, we may legitimately ask ourselves whether it is possible to reuse them in order to formalize the vocabulary of language. These dictionaries are also accessible via the Internet and can be consulted on CD or DVD (or even downloaded at no cost, in the case of Wiktionary). Could we automatically extract the information necessary for a formalized vocabulary from these dictionaries?

I am drawing here from an experiment described in [GRO 94] to show the inadequacy of editorial dictionaries for the linguistic project. Any project to formalize the vocabulary of a natural language must necessarily include a classification of nouns that distinguishes "human" nouns (e.g. *baker*) from "concrete" nouns (e.g. *apple*) and "abstract" nouns (e.g. *birthday*). For example, there are syntactic rules that apply only to human nouns:

– interrogative and relative pronouns *who* vs. *what* and *that:*

> *Who fell? The employee. The employee who fell left.*
> *What fell? The ashtray. The ashtray that fell broke.*

– pronominalizations into *him/her* or *it:*

> *I am thinking about my boss = I am thinking about her.*
> *I am thinking about the ashtray = I am thinking about it.*

– many verbs take arguments (subject or complements) which must be human:

> *This commercial amuses Joe.*
> ** This commercial amuses the truth.*
> ** This commercial amuses the pencil.*

These types of restrictions constitute the basis for a system of rules essential for processing semantic operations such as metaphor or metonymy. Thus, the following sentence:

> *The bank opposed his decision.*

makes no sense if *bank* refers to a building, but it becomes understandable if *bank* refers to a human organization:

> *= The bank officials opposed his decision.*

To analyze this sentence, we must perform an operation of metonymy. However, to even know that we need to perform this operation, we need to know that the noun *bank* is not "directly" human. Therefore we must distinguish human nouns such as *officials* from nouns "containing" humans, such as *bank*.

But is it truly possible to create a classification of nouns from these reference dictionaries by automatic extraction? Look, for example, at how the noun *artisan* is described in the *American Heritage dictionary*:

---

artisan
n.
A skilled manual worker; a craftsperson.

The entry *artisan* is associated with two synonyms: *skilled manual worker* and *craftsperson*. The first term is not a dictionary entry, but we can search for the lexical item *worker*, since a *skilled manual worker* is a *worker*:

---

worker
n.
1.a. One who works at a particular occupation or activity: *an office worker*.
  b. One who does manual or industrial labor.
2. A member of the working class.
3. A member of a colony of social insects such as ants, bees, wasps, or termites, usually a sterile female but often a sexually immature individual of either sex, that performs specialized work such as building the nest, collecting and storing food, and feeding other members of the colony.

Both definitions 1.a. and 1.b. start with the sequence "One who", which indicates that *worker* is a human noun.

Definition no. 2 of *worker* gives the synonym *member of the working class*. Of course, *member of the working class* is not a dictionary entry. However, if we search for *member*, we find nine uses, eight of which correspond to non-human nouns (for example *a part of a plant*), and 1 which corresponds to an indeterminate type (use no. 4).

---

member

n.

1. A distinct part of a whole, especially:

a. *Linguistics* A syntactic unit of a sentence; a clause.

b. *Logic* A proposition of a syllogism.

c. *Mathematics* An element of a set.

2. A part or an organ of a human or animal body, as:

a. A limb, such as an arm or a leg.

b. The penis.

3. A part of a plant.

4. One that belongs to a group or an organization: *a club member, a bank that is a member of the FDIC.*

5. *Mathematics* The expression on either side of an equality sign.

6. A structural unit, such as a beam or wall.

Definition no. 3 of *worker* gives three synonyms: *member of a colony of social insects, sterile female,* and *sexually immature individual of either sex.* None of these expressions is a dictionary entry. The first synonym refers back to *member*, which we do not know how to analyze. If we search for the noun *female*, we find three uses:

---

female

n.

1. A member of the sex that produces ova or bears young.

2. A woman or girl.

3. *Botany.* A plant having only pistillate flowers.

The first meaning of *female* refers back again to *member* (which we do not know how to analyze), while the second definition enables us to deduce that *artisan* is a human noun, but note that the analysis produced by artisan#1 + worker#3 + female#2 is incorrect:

artisan = skilled manual sterile (woman or girl).

The third meaning of *female* does not correspond to a human noun.

Now look at the second definition of *artisan*: *craftsperson*. If we search for this term in the dictionary, we find:

> **craftsperson**
> n.
> A craftsman or a craftswoman

Here we have no "one who" or "person" to help us figure out that *craftsperson* is a human noun[2]. So, we must search for the terms *craftsman* and *craftswoman*:

> **craftsman**
> n.
> A man who practices a craft with great skill.
> **craftswoman**
> n.
> A woman who practices a craft with great skill.

Here, we have mentions of "who" as well as the keywords "man" and "woman", which indicate that these are indeed human nouns.

In conclusion, to attempt to automatically extract the type of the noun *artisan* from the dictionary, we must explore a graph containing 38 analyses, 17 of which will produce an incorrect result (*artisan:* non-human noun), 16 that are undetermined (*artisan = member of a group*), and 5 which will produce the correct result (*artisan:* human noun), of which the analysis *artisan = skilled manual sterile woman or girl* is still incorrect:

– *craftsperson → craftsman → a man*

– *craftsperson → craftswoman → a woman*

– *a skilled manual worker → a worker → a sterile female → a woman or girl*

– *a skilled manual worker → a worker → one who works at a particular occupation or activity*

– *a skilled manual worker → a worker → one who does manual or industrial labor*

---

2 It might be tempting to conduct an orthographic analysis to see that *person* is present in the form *craftsperson* in order to deduce that *craftsperson* is a person, hence a human noun, but this analysis would not work for other nouns that contain the sequence *person* without being human nouns; for example *impersonation, personality, personnel, supersonic*, etc.

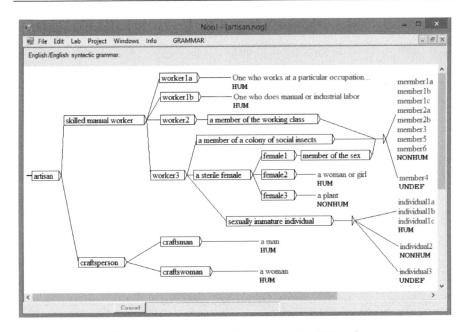

Figure 4.1. *Analysis of the lexical entry "artisan"*

In conclusion, a piece of information as basic as the noun type is not directly available in reference dictionaries. Other, more complex information, such as the number of complements a verb takes along with their type (human or non-human), as well as the possibility of passivization, possible derivations, etc. are beyond the scope of these dictionaries – which, remember, were designed to be used by human readers who already possess a good understanding of the language.

There are more precise dictionaries, used by linguists and language professionals (writers, terminologists, and translators). For example, thesauruses can provide synonyms or even translations for tens of thousands of words. WORDNET-type [FEL 14] dictionaries group words into *synsets* (sets of synonyms) and connect synsets by various semantic relationships (antonymy, meronymy, hyperonymy, causality, etc.). [LEV 93] describes and categorizes several thousand English verbs. The COBUILD (Collins Birmingham University International Language Database) dictionary was constructed from the *Bank of English corpus of contemporary texts* and offers descriptions that are somewhat more systematic than earlier general dictionaries[3]. The *Valency Dictionary of English*, also based on the *Bank of English corpus*, links each of its entries to complex syntactic and semantic descriptions but covers fewer than 1,500 entries [HER 04, FIL 08][4].

However, even the best dictionaries for linguists include a large number of implicit entries or items of information, and other experiments with these dictionaries have convinced me that it would be more reasonable to construct a new dictionary specifically designed to formalize the vocabulary of languages rather than to try to reuse the ones that were never designed for our project. The type of dictionaries we need are *electronic dictionaries*, in which each vocabulary element is explicitly associated with a set of fully defined linguistic properties.

In the private sphere there are numerous specialized electronic dictionaries used for various software applications; for example the spellcheckers in Microsoft Office software rely on dictionaries, and the Linguistic Data Consortium distributes the electronic dictionary COMLEX [MAC 94], which contains 37,000 entries associated with semantic information (predicates and their arguments). There are also some university dictionaries, such as the NomBank [MAC 04] group of dictionaries, constructed from Penn TreeBank and containing derivation information, and the OpenLogos [BAR 14] family of bilingual dictionaries used for automatic translation.

To date, however, there is no electronic dictionary that completely formalizes the standard English vocabulary, associating each vocabulary element with its morphological properties (inflection and derivation), syntactic properties (number of complements, preposition, restructuring), and semantic properties (distributional category of each complement, semantic class, and semantic domain).

---

3 For example, it contains numerous definitions such as: *chemist = a chemist is a person who…* But there are also a large number of definitions such as: *Catholic = a member of the Catholic church* or *professor = a professor in a British university is the most senior teacher…* These definitions are perfectly clear and usable for linguists and human language professionals, but are not sufficiently formalized to be used by automatic linguistic analysis applications.

4 Remember that the size of the standard vocabulary is estimated at around 250,000 elements.

I will now discuss the two resources closest to what would be needed to formalize the vocabulary of a language: the electronic dictionaries constructed by the LADL, and those constructed by Dubois and Dubois-Charlier.

4.2. LADL electronic dictionaries

The electronic dictionaries created by LADL in the 1990s are more formalized than editorial dictionaries and provide wider coverage than specialized dictionaries for linguists. They are divided into two parts: the lexicon-grammar [GRO 96] associating each of its entries with a set of syntactico-semantic properties, and the DELA, which associates each of its entries with its inflectional morphological properties.

4.2.1. Lexicon-Grammar

The *Lexique-Grammaire des verbes français* [LEC 05][5] (*Lexicon-Grammar of French Verbs*) is a database that lists more than 12,000 verbs and associates them ("+") or not ("–") with binary syntactico-semantic properties. Entries possessing a certain number of properties in common are naturally grouped together in tables. For example, intransitive verbs without complements (corresponding to the structure N_0 V) are all arranged in table number 31x; direct transitive verbs (the structure N_0 V N_1) are arranged in tables 4, 6 and 32x, etc.

There are lexicon-grammar tables for categories of words other than verbs, and also for languages other than French [LEC 98][6]. In particular, several lexicon-grammar tables have been constructed for English. For example, the sample table in Figure 4.2 describes the properties of 300 English verbs that take the two structures [SAL 83, SAL 04, FRE 85, MAC 10, MAC 12]:

N_0 V Prep N_1 = N_1 V with N_0

---

5 For an introduction to the classification of the entries of the *Lexicon-Grammar of French Verbs*.
6 For a list of references to works on lexicon-grammar.

Bees are swarming in the garden = The garden is swarming with bees

In this table, the first columns concern the semantic category of the subject (N_0), which can be +conc (e.g. *table*), +abs (e.g. *enthusiasm*), +anim (e.g. *insect*) or +hum (e.g. *council*). The next columns describe the syntactic structures of the locative phrase (L), the locative preposition used, the semantic class of the complement N_1, the structures of the phrase transposed, the possibility of adjectivization of the verb, etc.

		ABOUND	ACHE	ARC	BALLOON	BATTLE	BEAM	BEAT	BELCH	BERRY	BE BIG	BILLOW	BLAZE	BLEED	BLINK	BLISTER	BLOOM	BLOSSOM	BLOW	BLUSH	BOB	BOIL	BOIL OVER	BOIL OVER	BOOM	BOUNCE
N_0	conc	+	-	+	+	-	+	+	+	+	-	+	+	+	+	+	+	+	+	+	+	+	+	-	+	+
	plur	+	-	-	-	-	-	-	-	+	-	+	-	-	-	-	-	-	-	-	-	-	-	-	-	-
	abs	+	+	-	+	+	+	+	+	-	+	-	+	-	-	-	+	+	+	-	-	+	-	+	-	+
	plur	+	-	-	-	-	-	-	-	-	-	-	-	-	-	-	-	-	-	-	-	-	-	-	-	-
	anim	+	-	-	-	+	-	-	-	-	+	-	-	-	-	-	-	-	-	-	-	-	-	-	-	+
	hum	+	-	-	-	+	-	-	-	-	+	-	-	-	-	-	-	-	-	-	-	-	-	-	-	+
L form	N_0 V	+	-	-	-	-	+	+	-	-	-	-	+	-	+	+	+	+	-	-	+	-	+	-	+	+
	N_0 V P N_1	+	+	+	+	+	+	+	+	+	-	+	+	+	+	+	+	+	+	-	+	+	+	+	+	+
	N_0 be a-V P N_1	-	-	-	-	+	-	-	-	-	-	-	+	-	-	-	+	-	-	+	-	-	+	-	-	+
	about/around	-	-	-	-	-	-	-	-	-	-	-	-	-	-	-	-	-	+	-	+	-	-	-	-	+
PREPOSITIONS	in	+	+	-	-	+	+	+	-	-	-	-	+	-	+	-	+	+	-	+	-	+	+	+	+	+
	among	-	-	-	-	-	-	-	-	-	-	-	-	-	-	-	-	-	-	-	-	-	-	-	-	-
	from	-	-	-	+	-	-	-	+	-	-	+	-	+	-	-	+	-	+	-	-	-	+	-	-	-
	on	-	-	-	+	-	-	-	-	+	-	+	+	-	+	+	+	+	+	+	+	+	-	-	-	+
	over	-	-	+	+	-	-	-	-	+	-	+	-	-	-	-	+	+	+	-	+	-	-	-	-	+
	into	-	-	-	-	-	-	-	-	-	-	-	-	-	-	-	-	-	-	-	-	-	-	-	-	-
	through	-	-	-	-	+	-	-	-	-	-	-	-	+	-	-	-	-	-	-	+	-	-	-	-	-
	across	-	-	+	-	+	-	-	-	+	-	+	-	-	-	-	-	-	-	-	-	-	-	-	+	+
	along	-	-	+	-	-	-	-	-	+	-	+	-	-	-	-	-	-	-	-	-	-	-	-	+	+
	down	-	-	-	-	-	-	-	-	-	-	+	-	-	-	-	-	-	-	-	-	-	-	-	+	-
	off	-	-	-	-	-	-	-	-	-	-	-	-	-	+	-	-	-	-	-	-	-	-	-	+	+
	against	-	-	-	-	-	-	+	-	-	-	-	-	-	-	-	-	-	-	-	-	-	-	-	+	+
	out of	-	-	-	+	-	-	-	+	-	-	-	+	-	-	+	-	-	-	-	-	-	+	-	-	-
	at	-	-	-	-	-	-	-	-	-	-	-	-	-	-	+	-	-	-	-	-	-	-	-	-	-
N_1	hum	-	+	-	-	-	+	-	+	-	+	-	-	-	-	-	+	-	-	-	-	+	-	+	-	-
	plur	-	-	-	-	-	-	-	-	-	-	-	-	-	-	-	-	-	-	-	-	-	-	-	-	-
	Nbody	-	+	-	+	+	+	-	-	-	-	-	+	-	-	+	-	-	-	-	-	-	-	-	-	-
	conc	+	-	+	+	+	+	+	+	+	-	+	+	+	+	+	+	+	+	+	+	+	+	-	+	+
	abs	+	-	-	+	+	-	-	-	-	+	-	-	-	-	-	+	+	+	-	-	-	-	-	-	+
Tform	N_1 V	-	+	+	-	-	+	-	-	+	-	-	-	-	-	-	-	+	-	-	-	+	+	+	-	-
	N_1 V with N_0	+	+	+	+	-	+	+	+	+	+	+	+	+	+	+	+	+	-	-	+	+	+	+	+	+
	with → Ø	-	-	-	-	-	-	-	+	-	-	-	-	+	-	-	-	-	-	-	-	-	-	-	-	-
ADJ	N_1 be a-V P N_0	-	-	-	-	+	-	-	-	-	-	+	+	+	+	+	+	+	+	+	+	+	-	-	+	+
	V-y/V-ent	+	+	-	-	-	+	-	-	-	-	+	-	+	-	+	+	+	+	-	-	-	-	-	+	+
	N_1 be V-a P N_0	-	+	-	-	-	+	-	-	-	-	+	-	-	-	+	-	-	-	-	-	-	-	-	+	-
N_0	sound	-	-	-	-	-	-	+	-	-	-	-	-	-	-	-	-	-	-	-	-	-	-	-	-	-
	plur	+	+	-	+	+	+	+	-	+	-	+	+	+	+	+	+	+	+	+	+	-	+	-	+	+
Other PREP		IN			INTO			TO																		

Figure 4.2. *A lexicon-grammar table for English verbs*

There are lexicon-grammar tables for phrasal verbs and for frozen expressions. For example, Figure 4.3 is an extract from the table that contains 700 phrasal verbs using the particle *up* [MAC 10]:

$N_0 =:$ Nhum	$N_0 =:$ N-hum	Verb	Particle	Example of N_1	$N_1 =:$ Nhum	$N_1 =:$ N-hum	N_0 V N_1	N_1 V Part	N_1 V	Synonym
+	+	beam	up	the aliens	+	+	-	+	-	transport by energy
+	+	bear	up	the weight	+	+	+	-	-	support
+	+	beat	up	the door	-	+	-	-	-	damage
+	+	beat	up	the eggs	-	+	+	-	-	beat
+	-	beat	up	the child	+	-	+	-	-	attack physically & hurt
+	+	beef	up	the proposal	-	+	-	-	-	strengthen
+	+	bend	up	the credit card	-	+	+	-	-	bend completely
+	-	bind	up	the wound	+	+	+	-	-	put bandage on
+	+	block	up	the sink	-	+	+	+	-	obstruct
+	+	blow	up	the balloons	-	+	-	-	-	inflate
+	+	blow	up	the building	+	+	-	+	+	explode
+	+	blow	up	the photo	-	+	-	-	-	enlarge
+	+	blow	up	the scandal	-	+	-	+	-	exaggerate
+	-	boil	up	some water	-	+	+	-	+	boil
+	+	bolster	up	Max	+	+	+	-	-	give hope to
+	+	bolster	up	the theory	-	+	-	-	-	support
+	+	boot	up	the computer	-	+	+	+	+	start

Figure 4.3. *Lexicon-grammar table for phrasal verbs*

4.2.2. *DELA*

The LADL system of electronic dictionaries (DELA)[7] covers standard vocabulary as well as a large number of technical terms, and contains information limited to inflectional morphology. There are currently DELA dictionaries available for 20 languages[8], the essential components of which are the DELAS[9] dictionary, which describes simple words, and the DELAC[10] dictionary, which describes multiword units. For example, here is a typical entry from the English DELAS electronic dictionary:

```
abdicator,N+FLX=TABLE+Hum
```

This lexical entry describes the fact that the ALU *abdicator* is a noun that is inflected according to the TABLE paradigm (+FLX=TABLE), that is, inflected like the word *table*, which takes -*s* in the plural, and corresponds to a human noun (+Hum). Here is an example of an entry in the English DELAC dictionary:

```
absentee voter,N+XN+Hum+FLX=TABLE
```

Here too, the lexical entry is associated with a series of codes: N for "noun"; the structure XN, meaning that the multiword unit ends with a noun; "Hum", meaning that this noun designates a person, and FLX=TABLE, meaning that the multiword unit inflects following the TABLE inflectional paradigm.

---

7 See [COU 90b]. The "Resources" page on the website www.nooj4nlp.net makes available to the public NooJ modules for automatic text analysis in twenty languages, most of which contain a DELA dictionary. Henceforth I will use NooJ notation and formatting, though the DELA dictionaries were originally designed for use with the Intex software platform; see intex.univ-fcomte.fr [SIL 93a].
8 There are also dictionaries of technical terms in DELAC/NooJ, format; see for example [AOU 07], as well as dictionaries of proper names, for example [GRO 02].
9 See [AOU 07] for the French DELAS, [TRO 12] for the French NooJ dictionary, [KLA 91] for the English DELAS, and [MON 14] for the NooJ English dictionary.
10 See [SIL 90] for the French DELAC and [CHR 99] for the English DELAC.

The English DELAS dictionary contains more than 150,000 entries, while the English DELAC dictionary contains around 60,000.

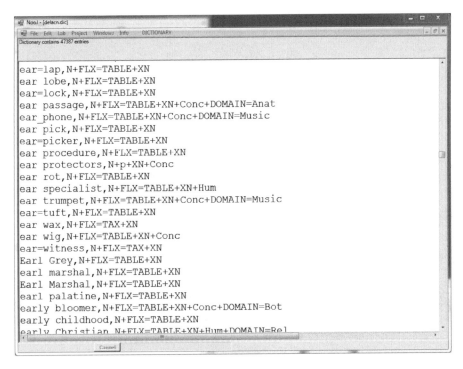

Figure 4.4. *Extract from DELAC dictionary (Nouns)*

4.3. Dubois and Dubois-Charlier electronic dictionaries

It is important to present the *Dictionnaire électronique des mots* (DEM) [DUB 10] [*Electronic Dictionary of Words*] and *Les verbes français* (LVF) [DUB 97] [*The French Verbs*] dictionaries by Dubois and Dubois-Charlier, even though they concern only the French language, because these two dictionaries, recently published and available to the public [SAB 13][11], represent the best attempt to formalize the vocabulary of a language to date:

---

11 See also the Internet links in the references.

– each lexical entry corresponds to one and only one vocabulary element; if a word has multiple meanings, each meaning is represented by a different lexical entry;

– each lexical entry is associated with a set of morphological properties (inflectional and derivational), syntactic properties (characterization of complements), and semantic properties (semantic category and domain).

4.3.1. *The Dictionnaire électronique des mots*

The *DEM* contains 145,135 entries.

```
                                    Nooj - [DEM v13.dic]                              – □ ×
 File   Edit   Lab   Project   Windows   Info       DICTIONARY                        – ₽ x
 Dictionary contains 111858 entries

Entrée           C...  Emp  FLX        DRV  G..  SynSem    DOM     CONT            OP     OP1    SENS
égalitairement   ADV                                      "SOC"   "adhér adv"     "st"   "C1g-" "d faç visant égalité"
égalitarisme     N          M_S             m   Nanime    "POL"   "adhér à N"     "syst" "C1g-" "égalité soc complète"
égalitariste     A          S_0             -   N+Hum     "POL"   "N q adhér"     "adp"  "U2b1" "pr égalitarisme"
égalité          N     01   F_S         f       Nanime    "RLA"   "rli qn p N"    "syn"  "U1a2" "parité etr humains"
égalité          N     02   F_S         f       Nanime    "POL"   "rli qn p N"    "syn"  "U1a2" "égal jurid etr citoyens"
égalité          N     03   F_S         f       Nanime    "MAT"   "val x p N"     "calc" "H3f1" "égal qc/qn en nbr"
égalité          N     04   F_S         f       Nanime    "RLA"   "rli qc p N"    "tech" "U3a1" "plan,uni d qc"
égard            N          M_S             m   Nanime    "SOC"   "éprouver N"    "sent" "P1j-" "considération,estime"
égards           N          M_PL+M_PL       m   Nanime    "SOC"   "f preuve N"    "car"  "H2a1" "marques d déférence"
égaré            A     01   S_E             -       "PSY"   "éprouv adj"    "ql"   "cv"   "affolé,hagard"
égaré            A     02   S_E             -       "LOC"   "preuve adj"    "st"   "c"    "(qn)q a perdu chemin"
égaré            A     03   S_E             -       "RLG"   "appart adj"    "st"   "c"    "(grp)hrs voie relig"
égarement        N          M_S             m   Nanime    "PSY"   "éprouver N"    "sent" "P1j-" "folie,déraison"
égayant          A          S_E             -       "PSYt"  "f épro adj"    "ql"   "cvt"  "q égaie,amusant"
égayement        N          M_S             m   Nanime    "PSY"   "éprouver N"    "sent" "P1j-" "joie"
égéen            A     01   S_DE            -   N+Hum     "REGm"  "N q orig d"    "hab"  "L1a1" "Egée (Grèce)"
égéen            N     02   M_SG            m   Nanime    "LAN"   "parler N"      "idio" "C1a3" "grec Egée anc"
égéide           A          S_0             -   N+Hum     "GREm"  "N q dirige"    "tit"  "H2i2" "descendant de Egée"
égérie           N          F_S         f       "PSYt"  "N q f épro"    "sent" "P2a1" "inspiratrice"
égermage         N          M_S             m   Nanime    "CUL"   "dmu qc p N"    "tech" "N3b1" "d égermer"
égesta           N          M_S             m   Nanime    "BIO"   "organe N"      "phys" "U3a1" "matiàres non absorbées"
égide            N          F_S         f       Nanime    "GRE"   "mun qn d N"    "arme" "N1a2" "bouclier d'Athéna"
égidien          A          S_DE            -       "ECN"   "val adj"       "st"   "cn"   "(pièce)comte d Toulouse"
éginète          A          S_0             -   N+Hum     "GREm"  "N q rési à"    "hab"  "L1a1" "Egine"
éginétique       A          S_0             -       "GEG"   "struct adj"    "st"   "cn"   "d Egine"
églantier        N          M_S             m   Nanime    "SYL"   "cultiv N"      "arb"  "R3a1" "rosacée,rosier sauvage"
églantine        N          F_S         f       Nanime    "BOT"   "organe N"      "org"  "U3a1" "fleur d'églantier"
églefin          N          M_S             m   Animal    "PIS"   "an mov eau"    "qadi" "M1a1" "gadidé,morue,cabillaud"
églestonite      N          F_S         f       Nanime    "GEL"   "extrac N d"    "sol"  "E3c-" "oxychlorure mercure"
                  Cancel
```

Figure 4.5. *Le Dictionnaire électronique des mots*

Each entry in the *DEM* is associated with the following seven properties[12]:

– CAT: syntactic category, for example Adverb, Verb, etc. This information also represents distribution for nouns and adjectives; for

---

12 I have replaced each original code with a more understandable English code.

example "masculine, human noun". In addition, CAT can have a double value: Noun + Adjective, for example for the entries *artist* [artist/artistic] or *plastic* [plastic]. This means that we do not have to duplicate a vocabulary element, and therefore fulfills the needs of the "1 ALU = 1 lexical entry" constraint. The *DEM* contains 7,043 adverbs, 12 conjunctions, 1,178 interjections, 17,138 verbs, 21,793 adjectives, 13,836 entries with the double function of being a Noun and an Adjective and 84,135 nouns.

– USE: when a word has multiple meanings, these are distinguished and numbered, and each use is described by a separate lexical entry. Here again, the dictionary complies with our requirement for "1 ALUs = 1 lexical entry". For example, the most ambiguous word described in the *DEM* is the word *blanc* [white], with 14 lexical entries.

– SYNONYMS: one or more synonymous terms or expressions, which help linguists in distinguishing between the different uses of a word.

– DOM: the semantic domain of the entry. 122 domains are given; for example "ALI" (Alimentation) or "MED" (Medicine). DOM also gives information about language style of (familiar, for example) and regionalisms (such as Canadian French).

– CONT: prototypical semantico-syntactic schema of the term. For example, the noun *boulanger* [baker] is associated with the schema "N q exerce" [N whose job is to], which corresponds to the schema associated with around 1,000 nouns of profession, while the adjective *fiable* [reliable] is associated with the schema "preuve adj" [prooves adj] associated with around 2,000 qualifying adjectives such as *bon* [good], *boiteux* [lame], *brillant* [bright], etc.

– CLASS: completes the CONT field by adding specialized information. For example, the noun *désespoir* [despair] is associated with the CONT property "éprouver N" [to feel N] and the CLASS code "sent" associated with around 2,000 sentiment [feeling] nouns.

– CLASSV: semantic class of the verb typically associated with the entry. For example, the noun *pizza* is associated with CLASSV="S3j", which contains around 200 "eat" verbs, such as *avaler* [swallow], *bouffer* [gobble], *croquer* [crunch], *manger* [eat], *picorer* [nibble], etc.; see the CLASSV field in the *Les Verbes Français* dictionary in Figure 4.6.

4.3.2. *Les Verbes Français (LVF)*

The *Les Verbes Français* (*LVF*) [*The French Verbs*] dictionary contains 25,609 entries.

Entrée	Catégorie	Emploi	DOMAINE	AUX	FLX	SynSem	LEXI
abaisser	V	01	LOC	AVOIR	CHANTER	T1308+P3008	2
abaisser	V	02	TEC	AVOIR	CHANTER	T13g0+P30g0	2
abaisser	V	03	QUA	AVOIR	CHANTER	T1306+P3006	2
abaisser	V	04	MON	AVOIR	CHANTER	T1306+P3006	2
abaisser	V	05	MED	AVOIR	CHANTER	T1308+P3008	5
abaisser	V	06	PSYt	AVOIR	CHANTER	T1108+P1000	5
abaisser	V	07	PSY	AVOIR	CHANTER	P10a0	5
abaisser	V	08	VEH	AVOIR	CHANTER	P3001	5
abaisser	V	09	PSY	AVOIR	CHANTER	P10a0+T11a0	5
abalourdir	V	-	PSYt	AVOIR	FINIR	P1000+T9106	6
abandonner	V	01	DRO	AVOIR	CHANTER	T13a0	1
abandonner	V	02	MAR	AVOIR	CHANTER	T13a8+P30a8	5
abandonner	V	03	EQU	AVOIR	CHANTER	T1300	5
abandonner	V	04	PSY	AVOIR	CHANTER	T1300	1
abandonner	V	05	SOC	AVOIR	CHANTER	T1300+A10	1
abandonner	V	06	SPO	AVOIR	CHANTER	T1300+A10	1
abandonner	V	07	COM	AVOIR	CHANTER	T13k0	5
abandonner	V	08	SOC	AVOIR	CHANTER	T1307	5
abandonner	V	09	LOC	AVOIR	CHANTER	T1101	5
abandonner	V	10	SOC	AVOIR	CHANTER	T1300+A10	5
abandonner	V	11	SOC	AVOIR	CHANTER	T3100	5
abandonner	V	12	PSY	AVOIR	CHANTER	P10a0	5
abandonner	V	13	LANt	AVOIR	CHANTER	P1006	5

Figure 4.6. *Les Verbes Français dictionary*

Each entry in the *LVF* dictionary is associated with the following eleven properties:

– USE: when a verb has multiple uses, these are distinguished from one another and each use is described by a separate lexical entry. For example, the entry "*abaisser 06*" [to humiliate] represents a different ALU from that of "*abaisser 01*" [to lower]. Here again, the principle "1 ALU = 1 lexical entry" is followed.

– DOMAIN: the semantic domain of the ALU (for example "POL" for politics). As in the *DEM*, the domain is sometimes associated with a style of language. For example, the DOM code "SOCt" represents the domain of sociology with a literary style, as in *un malheur s'abat sur la famille* [a tragedy struck the family].

– CLASS: the semantic class of the ALU, for example "P1c" for psychological verbs with human subjects expressing mental activity, as in: *On s'accommode de la situation* [one adapts to the situation], *ils bavent d'envie* [they're drooling with envy], *il blanchit de colère* [he turned white with rage].

– SEMANTICS: syntactico-semantic schema describing the predicative structure of the ALU. For example, the ALU *"accorder 07"*, as found in *Joe accorde sa confiance à Lea* [Joe places his trust in Lea] is described by the schema "dat abs A qn": "dat" denotes dative predicates, "abs" describes abstract complements, "A" the preposition *à*, and "qn" human complements.

– SYNONYMS: one or more verbs synonymous with the lexical entry. This field helps linguists differentiate between the different uses of a verb.

– EXAMPLE: one or more examples of use of the ALU.

– CONJUGATION: the conjugation model of the verb as well as its auxiliary verb. For example, the verb *acheter* [to buy] is associated with the code "1jZ": a verb from the first group (1), subtype "j" (representing the addition of the grave accent in *il achète*), and takes the auxiliary verb *avoir* in transitive structures and the auxiliary verb *être* in pronominal structures (code "Z"): *il a acheté un livre* [he bought a book]; *il s'est acheté un livre* [he bought himself a book].

– SYNTAX: the characteristic syntactic construction(s) of the ALU. For example, the unit "admirer 02" from *Lea admire un tableau* [Lea admires a painting] is associated with the construction "T1306": direct transitive structure (T), human subject (1), the direct object complement is a thing (3), there is no prepositional complement (0), a circumstantial modality is accepted (6), for example *Lea admire beaucoup ce tableau* [Lea admires this painting a lot].

– DERIVATION: this field describes four potential nominal and/or adjectival derivational paradigms of the ALU. For example, the aforementioned unit "admirer 02" is associated with the derivational code "--RBRB-" which represents the only two derivations: *admiration*, *admirateur* [admirer].

– NOUN: possible indication of the noun from which the verb was constructed. For example, for the entry "agoniser 01", NOUN = "3e", which means that the verb *agoniser* [to agonize] is taken from the noun *agonie* [agony] (its base nominal form is obtained by erasing its last 3 letters and adding an "e").

– LEVEL: language level. For example, the entry "abattre 01" from *Joe a abattu un arbre* [Joe felled a tree] belongs to standard vocabulary (code "1"), while the entry "abattre 05" from *Ils ont abattu l'avion avec un missile* [they shot down the plane with a missile] belongs to technical vocabulary (code "5").

4.4. Specifications for the construction of an electronic dictionary

A dictionary designed to formalize the vocabulary of a language must list and describe in a unified manner all the vocabulary elements; that is, the four types of ALU: affixes, simple words, multiword units, and expressions. Ideally, such a dictionary must have coverage similar to those of the DELA dictionaries, contain the syntactic information given in Lexicon-Grammar tables, and the derivational and semantic information of the Dubois and Dubois-Charlier dictionaries.

Unfortunately, the DELAC dictionaries for English are far from being complete; lexicon-grammar tables for English remain to be created, and there are simply no equivalents of the Dubois and Dubois-Charlier dictionaries for English.

In the next section I will describe the specifications of the ideal English electronic dictionary, basing my description on the DELA English dictionaries that have already been constructed and I will discuss how such a dictionary could be used by NLP applications.

4.4.1. *One ALU = one lexical entry*

> Each entry in an electronic dictionary must correspond to one (and only one) vocabulary element: an ALU.

Like lexicon-grammars and the dictionaries of Dubois and Dubois-Charlier, an electronic dictionary must describe each element of vocabulary using one and only one lexical entry.

Homographs are separate elements of vocabulary that are spelled in the same way. Some homographs are related by morphological, metaphorical, or etymological relationships; for example the verb *to hit* (as in *Apple will hit a post-split $100 per share*) is probably linked by a metaphorical relationship to the verb *to hit* (in *Lea hit Ida with a ball*). For our project, these two uses must be treated as independent from one another. More generally, if a "word" has multiple meanings, it corresponds to multiple vocabulary elements and must therefore be described by multiple lexical entries.

4.4.2. *Importance of derivation*

> An electronic dictionary must link each lexical entry to its derived forms.

Forms derived from an ALU must not be described separately from one another. Therefore, it would be absolutely necessary to add to the electronic dictionary a formalization of derivations (which is not done in DELA dictionaries). For example, we must have a single lexical entry to describe the verb *to demonstrate*, the abstract noun *a demonstration* and the human noun *a demonstrator*. In this way we can link the sentences:

> *There were a lot of people demonstrating against the war*
> *= There were a lot of demonstrators against the war*
> *= A lot of people had a demonstration against the war.*

In the NooJ system, this lexical entry would be associated with its derived forms in the following way:

```
demonstrate,V+FLX=ATE+DRV=ATION:TABLE+DRV=ATOR:TABLE
```

This entry represents the vocabulary element *to demonstrate*, which is a verb (V), conjugates according to the model ATE (+FLX=ATE)[13], and which is used to derive *demonstration* (+DRV=ATION:TABLE) and *demonstrator* (+DRV=ATOR:TABLE); these two derived forms themselves inflect according to the TABLE model (taking an *-s* in plural form).

---

13 We will see how FLX and DRV paradigms are implemented in Chapter 11.

Addressing derivation makes it possible to construct sophisticated NLP applications; for example, a search engine able to find in a text all the occurrences of the ALU *to demonstrate*, including when this linguistic unit appears in the forms *demonstrating, demonstration,* or *demonstrators.*

Note, however, the limitations of derivation that we discussed in section 3.2.3: derived forms that have become autonomous (e.g. *globalization*) must be described by separate lexical entries.

4.4.3. *Orthographic variation*

> An electronic dictionary must address the spelling variants of each ALU by linking them, either by rules or explicitly.

An electronic dictionary must link together all of the spelling variants that a given ALU may take in texts, either using rules in the case of productive alternations, or explicitly in the case of idiosyncratic variations. NooJ uses several conventions, in particular regarding the use of case (lower-case/upper-case), hyphens, and separators. For example, in the following entry from a NooJ dictionary:

```
john,N+FLX=TABLE
```

the word *john* is written in lower-case to represent the common noun *a john*, which can appear in both lower-case and upper-case, and both singular and plural. The six forms below are therefore recognized by NooJ:

john, johns, John, Johns, JOHN, JOHNS

Conversely, the following lexical entry:

```
John,FIRSTNAME+m+s
```

is entered in capitals to represent the masculine first name, which can only appear with the first letter capitalized, and only in singular form. Thus, only the two forms *John* and *JOHN* are represented by this lexical entry.

We must also be able to force the case of a term. For example, the lexical entry below:

```
"dnaC",TERM+s
```

represents only the orthographic form "dnaC"; neither the form "DNAC", nor the form "dnac", nor any other form will be recognized by NooJ.

There are also regular variations of the use of spaces and hyphens. For example, consider the following entries from a NooJ dictionary:

```
audio_visual,A
Advocate=General,N
```

The special character "_" represents alternation between agglutination (e.g. *audiovisual*), hyphenation (e.g. *audio-visual*), and spacing (e.g. *audio visual*). The special character "=" represents alternation between hyphenation (e.g. *Advocate-General*) and spacing (e.g. *Advocate General*). The two lexical entries above link all of these orthographic variants to their corresponding ALU. The two special characters "_" and "=" guarantee that each ALU is described by a single lexical entry; thus there is a biunivocal correspondence between vocabulary elements and dictionary entries, while taking orthographic variation into account.

Sometimes it is not possible to use rules to unify the variants of an ALU. In this case the variants are linked explicitly. For example, Google Search produces around 600,000 results for the request "tzar", but almost 17 million for the request "czar". The four variants *csar*, *czar*, *tsar*, and *tzar* can be linked as follows:

```
tsar,N+FLX=INAS
csar,tsar,N+FLX=INAS
czar,tsar,N+FLX=INAS
tzar,tsar,N+FLX=INAS
```

This notation represents the fact that the single ALU is represented by the lexical entry *tsar*, while the other lexical entries are not separate ALUs but rather alternate forms of the same ALU. Thanks to these lexical entries, all the inflected forms of all the variants (for example *czarina*) will be analyzed as occurrences of the ALU *tsar*.

4.4.4. *Inflection of simple words, compound words, and expressions*

> An electronic dictionary must address, simply and in a unified manner, the inflection and derivation of simple words, multiword units, and expressions.

An ideal electronic dictionary would make it possible to describe the inflection and derivation of lexical entries using a unified mechanism[14]. For example, NooJ includes the two lexical entries:

```
campaign,N+FLX=TABLE
presidential campaign,N+FLX=TABLE
```

The TABLE inflection model is identical for the simple noun *campaign* and the compound noun *presidential campaign*: in both cases, an "s" is added to the lexical entry to produce the plural form[15].

The situation is different for multiword units that contain several inflecting components. Consider the following three lexical entries:

```
farmer,N+FLX=TABLE
gentleman,A+FLX=MAN
gentleman farmer,N+FLX=TABLE<P>MAN
```

To inflect the compound noun *gentleman farmer*, we first apply the TABLE inflectional model (i.e. we add an "s" to create the plural) to inflect *farmer*, and then we apply the MAN model (replacing "an" with "en" to create the plural) to inflect *gentleman*. NooJ automatically takes into account the mandatory agreement between the two components to block incorrect forms such as "gentlemen farmer"[16].

---

14 For technical reasons, the inflection of multiword units in DELAC was not integrated with those of simple words in DELAS. [SIL 93a] describes the procedure for the inflection of the DELAC dictionary.

15 Inflectional and derivational models are described in section 11.3.

16 The "Check Agreement" option makes it possible to automatically eliminate forms whose constituents do not agree. It is not always necessary to activate this function; for example the compound noun *master of illusion* can take four forms: *a master of illusion, a master of illusions, masters of illusion, masters of illusions*.

4.4.5. *Expressions*

| An electronic dictionary must contain expressions.

An electronic dictionary must necessarily manage all types of ALU, including discontinuous expressions. Consider, for example, the predicative noun *class*, which is used with the light verb *to take* to form the expression *to take a class*. In a NooJ dictionary, this expression is described based on the following lexical entry[17]:

```
class,N+FXC+NPred1+VSup="take"
```

The feature +FXC means that the entry *class* described here is not an independent word, but rather a non-autonomous constituent of an expression; in other words, that this lexical entry must be taken into account only in a certain context described by a syntactic grammar. The syntactic grammar uses then the feature +NPred1 to verify that the entry corresponds to the object complement of the light verb, as well as the property +Vsup="take" (to verify the value of the light verb).

This verification mechanism is the same as the one used for so-called "free" verbs. For example, when a syntactic analysis is made of a sentence containing the ALU *to run* associated in the dictionary with the feature +i (intransitive), we apply a grammar in which the feature +i disables the presence of a direct object complement. This verification makes it possible to analyze the sentence *She will run Monday* while preventing the term *Monday* from being analyzed as a direct object complement of the verb *to run*.

4.4.6. *Integration of syntax and semantics*

We saw in section 4.3.1.1 that words with multiple meanings or uses must be described with multiple lexical entries. For example, consider the five uses of the verb *abriter* described in the French dictionary *LVF*:

– abriter1 (T11b8, P10b8): *Joe abrite Lea de la pluie avec un parapluie*

---

17 See for example [SIL 08] for the formalization in NooJ of French frozen expressions; [VIE 08] for the formalization of Italian frozen expressions; and [MAC 12] for the formalization of English phrasal verbs.

[Joe shields Lea from the rain with an umbrella]

– abriter2 (T1101, P1001): *Lea abrite des réfugiés chez elle*

[Lea shelters refugees in her home]

– abriter3 (T3100): *Cet immeuble abrite les services du ministère*

[This building houses the Ministry's offices]

– abriter4 (P10b1): *Joe s'abrite des ennuis derrière ses supérieurs*

[Joe hides behind his superiors]

– abriter5 (T13b8): *On abrite le port des vagues avec des digues*

[The city protects the harbor from the surf with a dike]

Each of these uses is associated with different syntactic structures: for use no. 1, for example, T11b8 represents a transitive syntactic construction (T), with a human subject and a human direct object complement (11) and a tool as a prepositional complement (b8). For use no. 3, T3100 represents a transitive syntactic construction with a non-human subject and a human direct object complement (T31), etc.

Here is the NooJ dictionary lexical entry corresponding to the first use:

```
abaisser,V+EMP=01+DOM=LOC+AUX=AVOIR+FLX=CHANTER
+CLASS=T3c+T1308+P3008+LEX=2+DRV=BASE1+DRV=ABLE+DRV=MENT
+DRV=EUR+OPER="r/d bas qc"
```

abaisser is a verb (V) for which the entry describes one of its uses (EMP=01); this is a locative use (DOM=LOC) belonging to class T3c which corresponds to the semantic schema "r/d bas qc" ("*on rend quelque chose bas*"). The verb is conjugated using the *chanter* model (FLX=CHANTER) with the auxiliary verb *avoir* (AUX=AVOIR). It falls within both of the following syntactic constructions:

T3108: Human Subject + Verb + Inanimate Object + Instrumental adverb
P3008: Inanimate Subject + Reflexive Verb + Instrumental adverb

This verb takes three derivations: the verb *abaissable* (DRV=ABLE), the noun *abaissement* (DRV=MENT), and the noun *abaisseur* (DRV=EUR). The verb is also associated with the noun *abaisse*, which is part of the base French vocabulary (LEX=2).

In the *LVF* dictionary, each entry is associated with one or more syntactic constructions:

– A: pure intransitive constructions;

– N: intransitive constructions with prepositional complement;

– P: pronominal constructions;

– T: direct transitive constructions.

For example, Figure 4.7 shows an extract from NooJ grammar T, which addresses direct transitive constructions.

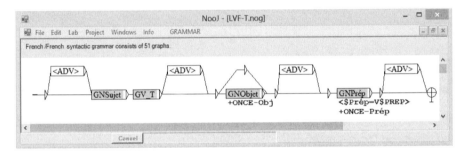

Figure 4.7. *T grammar of constructions*

We will look at syntactic analysis in Chapter 12. By applying the *LVF* dictionary together with grammar T to a corpus of 7,000 articles taken from the newspaper *Le monde diplomatique*, we get the following concordance[18]:

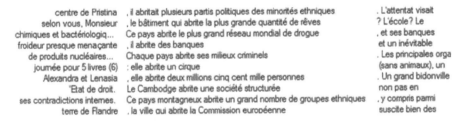

Figure 4.8. *Occurrences of the verb* abriter
in a direct transitive construction (T)

18 The incorporation of the dictionary *Les Verbes Français* into NooJ, as well as the construction of corresponding morphological and syntactic grammars, is described in [SIL 15].

Here we see occurrences of use *abriter3*, while the uses *abriter1*, *abriter2* and *abriter5* are excluded since they require prepositional complements that are not present in the sentences found. Likewise, if we apply grammar P, we get the complementary concordance shown in Figure 4.9.

première fois aussi	. le premier ministre israélien ne s'abrita pas derrière les slogans traditionnels	- "Jérusalem u
désarmé. En Europe	. il s'abrite derrière les pressions exercées	par le Luxemb
la corruption endémique.	Les responsables politiques s'abritent derrière le carcan traditionnel	des "valeurs a
prend pas parti.	Il s'abrite derrière sa tâche d'homme	de théâtre qui
dissimuler le fond	. il s'abrite en général derrière des considérations de forme.	et remet tout
système financier international.	Il s'abrite derrière le contentieux colonial,	dont il exige
à visage découvert	. ils s'abritent derrière des notables traditionnels	qui les utilisent

Figure 4.9. *Occurrences of the verb "abriter" in a pronominal construction (P)*

This time use *abriter2* is recognized, while use *abriter1* (P10b8) and use *abriter4* (P10b1) are excluded because there is no *de* prepositional complement in these sentences.

Readers can appreciate the qualitative difference between a search engine that looks up orthographic forms and an application that would use a formalized description of the vocabulary, capable of finding unambiguous vocabulary elements (ALU) using their morphological, syntactic, and semantic properties.

4.5. Conclusion

To formalize the vocabulary of a language, it is necessary to construct an electronic dictionary that implements a biunivocal correspondence between an ALU and a lexical entry, which requires a dictionary capable of integrating the morphological, syntactic, and semantic properties of each ALU. Such a dictionary could be used by revolutionary NLP applications to distinguish between the various meanings of each word.

No electronic dictionary able to formalize the standard English vocabulary and available to all currently exists. However, the experiments conducted for French in the 1990s prove that constructing such a dictionary is quite possible[19].

4.6. Exercises

1) In a dictionary, read the definitions associated with the nouns *appogiatura*, *banjo*, *castrate*, *diaphone*, and *electro-pop*. Is there any explicit information in the definition of these terms that would allow us to automatically extract them, as well as any musical term, while rejecting all non-musical terms?

2) In a dictionary, read the definitions associated with the verbs *to alienate someone*, *to bother someone*, *to confuse someone*, *to discourage someone*, and *to enrage someone*. Is there any information in the definitions of these terms that would allow us to automatically extract these verbs, as well as all the semantically similar verbs; that is, the verbs that express that someone or something is producing a psychological effect on a person?

3) Identify and describe the fifteen ALUs potentially present in the sentence: *This Attorney General threw out the results of the electoral vote.*

4.7. Internet links

Non-specialized editorial dictionaries are available on the Internet:

– *American Heritage Dictionary*: www.ahdictionary.com

– *Collins Cobuild Dictionary*: www. mycobuild.com

– *Merriam-Webster Unabridged Dictionary*: unabridged. merriam-webster.com

– *Oxford English Dictionary*: www.oed.com

---

19 I estimate that it would take a staff of five linguists five years to complete this project. Perhaps in the foreseeable future, organizations or companies such as the National Science Foundation, National Institutes of Health, Linguistic Data Consortium, Google, Microsoft, or Apple will understand the advantages of, and fund such a complete formalization of the English vocabulary.

– Wiktionary: en.wiktionary.org

– WORDNET: wordnet.princeton.edu

The Proteus project website at nlp.cs.nyu.edu/projects contains lexical resources that can be used by NLP applications.

The French *DEM* and *LVF* dictionaries by Jean Dubois and Françoise Dubois-Charlier can be downloaded from the website: www.modyco.fr.

Electronic dictionaries in NooJ format are available on the "Resources" page of the NooJ website: www.nooj4nlp.net.

PART 2

Languages, Grammars and Machines

We have seen how to formalize the base elements of language: the letters and characters that constitute the alphabet of a language, and the Atomic Linguistic Units (ALUs) that constitute its vocabulary. I have shown in particular that it is necessary to distinguish the concept of an ALU from that of a *word form*: ALUs are elements of vocabulary (affixes, simple and multiword units, and expressions); they are represented by entries in an electronic dictionary, and are the objects around which phrases and sentences are constructed.

We turn now to the mechanisms used to combine the base linguistic units with one another. Combining letters, prefixes, or suffixes to construct word forms uses morphological rules, while combining ALUs to construct phrases or sentences uses syntactic rules. Note that unifying the types of ALUs has freed us from the arbitrary limits imposed by the use of space delimiters, and so it is all of a language's rules (both morphological and syntactic) that constitute its grammar. This part of the book is dedicated to the study of grammars.

In his seminal book, [CHO 57] first posed the problem of the formalization of grammars and their adequacy for describing natural languages. The study of formal grammars and of the machines that implement them is part of the standard curriculum of computer science departments in universities today.

In Chapter 5, I will define the base concepts (language, grammar, machine) and then present the four types of grammars that make up the Chomsky-Schützenberger hierarchy. Each of the chapters after that will be dedicated to types of languages/grammars/machines: regular grammars (Chapter 6), context-free grammars (Chapter 7), context-sensitive grammars (Chapter 8), and unrestricted grammars (Chapter 9).

Languages, Grammars, and Machines

In this chapter I will define the theoretical base concepts *alphabet*, *language*, *grammar*, and *machine*, and then introduce the four types of grammars that make up the Chomsky-Schützenberger hierarchy introduced by [CHO 57].

5.1. Definitions

5.1.1. *Letters and alphabets*

We begin by defining the smallest possible units.

The term *alphabet* designates any finite set of elements. These elements are called the *letters* of the alphabet.

For example, the following set:

$$\Sigma = \{a, e, i, o, u\}$$

is an alphabet that contains 5 letters. Likewise, the set Σ_F below:

$$\Sigma_F = \{a, b, c, d, e, f, g, h, i, j, k, l,$$
$$m, n, o, p, q, r, s, t, u, v, w, x, y, z,$$
$$à, â, ä, ç, é, è, ê, ë, î, ï, ô, ö, ù, û, ü\}$$

is an alphabet that contains 41 letters[1]. All written languages use an alphabet of finite size[2], and there are simple techniques for transcribing non-written languages, for example using a phonetic alphabet or one composed of symbols[3].

5.1.2. *Words and languages*

Using a given alphabet, we can construct sequences composed of a finite number of letters; these sequences are called *words*. Any set of words is called a *language*.

| A *language* is a set of *words* constructed using an *alphabet*.

Here is a language constructed using the alphabet Σ_F above:

```
{"love", "loves", "loving", "loved"}
```

This language contains four words[4].

5.1.3. *ALU, vocabularies, phrases, and languages*

The terms *alphabet*, *letter*, and *word* are well suited for typographical, orthographic, and morphological descriptions, while we use the corresponding terms *vocabulary*, *ALU*, and *sentence* for syntactic and semantic description. In syntax, we would say:

| A *vocabulary* is a finite set of ALUs. A *language* is a set of
| *sentences* constructed using a *vocabulary*.

---

1 This alphabet constitutes an approximation of the French alphabet, to which we should add the ligatures (for example "œ") and foreign letters (for example "ñ") often found in French journalistic texts, as well as the corresponding capital letters.
2 Nevertheless some alphabets are very large – for example the traditional Chinese alphabet contains more than 100,000 characters.
3 The international phonetic alphabet (IPA) contains around 100 characters, while the dactylological alphabet used to transcribe French sign language (FSL) and American sign language (ASL) contains 26 signs.
4 Henceforth I will use quotation marks to distinguish words that contain only one letter (for example "a" is a determiner) from the letters themselves (for example *a* is the first letter of the alphabet).

Here is an example of vocabulary:

Σ_V = {cat, dog, the, sees}

The vocabulary Σ_V contains four ALUs. The entire set of correct English sentences that can be constructed from vocabulary Σ_V is the following language:

{"the cat sees", "the cat sees the cat", "the cat sees the dog", "the dog sees", "the dog sees the cat", "the dog sees the dog"}

Languages may be infinite in size, as we saw in Chapter 1. For example, based on alphabet Σ_F, we could define the language containing all the words (not necessarily English) that contains only vowels:

{"a", "eu", "éééé", "ouuuuuuie", "ouou", "aïeaïeaieaïe", …}

The word "aaaaaaaaaaaaaaa" is part of this language, while the word "aaabaaaa" is not. This language is infinite in size since it is impossible to limit the length of its words, even though each of the words in the language is finite in size.

5.1.4. *Empty string*

There is a particular word called an *empty string*. The empty string does not contain any letter; in other words, it has a length of zero. In computer programming languages, the empty string is written as "", while mathematicians and some linguists write it as ε; in this book I will use the NooJ notation: <E>.

| The *empty string* is a word composed of 0 letters.

Be careful not to confuse the empty language (that is, a set containing no words), written as { } or Ø, the empty string <E> (which is a word, not a language), and the language {<E>} which is the set containing one element: the empty string.

5.1.5. *Free language*

The language containing all the words that can be constructed over an alphabet Σ is called the free language, is infinite in size and is written as Σ^*. For example, using the English alphabet Σ_E, the following language can be constructed:

```
ΣE* = {<E>, "a", "b", "c", …, "z", "aa", "ab", "ac",
…, "à", "ba", "bb", "bc", …, "ca",… , "zz", "aaa",
"aab", … , "zzz", "loves", …, "zero", …}
```

The empty string <E> is an element of the language Σ_E^*.

Likewise, the language containing all the sentences (even grammatically incorrect ones) that can be constructed using the aforementioned vocabulary Σ_V is called the free language, and is infinite in size:

```
ΣV* = {"sees", "dog sees", "the sees cat", "cat cat
dog", "the", "dog", "dog the sees cat the cat dog
dog", "the the dog dog cat sees sees the sees", …}
```

In linguistics, we are more interested in subsets of free languages – for example the subset of Σ_E^* that contains only orthographically correct forms, or the subset of Σ_V^* that contains only well-formed sentences.

5.1.6. *Grammars*

Defining a set means being able to characterize all its elements: being able to prove whether or not an element belongs to this set on the one hand, and being able to produce each of its elements at will on the other. The objective of the project described in this book is to define a language containing all linguistically correct sentences. To define a language of finite size we could inventory all its elements, which poses no problem in theory[5]. On the other hand, to describe a language of infinite size, we must construct

---

5 However, if the number of elements is too large, it is preferable to treat the language as if it were infinite. Thus we could limit the linguistic project to the characterization of all sentences containing a maximum of fifty words. In English, there are around 200,000 word forms, so it would be necessary to verify the grammatical correctness of around $200,000^{50}$ sentences (that is approximately 10^{265}). But this number – which is much higher than the number of atoms in the universe: 10^{80} – is much too large for an exhaustive inventory to be feasible.

a system capable of recognizing whether a given text sequence belongs to the language or not (using a *parser*) and capable of producing any sentence in the language at will (using a *generator*). Such a system relies on the *grammar* of a language.

> A *grammar* is a set of rules that can be used to recognize the sentences of a language as well as to produce any sentence of the language at will.

It is a matter, then, of defining a set of rules that can be used both to characterize each correct sentence (for example to verify whether a sequence of ALUs is well formed or not), and to produce any correct sentence at will.

5.1.7. *Machines*

Machines are devices that process data (as input) and automatically produce results (as output). For example, a scale produces a measurement of weight according to the pressure put on its pan; a calculator produces the result of a calculation according to the numbers and operations that have been entered, etc. In this case, we want to construct a "linguistic machine" – that is, a machine capable of recognizing automatically whether a sentence belongs to a given language or not, and also of automatically producing all of the sentences in this language.

In more prosaic terms, if we provide a sequence of ALUs as input to a machine designed to recognize a given language, this machine will produce a binary result as output (for example "YES" or "NO") to indicate whether or not this sequence belongs to this language.

> *Joe is eating an apple* → *YES*
> *Joe an eating is apple* → *NO*

I will discuss parsers in Part 3 of this book. Conversely, a machine must be able to produce all of the sentences in the language at will, and only those sentences satisfying a series of criteria. I will discuss generators in Chapter 13.

Machines must therefore be capable of processing grammars that describe languages, and so we have a perfect correspondence between languages, grammars, and machines. Today, in practice, these machines are only rarely built[6]: their functioning is simulated using software platforms which themselves are executed by computers; in other words, the computer is a real machine which simulates linguistic machines.

5.2. Generative grammars

> A *generative grammar* is a set of *rewriting rules* composed of two sections: each left-hand section is rewritten into the right-hand section. A generative grammar contains one and only one starting symbol.

For example, Figure 5.1 shows a generative grammar composed of eight rewriting rules, and the starting symbol of which is SENTENCE:

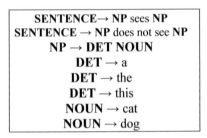

Figure 5.1. *A generative grammar*

The first rule expresses the fact that a sentence (*SENTENCE*) can be composed of a noun phrase (*NP*) followed by the ALU *sees,* and then by another noun phrase. The second rule expresses the fact that a sentence (*SENTENCE*) can be composed of a *NP* followed by the sequence of ALUs *does not see,* and then by another *NP*. The third rule expresses the fact that a *NP* can be composed of a determiner (*DET*) followed by a noun (*NOUN*). The next three rules define the determiners, and the last two rules define two nouns.

Two types of symbols may be used in both sides of each rewriting rule: *terminal symbols* representing ALUs (in this case *a, cat, does, dog, not, sees,*

---

6 In 1986 I worked at the Bull Research Center in Louveciennes on the construction of a true finite-state machine implemented in the form of a specialized integrated circuit capable of recognizing all French word forms. There are websites that simulate Turing Machines, see the Internet links at the end of the chapter.

the and *this*) and *auxiliary symbols* (in this case *SENTENCE, NP, DET,* and *NOUN*).

If we write the first auxiliary symbol of the grammar (*SENTENCE* in this case), and then arbitrarily use the grammar rules to rewrite all of the auxiliary symbols until none are left, we obtain a sequence of ALUs described by the grammar. In this case we say that the grammar has generated the sentence (hence the term *generative grammars*). For example, here is one possible generation[7]:

SENTENCE → <u>NP</u> sees NP → **DET** NOUN sees NP → <u>the </u>**NOUN** sees NP
→ the <u>cat</u> sees **NP** → the cat sees **DET** NOUN → the cat sees <u>a </u>**NOUN**
→ the cat sees a <u>dog</u>

Figure 5.2. *Generation of the sentence "the cat sees a dog"*

A sequence of applied rewritings such as the one shown above is called a *derivation.*

By choosing other derivations than the previous one, we can see that the grammar in Figure 5.1 can generate 16 sentences, thus defining the following language:

```
{"a cat sees a cat", "a cat sees a dog", "a cat
sees the cat", "a cat sees the dog", "the cat sees
a cat", "the cat sees a dog", "the cat sees the
cat", "the cat sees the dog", "a dog sees a cat",
"a dog sees a dog", "a dog sees the cat", "a dog
sees the dog", "the dog sees a cat", "the dog sees
a dog", "the dog sees the cat", "the dog sees the
dog"}
```

5.3. Chomsky-Schützenberger hierarchy

Just as we have distinguished languages of finite size from languages of infinite size, we need to distinguish between multiple types of infinite languages according to the complexity of the grammars that describe them.

---

7 Left members of the rule to be applied appear in bold, sequences that have just been produced are underlined.

The Chomsky-Schützenberger hierarchy is used to describe four types of generative grammars [CHO 57], with each type of grammar corresponding to one type of language:

– Type 3: *regular grammars* are generative grammars containing only rules in which the left-hand section is composed of one single auxiliary symbol, and the right-hand section contains either a single terminal symbol (e.g. NOUN → cat), or the empty string (e.g. NP → <E>), or a single terminal symbol followed by a single auxiliary symbol (e.g. NOUN → cat *ADJECTIVE*). Regular grammars describe *regular languages*.

The generative grammar shown in Figure 5.1 is not a regular grammar, since in the first rule, the right-hand section contains two auxiliary symbols (NP, twice);

– Type 2: context-free grammars contain rules in which the left-hand section is composed of a single auxiliary symbol and the right-hand section is any combination of terminal symbols and auxiliary symbols, for example:

SENTENCE → NP sees NP

Context-free grammars describe *context-free languages*. The grammar shown in Figure 5.1 is a context-free grammar;

– Type 1: *context-sensitive grammars* contain rules in which we can add a context to the two sections of a rule; for example the context PLURAL in the contextual rule:

PLURAL SENTENCE → PLURAL NP see NP

This rewriting rule will not touch the symbol PLURAL. It is present only to "activate" the rule and is still there after the rewriting of PLURAL SENTENCE. A context can be an auxiliary or terminal symbol and can be located on the right of the two sides of the rule, or on the left of the two sides of the rule. Context-sensitive grammars describe *context-sensitive languages*.

– Type 0: *unrestricted grammars* contain rules without any restriction; that is, with any combination of auxiliary and terminal symbols in each of their two sides. Unrestricted grammars can describe any recursively enumerable language[8].

The set of all regular languages is included in the set of all context-free languages; the set of all context-free languages is included in the set of all context-sensitive languages; and the set of all context-sensitive languages is included in the set of all recursively enumerable languages.

Likewise, all regular grammars are context-free grammars, all context-free grammars are context-sensitive grammars, and all context-sensitive grammars are unrestricted grammars[9].

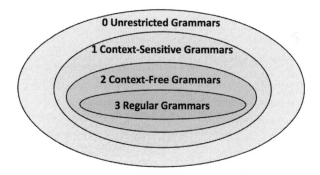

Figure 5.3. *Chomsky-Schützenberger hierarchy*

With each type of generative grammar, we associate a type of machine capable of automatically applying this grammar to verify whether a given sentence belongs to the language described by the grammar, as well as produce at will any sentence of the language described by the grammar. This gives us the following four correspondences:

– Regular grammars ⇔ Finite-state automata (FSA);

– Context-free grammars ⇔ Push-down automata (PDA);

---

8 There are languages that are not recursively enumerable, but these languages are exotic mathematical constructs that have no potential linguistic application, such as the language obtained by diagonalization of the (infinite) set of all recursively enumerable languages, see the Internet link at the end of the chapter.

9 This inclusion is also true for NooJ grammars, but it is not true for most formalisms used in NLP, as grammars written with less powerful formalisms are not compatible with more powerful formalisms (for example HPSG cannot read XFST grammars).

– Context-sensitive grammars ⇔ Linear-bounded automata (LBA);

– Unrestricted grammars ⇔ Turing machines (TM).

Any machine capable of processing unrestricted grammars is capable of processing context-sensitive grammars; any machine capable of processing context-sensitive grammars is capable of processing context-free grammars, and any machine capable of processing context-free grammars is capable of processing regular grammars.

From a computational point of view, FSA are more efficient than PDA, that are more efficient than LBA that are more efficient than TM[10].

Typically, then, it is advantageous to use regular grammars to describe the linguistic phenomena that lend themselves to it, and to use the more powerful grammars to describe linguistic phenomena that cannot be described by regular grammars.

Note that from a linguistic point of view, the question is not one of knowing what type of grammars are needed to describe all the phenomena of all natural languages (unrestricted grammars are adequate), but rather which types of grammars are best suited to describing which types of linguistic phenomena.

5.3.1. *Linguistic formalisms*

Generative grammars are simple mathematical objects; their classification is elegant, and they have been used to prove important results having to do with languages, calculability, and complexity. However, these grammars are not really adapted to the linguistic description project, because they very quickly become illegible, to the extent that the description even of trivial linguistic phenomena becomes humanly impossible.

---

10 Actually, TMs are not even good at processing recursively enumerable languages because of the halting problem: when applying an unrestricted grammar to a text, it is not always possible to predict if and when the TM will stop at one point, or if it will run forever.

For this reason, dozens of notations have been created since the 1950s for writing grammars better suited to linguistics[11]. These notations constitute *linguistic formalisms*. In general, these formalisms align more or less with the Chomsky-Schützenberger hierarchy: the best known formalisms are those of the *Xerox Finite State Tool* (XFST) for regular grammars, *Backus Naur Form* (BNR), *Yet Another Compiler Compiler* (YACC) [JHO 12][12], and *Generalized Phrase Structure Grammar* (GPSG)[13] for context-free grammars, *Lexical Functional Grammar* (LFG) [KAP 82] for context-sensitive grammars, and *Head Driven Phrase Structure Grammar* (HPSG) [POL 94] for unrestricted grammars.

In general, the higher up we go in the hierarchy of formalisms, the slower the corresponding machines become. This is probably a reason why some researchers have tried to find a "good compromise" between power and efficiency, which has given rise to "mildly context-sensitive" formalisms such as *Combinatorial Categorical Grammars* (CCGs) [MOO 97], *Head Grammars* (HGs) [POL 84], *Linear Indexed Grammars* (LIGs), and *Tree Adjoining Grammars* (TAGs)[14]. Such compromises are reasonable in the context of the construction of NLP software applications, as they make it possible to construct software applications that are rapid enough to be usable. However, the goal of the project described in this book is to formalize languages completely. Limiting the power of grammars *a priori* for the sake of efficiency does not make any sense for us.

A more reasonable scientific approach would be to use the most powerful formalism possible (for example HPSG) and to process all linguistic phenomena with this tool. This approach makes sense theoretically, but it has two drawbacks:

---

11 This situation is no different from that of programming, in which no-one programs TMs, and most programmers do not even know which language is actually used by their computer's processor. There are hundreds of programming languages today that provide programmers with functionalities suited to their needs.

12 BNR, YACC, and BISON are used to formalize programming languages and construct compilers for these languages.

13 GPSG contains a mechanism making it more powerful than context-free grammars.

14 Some users of these formalisms add functionalities (called "metagrammars", "metarules", or "metacompilers") to compensate for the inadequacies of these formalisms, which were initially deliberately limited.

– HPSG parsers are not efficient enough to be used in real conditions (it is impossible in practice to apply an HPSG grammar to large texts, in real time);

– grammars constructed with HPSG are heavy and difficult to understand, maintain, and accumulate, which makes them unsuitable for formalizing large numbers of linguistic phenomena, especially very simple ones such as orthographic variation, inflection, derivation, multiword units, etc.

An alternative solution consists of using various formalisms to describe various linguistic phenomena; for example, we would describe verb conjugation with simple regular grammars, while using context-free grammars to describe sentence structure; context-sensitive grammars to verify agreements. Unfortunately, existing formalisms are largely incompatible with one another. We cannot insert an XFST regular grammar into an LFG grammar, for example, or merge the rules of a YACC grammar with the rules of an HPSG. In practice, these linguistic formalisms force linguists to unify all descriptions – for example, to describe lexical entries like grammar rules (or even using syntactic trees), or to describe orthographic phenomena like syntactic phenomena, or even to bypass dictionaries and grammar rules all together and use only AVMs, etc.

It is precisely because any project to describe natural languages in their entirety necessarily involves the formalization of numerous and diverse linguistic phenomena that I constructed the NooJ platform.

5.4. The NooJ approach

5.4.1. *A multifaceted approach*

With NooJ, it is possible to construct regular grammars, context-free grammars, context-sensitive grammars, and unrestricted grammars. Linguists can thus use the tool best-suited for describing each linguistic phenomenon.

NooJ's multifaceted approach is scientifically justified: we do not describe the vocabulary of a language in the same way as we do its grammar; and orthographic phenomena are very different from syntactic phenomena. NooJ therefore offers different tools to process different types of linguistic phenomena. In NooJ, we have descriptions of alphabets (for example to describe ligatures or orthographic variation), dictionaries, inflectional and derivational grammars, grammars of agglutination, local syntactic grammars, structural syntactic grammars, and transformational grammars. We do not need to describe orthographic variation in Chinese with the same tool as verb conjugation in French, and agglutination in Semitic languages is not processed with the same tool as derivation in Romance languages, etc.

This multifaceted approach has the advantage of being simple, since for each type of phenomenon to be described, linguists have one or more specifically adapted tools: each description is thus more natural, and thus simpler. From a scientific point of view, this approach seems to be validated by some recent work in neurolinguistics, which tends to show that when the brain analyzes statements, different parts of the brain are activated to process different levels of linguistic analysis; see for example [FRI 03]:

> *Temporal regions support identification processes, with syntactic processes involving the left anterior STG, semantic processes recruiting the left MTG and prosodic processes involving the right posterior STG. Frontal regions, by contrast, support the formation of relationships, with syntactic relationships involving BA 44 and the frontal opercular cortex, and semantic relationships recruiting BA 45/47.*

If humans themselves use different parts of their brain to process the various levels of a linguistic analysis (lexical, prosodic, syntactic, and semantic), then the multifaceted approach seems logical.

5.4.2. Unified notation

The multifaceted approach would not be viable if the different types of parsers could not communicate with one another. We will see in Chapter 10 that all NooJ parsers communicate via a data structure (the TAS) in which all linguistic analyses are stored and can be consulted.

Finally, the multifaceted approach makes it possible to use the same notation to construct regular grammars, context-free grammars, context-sensitive grammars, and unrestricted grammars. This unified notation (that is, "NooJ formalism") grows richer in an ascending manner, meaning that a NooJ regular grammar can be integrated without modification into a context-free grammar, a context-sensitive grammar, or an unrestricted grammar.

Using a single notation to describe the whole range of linguistic phenomena is of particular interest for educational purposes[15]; NooJ also has four crucial advantages for the project of exhaustive formalization of languages:

– *Suitability*: there are many linguistically mundane phenomena that would be very difficult to describe with generative grammars. We will see that NooJ offers multiple mechanisms (variables, agreement restrictions, special features) that make it possible to describe simple linguistic phenomena in a natural and immediate way.

– *Flexibility*: a NooJ context-free grammar is nothing more than a regular expression to which an additional mechanism has been added (recursion). Likewise, a context-sensitive grammar is a regular or a context-free grammar to which contextual constraints have been added. Linguists describing a particular phenomenon can thus begin their descriptive work with a regular expression, and then add one or several more powerful mechanisms as needed, without having to start over again from scratch. Or, conversely, they can begin using powerful tools and then simplify the description when they realize they can do without certain powerful mechanisms.

– *Compatibility*: the compatibility of the four grammar types makes it possible to accumulate a large amount of data on languages simply by merging grammars, whatever their type. For example, we can integrate into an unrestricted grammar that produces paraphrases (for example *I am doing the shopping in the supermarket* → *I am shopping in the supermarket*) a context-free grammar that describes the structure of the sentences (e.g. $[I]_{Subject}$ $[shop]_{Verb}$) and a regular grammar that addresses morphological derivations (e.g. *to shop* → *the shopping*).

– *Computer efficiency*: offering linguists the ability to choose the tool best suited for each phenomenon allows us to gain in both efficiency and power: if a grammar contains neither recursive rules nor contextual constraints, NooJ uses a highly efficient parsing algorithm that applies a finite-state automaton. Conversely, NooJ is not limited to the processing of regular linguistic phenomena, since we can always add mechanisms to an initially regular expression to make it more powerful. It is only when it encounters these more powerful operators that NooJ uses a more powerful (and thus slower) machine. In practice, this dynamic architecture enables NooJ to process large corpora in real time.

---

15 This also makes it much simpler to read this book!

5.4.3. *Cascading architecture*

NooJ has a unique architecture among automatic parsers: instead of unifying all levels of linguistic analysis and processing them together (that is, with a single parser in one pass), NooJ uses a "cascading" or "pipeline" architecture in which different parsers process the text level-by-level, one after another, starting from character analysis and ranging up to semantic analysis.

NooJ's sequential approach may seem strange or complex, but it is natural: we have known for a decade that the human brain also processes statements sequentially. For example [FRI 03] has compared the electrophysiological brain response of testers when they hear well-formed statements, statements that are lexically poorly formed, statements that are syntactically poorly formed, and statements that are semantically absurd. This study revealed three sequential phases:

– a lexically incorrect category (for example the sentence *the ice was in the ate*) produces a reaction in between 100 and 300 ms (this is the ELAN signal);

– a distributional variation (e.g. *Jenny put the candy in her mouth after the lesson* versus *Jenny put the candy in her pocket after the lesson*) produces different reactions in around 400 ms (this is the N400 signal);

– an absurd statement (e.g. *the volcano has been eaten*) produces a reaction in around 600 ms (this is the P600 signal).

The fact that different types of linguistic phenomena produce reactions in the brain at very separate times seems to me to be a good argument in favor of sequential architecture like that of NooJ.

5.5. Conclusion

In this chapter I have introduced the concepts of formal languages, generative grammars, and machines. The Chomsky-Schützenberger hierarchy describes four types of languages, which can be described by four types of generative grammars and automatically processed by four types of machines.

There are numerous formalisms used in NLP (from LEX to HPSG), each of which can be situated in relation to the Chomsky-Schützenberger hierarchy. However, in practice these formalisms are largely incompatible with each other, and their complexity does not make them very practical for an exhaustive language formalization project.

NooJ, unlike these formalisms, offers a system of description in which the four types of grammars exist side by side. This multifaceted system considerably simplifies the description of simple linguistic phenomena, and also gives great flexibility to linguists, who can "adjust" the power of their grammars at will. NooJ's parsers work in cascade while communicating thanks to a data structure that contains all of the analyses produced at all linguistic levels. In this book, I will therefore use NooJ notation to present regular grammars, context-free grammars, context-sensitive grammars, and unrestricted grammars. Of course, it is possible to transcribe any NooJ regular grammar into any other regular formalism (LEX, PERL, XFST, and others) and NooJ context-free grammars into any other suitable notation (BNR, GPSG, YACC, etc.). Some context-sensitive grammars that I will introduce could be written with "mildly context-sensitive" formalisms such as CCG, HG, LIG, or TAG, and others with more powerful formalisms such as LFG. The unrestricted grammars I will introduce can be rewritten in the form of HPSG grammars.

5.6. Exercises

Take the following generative grammar with the starting symbol S:

$S \rightarrow N\ V$
$S \rightarrow N\ V\ N$
$N \rightarrow Joe$
$N \rightarrow Lea$
$V \rightarrow sees$
$V \rightarrow is\ waiting\ for$

1) What vocabulary does this grammar cover? What language does this grammar describe?

2) Is this grammar regular, context-free, context-sensitive, and/or unrestricted?

3) Construct a regular grammar equivalent to this grammar.

5.7. Internet links

A good introduction to formal languages, generative grammars, and machines is available at the Wikipedia pages:

– en.wikipedia.org/wiki/Formal_language;

– en.wikipedia.org/wiki/Chomsky_hierarchy.

Most programming departments offer a course on these three concepts, often in tandem with the programming concept of *calculability* and the mathematical concept of *decidability*.

There are a number of websites that simulate the behavior of Turing Machines, for instance:

– morphett.info/turing/turing.html;

– ais.informatik.uni-freiburg.de/tursi;

– www.turing.org.uk/book/update/tmjavar.html.

A course on formal grammars and machines is available on Apple iTunes: Lewis H.R., McKay G., 2007, CSCI-E207: *Introduction to Formal Systems and Computation*, Harvard Extension School.

Jeff Ullman (Stanford University) teaches a course on the algorithmic aspects of the use of finite-state automata, pushdown automata, and Turing machines on Coursera at: www.coursera.org/course/automata.

An important application of the formalization of formal grammars is the construction of computer language compilers. A course is available on Coursera: Alex Aiken, Stanford University: *Compilers*.

On recursively enumerable languages, see:

– www.seas.upenn.edu/~cit596/notes/dave/relang0.html;

– en.wikipedia.org/wiki/Recursively_enumerable_language.

6

Regular Grammars

Rather than using plain type-3 generative grammars as seen in section 5.3, NooJ uses two equivalent types of tools to formalize regular languages: *regular expressions* and *finite-state graphs*.

Many Unix-based tools (awk, grep, perl, sed, etc.) use regular expressions to find or modify texts. LEX is used to describe programming language keywords with the help of regular expressions, and is used by programming language compilers [AHO 87]. There are also numerous applications of regular languages for NLP [ROC 97]. For example, the linguistic analyzers INTEX [SIL 93a] and XFST [KAR 97] are used to compile regular expressions into finite-state graphs in order to parse texts.

6.1. Regular expressions

A regular expression is composed of four types of elements:

1) *A regular expression can contain one word.* Any word constructed over the alphabet constitutes a valid regular expression. The regular expression represents the language containing this single word. For example, from the alphabet Σ_E, we can construct the word "loving". This word constitutes a valid regular expression:

```
G = loving
```

which itself represents the following language L:

```
L = {"loving"}
```

Be careful to distinguish the meta-language used in grammars (without quotation marks) from the described language (all words written between quotation marks).

The empty string (written as <E>) also constitutes a valid regular expression. Thus, the following regular expression:

$$G_E = <E>$$

represents the language containing one element: the empty string.

$$L_E = \{""\}$$

(2) *A regular expression can contain a disjunction.* Using two regular expressions G_1 and G_2, which represent the two languages L_1 and L_2, respectively, we can construct the regular expression $G_1 | G_2$, which represents the union of the two languages L_1 and L_2; that is, the language containing all the words in L_1 and all the words in L_2. For example, using alphabet Σ_E, we can construct the following two grammars:

$$G_1 = \text{eat}; \quad G_2 = \text{eats}$$

Using these two regular expressions, we can construct a third regular expression using the disjunction operator written as "|":

$$G_3 = G_1 | G_2 = \text{eat} | \text{eats}$$

The regular expression G_3 thus represents the following language:

$$L_3 = L_1 \cup L_2 = \{"eat", "eats"\}$$

Disjunction is an associative operation. To describe the following language:

```
{"eat", "eats", "eating", "ate", "eaten"}
```

all we have to do is construct the following expression:

```
eat | eats | eating | ate | eaten
```

3) *A regular expression can contain a concatenation.* Using the two regular expressions G_1 and G_2, which represent the two languages L_1 and L_2, respectively, we can also construct the regular expression $G_1 \, G_2$, which represents the concatenation of the two languages L_1 and L_2; that is, the language containing all the words composed of any word in L_1 followed by any word in L_2. For example, using alphabet Σ_F, we can construct the following two expressions:

$$G_1 = \text{lov}; \quad G_2 = \text{e|es|ing|ed}$$

which represent the following two languages, respectively:

$$L_1 = \{\text{"lov"}\}; \quad L_2 = \{\text{"e"}, \text{"es"}, \text{"ing"}, \text{"ed"}\}$$

We can then compute the concatenation of these two expressions:

$$G_3 = G_1 \, G_2 = \text{lov (e|es|ing|ed)}$$

Concatenation distributes over disjunction and takes priority over disjunction. Expression G_3 represents the following language:

$$L_3 = L_1 \, L_2 = \{\text{"love"}, \text{"loves"}, \text{"loving"}, \text{"loved"}\}$$

L_3 contains all of the words composed of the word "lov" followed by any word in L_2.

Here is another example, this time in syntax: using English vocabulary, we can construct the following two grammars:

```
DET = my|your|his|her|its; NOUN = key|pen
```

We can then compute the concatenation of these two grammars:

```
NP = DET NOUN = (my|your|his|her|its) (key|pen)
```

The grammar NP represents the following language L$_{NP}$:

```
L_NP = {"my key", "your key", "his key", "her key", "its
key", "my pen", "your pen", "his pen", "her pen", "its
pen"}
```

L$_{NP}$ represents all of the sequences we can construct by concatenating an element of the language described by DET with an element of the language described by NOUN.

In many languages, the concatenation of two ALUs generally involves the insertion of a space between the ALUs; thus, in English we write "my key" and not "mykey". In some languages (Chinese, for example), ALUs are concatenated without spaces, while in other agglutinative languages (including Germanic and Semitic languages) ALUs are sometimes concatenated with a space and sometimes without. We will see in Chapter 11 that these typographical specificities do not concern NooJ's syntactic parsers, because all four types of ALUs are represented in a unified way after lexical analysis.

Concatenation is an associative operation. For example, to search in a corpus of texts for the three-ALU sequence "the", "young", and "lady", we simply write the regular expression the young lady. Concatenation has some interesting properties:

– it is not commutative: for example the two sequences *race car* and *car race* are not equivalent;

– it has a neutral element: the empty string, written as <E> in NooJ. For any grammar G, we have the double equality:

```
G <E> = <E> G = G
```

In other words, we can always concatenate the empty string within any word (in morphology) or any phrase (in syntax) without modifying them.

The empty string is very useful in linguistics: we use it to note that an element is optional. For example, the following regular expression:

```
the (young | <E>) lady
```

recognizes the two sequences *the young lady* and *the lady*. In other words, the adjective modifier *young* is optional;

4) *A regular expression can contain a Kleene operation.* Using a grammar G that represents the language L, we can construct a grammar G* which represents the language L* containing all the words that can be constructed by concatenating at will the words in L, including the empty string. For example, using the English alphabet, we can define the following two grammars:

$$G = \texttt{re};\ G_{\text{VERB}} = \texttt{acquire|build|calibrate|do}$$

We can then define the grammar G* which represents the set of all words that we can construct by concatenating the word *re* any number of times (including 0 times), which defines the following language L*:

$$L^* = \{\texttt{""}, \texttt{"re"}, \texttt{"rere"}, \texttt{"rerere"}, \texttt{"rererere"}, \ldots\}$$

The following grammar G_2:

$$G_2 = G^*\, G_{\text{VERB}} = \texttt{(re)*(acquire|build|calibrate|do)}$$

thus represents the following language L_2:

$$L_2 = L^*\, L_{\text{VERB}} = \{\texttt{"acquire"}, \texttt{"build"}, \texttt{"calibrate"}, \texttt{"do"},$$
```
"reacquire", "rebuild", "recalibrate", "redo"
"rereacquire", "rerebuild", "rerecalibrate",
"reredo"
"rerereacquire", "rererebuild", "rererecalibrate",
"rereredo" ...}
```

that is, the infinite set containing the four verbs in the language L_{VERB} preceded by any number of prefixes *re*.

6.1.1. *Some examples of regular expressions*

The following regular expression describes a set of orthographic variants:

$$E_1 = \texttt{(c|t) (s|z) ar}$$

It represents the following language:

$$\{\texttt{"csar"}, \texttt{"tsar"}, \texttt{"czar"}, \texttt{"tzar"}\}$$

i.e. all the spelling variants of the word *tsar*. Here is an example of a regular expression used to describe a set of conjugated forms:

$$E_2 = \text{help } (<E>|s|ing|ed)$$

This grammar represents the five conjugated forms of the verb *to help*, or the language:

```
{"help", "helps", "helping", "helped"}
```

Here are other examples, this time in syntax: here is a regular expression used to describe a term and its variants:

$$E_3 = (ATM \mid bank \mid cash \mid credit \mid debit) \ card$$

Here is a regular expression that describes a set of noun phrases:

$$E_4 = (the|a|this) \ (young|old) \ (lady|woman)$$

If we apply this grammar to the text of *The Portrait of a Lady* (Henry James, 1881), we get the concordance in Figure 6.1.

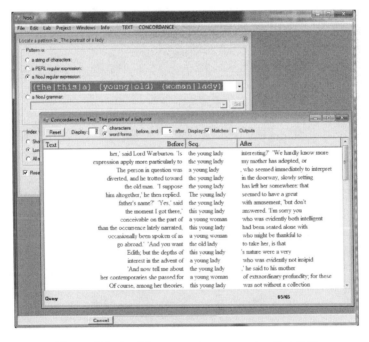

Figure 6.1. *Applying a regular expression to a text*

In practice, regular expressions are typically used to enter simple queries. It is easy to imagine that overly complex regular expressions will become unmanageable: beyond the few dozen lines and few levels of embedded parentheses, they will be very difficult to read. The use of a graphic tool is often preferred for the construction of more complex grammars.

6.2. Finite-state graphs

Some software platforms used in NLP to write regular expressions can also be used to construct finite-state graphs (for example HFST, SFST, and XFST). Unfortunately, these software platforms do not always allow these graphs to be displayed and edited "graphically".

```
xfst[1]: print net
Sigma:
0 1 2 3 4 5 6 7 8 9
Size: 10
Net: ["0" | 1 | 2 | 3 | 4 | 5 | 6 | 7 | 8 | 9];
Flags: deterministic, pruned, minimized, epsilon_free
Arity: 1
s0:0 -> fs1, 1 -> fs1, 2 -> fs1, 3 -> fs1, 4 -> fs1, 5
-> fs1, 6 -> fs1, 7 -> fs1, 8 -> fs1, 9 -> fs1.
fs1: (no arcs)
```

Figure 6.2. *Display of a graph using XFST*

The graph in Figure 6.2 contains two states (called "s0" and "fs1") and ten connections of state "s0" to state "fs1", tagged by ten numbers.

I now present finite-state graphs in NooJ notation[1].

A NooJ *finite-state graph* is defined by:

– a set of nodes, with each node being tagged by a regular expression constructed over an alphabet (in morphology) or a vocabulary (in syntax);

---

1 NooJ finite-state graphs are the same as INTEX graphs, introduced in [SIL 93]. They correspond to *expression automata*, which are a generalization of the *generalized finite-state automata* of [EIL 74] and are equivalent to traditional finite-state automata. In order to construct the finite-state automaton equivalent to a NooJ graph, one has to add a state before each node on the NooJ graph, and replace each node containing a regular expression with its corresponding finite-state automaton.

– the set of nodes must include one initial node and one terminal node;

– nodes may be connected or not; connections are unidirectional.

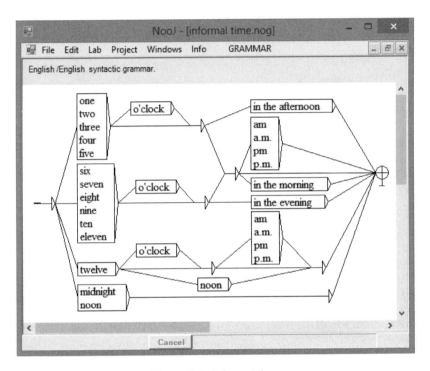

Figure 6.3. *Informal time*

Figure 6.3 shows an example of a NooJ finite-state graph describing some expressions of time. Vertically-aligned nodes are disjunctions, for example:

```
one | two | three | four | five
```

This graph compactly identifies a set of 167 time expressions[2], for example:

one o'clock, two in the afternoon, three o'clock am, ten o'clock in the evening

---

2 The NooJ command GRAMMAR>Generate Language produces the list of sequences recognized by a grammar.

while rejecting a number of incorrect sequences, such as:

twelve in the morning, ten in the afternoon, midnight o'clock

6.3. Non-deterministic and deterministic graphs

Consider the graph shown in Figure 6.4, which recognizes the five word forms *abduct*, *abort*, *accept*, *adjust*, and *adopt*.

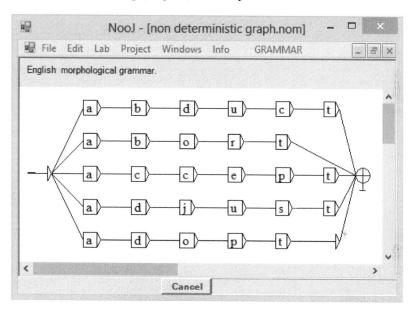

Figure 6.4. *A non-deterministic graph*

This graph contains repetitions that are problematic during parsing. For example, when we read the sequence "ab", we do not know if we must follow the top path (which leads to *abduct*) or the next path (which leads to *abort*). Likewise, the prefix "ad" can lead to two verbs: *adjust* and *adopt*. This graph is referred to as non-deterministic.

In practice, non-deterministic graphs are not efficient, because when they are applied to a text, a large number of intermediary paths must be remembered even if they will be eliminated later. In the graph above, for example, when we read the first letter "a", we must consider five potential paths. Then, when we read the second letter "d", we can eliminate three paths, but there are still two potential ones. We have to wait for the third letter, "o", before we can select the only correct path.

A deterministic version of the above graph is given in Figure 6.5.

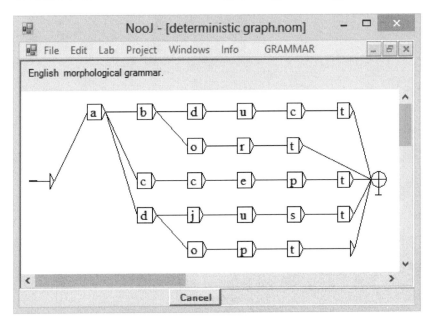

Figure 6.5. *A deterministic graph*

This deterministic graph is much more efficient than the non-deterministic graph before, since this time when we read a word letter by letter, we have a single path to consider at all times.

Non-deterministic graphs are generally used to present more clear and natural grammars, while deterministic graphs are much more efficient when used to parse texts.

An important result is that it is possible to automatically construct a deterministic graph equivalent to any given non-deterministic graph[3]. Consequently, linguists can construct the most readable grammars possible, without paying attention to potential redundancies; tools like NooJ are

3 For example, using the Power Set Construction algorithm, see [HOP 79].

capable of compiling these grammars into a more efficient deterministic version in order to parse large texts rapidly.

6.4. Minimal deterministic graphs

Note that we can further optimize the graph of Figure 6.5.

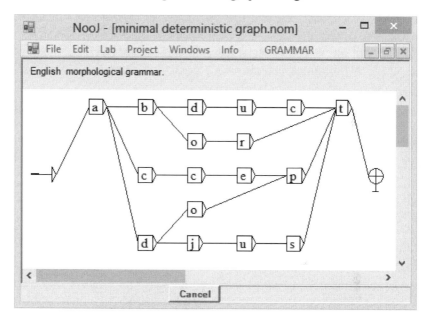

Figure 6.6. *A minimal graph*

This minimal deterministic graph is much more compact than the initial one because it factorizes the suffixes of each word. This graph has 19 nodes, while the original graph had 30 nodes. An important result is that it is possible to automatically minimize a deterministic graph[4].

Numerous languages make use of productive suffixes; for example, virtually all English verbs accept the suffix –*ing*, a large number of plural nouns end with –*s*, many nouns have the suffix –*ation*, etc. Linguists can construct dictionaries without worrying about the many shared prefixes and suffixes; software tools can then convert the resulting dictionaries into a

---

4 For example, using the Moore algorithm, see [MOO 56].

minimal deterministic graph in which the prefixes and suffixes have been factorized.

The richer the morphology of a language, the larger the number of word forms. For example, there are 200,000 word forms in English, 1 million word forms in French, and 150 million word forms in Hungarian. However, the larger the number of word forms, the more word forms there are that share prefixes and suffixes, and thus the more efficient determinization and minimization algorithms become. Consequently, dictionaries containing the word forms of any language, whether English, French or Hungarian, are all represented by minimal deterministic graphs of comparable size (a few Megabytes).

6.5. Kleene's theorem

The theorem put forth by [KLE 56] proves that equivalence exists between regular expressions and finite-state graphs. By equivalence, we mean that regular expressions and finite-state graphs can describe exactly the same language.

This is a very significant result, as it gives linguists the ability to choose the tools best suited to their needs. This theorem can be proved in two steps: first by showing how to construct a finite-state graph from any regular expression, and second by showing how to construct a regular expression from any finite-state graph.

There are several methods of construction for a finite-state graph, with the simplest being the one described by [THO 68]: it consists of constructing a basic graph for each letter (or ALU) contained in the regular expression, and then connecting the basic graphs, either in parallel when the expression contains a disjunction, in series for a concatenation, or in a loop for the Kleene operator.

For example, from the syntactic regular expression:

```
the very* pretty (chair | table)
```

we can construct the five basic graphs represented in Figure 6.7.

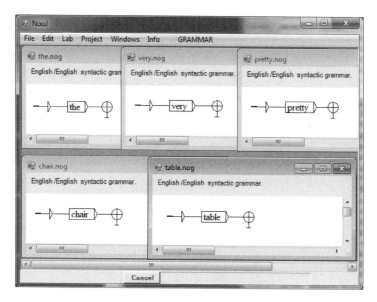

Figure 6.7. *Five basic graphs*

The words chair and table are linked by a disjunction (the operator "|" in the regular expression), so we connect the two corresponding graphs in parallel. We replace the Kleene operator in the expression very* with a loop. We compute the graphs in Figure 6.8.

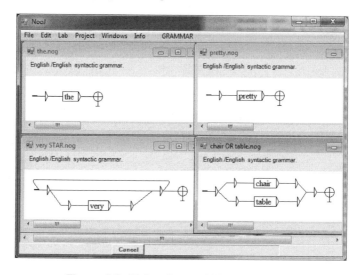

Figure 6.8. *Disjunction and Kleene operator*

Finally, we connect the graph starting with the word form the followed sequentially by the graph for very*, the word form pretty, and the graph for chair|table, to get the final graph equivalent to the complete regular expression (Figure 5.9).

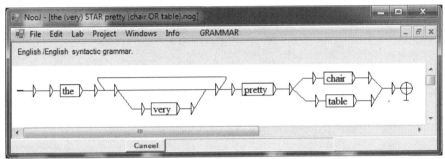

Figure 6.9. *Graph equivalent to a regular expression*

This equivalence means that linguists will always have the ability to construct a finite-state graph equivalent to a regular expression. Developers of large resources use this result on a daily basis, as graphs are much more scalable than the equivalent regular expressions.

There are several methods of constructing the regular expression equivalent to a given finite-state graph. The simplest consists of completing each node in the graph by transferring into it the regular expression of its continuations (meaning the expressions in the nodes that follow it), until the graph contains only one initial node and one terminal node, in which case the label of the initial node constitutes the regular expression equivalent to the original graph. For example, consider Figure 6.10.

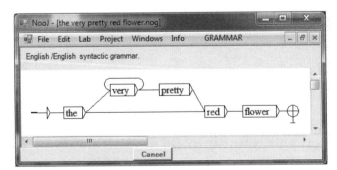

Figure 6.10. *A finite-state graph*

We can complete the node tagged "red" by incorporating its continuation:

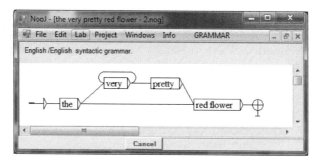

Figure 6.11. *Incorporating the node "red"*

Next we complete the node "pretty" by incorporating its continuation:

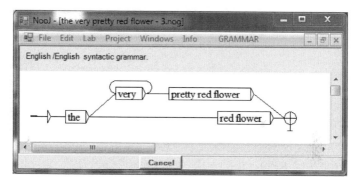

Figure 6.12. *Incorporating the node "pretty"*

Next we include the node "very":

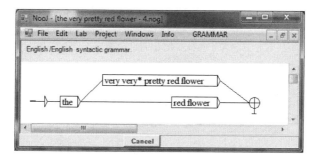

Figure 6.13. *Completeing the node "very"*

And finally we complete the graph with the node tagged "the" (Figure 6.14).

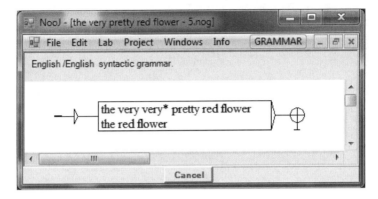

Figure 6.14. *Final graph*

The regular expression thus constructed:

```
the very very* pretty red flower | the red flower
```

represents the same language as the starting finite-state graph. The two advantages of using regular expressions rather than graphs are:

– when the query is very simple (for example a sequence of a few words), it is much quicker to enter it directly rather than opening the graph editor;

– regular expressions can be easily constructed automatically by computer programs. A NLP application could apply a regular expression to a technical text in order to find a few terms characteristic of a technical domain, and then reinsert parts of the resulting index into the initial regular expression to expand it (to find other terms), re-applying and enriching the regular expression until a fixed point is reached, at which point the final regular expression recognizes a large set of technical terms found in the text.

6.6. Regular expressions with outputs and finite-state transducers

As grammars define sets of sequences (of letters or of ALUs), we can use corresponding parsers to find these sequences automatically in texts. When a parser applies a finite-state graph to a text (whether entered via NooJ's graphical editor, or compiled from a regular expression), it typically produces the list of matching sequences, in the form of a concordance like the one in Figure 6.1 (in section 6.1.1). However, simply recognizing sequences is generally not enough; we want to be able to associate the sequences recognized by a grammar with some specific analysis.

To do this, we must add to grammars the ability to produce results.

Regular expressions which associate a set of recognized sequences with their analysis are called *enhanced regular expressions*. Finite-state graphs containing outputs are called *finite-state transducers*[5].

For example, the grammar in Figure 6.15 recognizes four spelling variants, and produces the corresponding canonical form *tsar* as output. This grammar could be used to impose spelling consistency in a book (for example to ensure that all the occurrences of a term are written in the same way), to index all the variants of a term under the same index key, or to consolidate the results of a search engine.

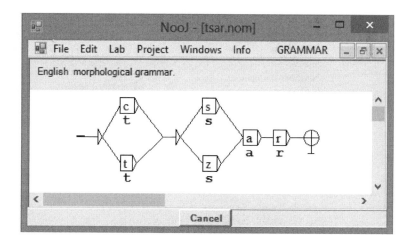

Figure 6.15. *An spelling transducer*

---

5 NooJ actually treats finite-state graphs as finite-state transducers that produce the empty string <E> as their output.

The finite-state graph in Figure 6.16 recognizes 43 terminological variants and produces the generic term "bank card" as a result. This grammar could be used by a search engine to find occurrences of all these terms based on the query "bank card".

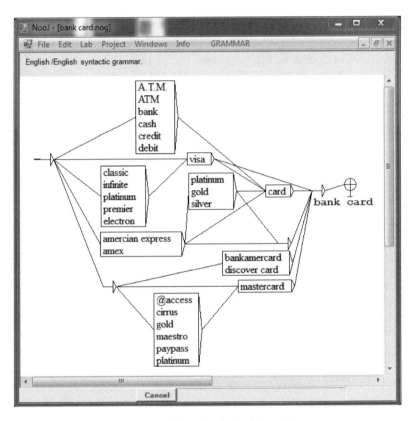

Figure 6.16. *A terminological transducer*

The following grammar produces the morphological analysis of the conjugated forms of the verbs *to abduct, to abort, to accept, to adjust,* and *to adopt*. For example, it recognizes *adjusting* and produces the output "G", which represents the analysis "Gerundive". The grammar recognizes the form *accepted* twice; once by producing the analysis "PT" (Preterite), and once by producing the analysis "PP" (Past Participle). When a grammar produces multiple different results for a matching sequence, we say that the sequence is ambiguous.

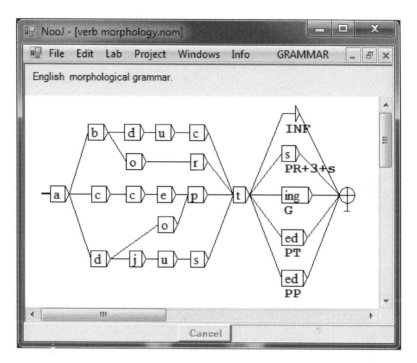

Figure 6.17. *A morphological transducer*

Note that adding a verb to this grammar can be done with minimal cost: for example, to add the verb *to adopt* to the graph, all we had to do is add a single "o" node. The graph in Figure 6.17 can easily be completed by inserting the 5,000 English verbs with the same conjugation paradigm. Then we could add all of the other words (verbs, nouns, adjectives, etc.), this time adding other suffixes and outputs. The result would be a transducer containing all the English word forms, associated with their morphological analysis[6].

The grammar shown in Figure 6.18 recognizes a few English expressions and produces their French equivalent.

---

6 This is precisely what NooJ does: when it "compiles" a dictionary, it actually constructs the equivalent finite-state transducer; see [MES 08b].

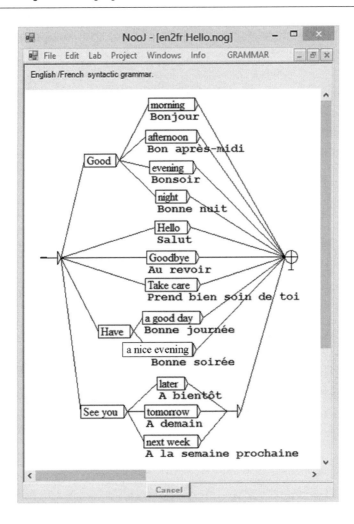

Figure 6.18. *A transducer for translation*

We will see in Part 3 of this book that grammars' outputs can be annotations that represent information on structures (e.g. <NP> for noun phrases), highlight named entities such as expressions of date (<DATE>) and names of organizations (<ORG>) or places (<LOC>), or even produce logic formulae such as "BUY (IBM, LOTUS)" to represent semantic predicates.

6.7. Extensions of regular grammars

Most software platforms that process regular grammars offer users the ability to use abbreviations to simplify writing. For example, Lex and Perl use the special symbol "." to represent any character; the "Find" function in Microsoft Word uses special symbol "^#" to represent any number, etc.

NooJ also offers a dozen special symbols; for example, in morphological grammars, the symbol <U> represents any capital letter; the symbol <V> any vowel. In syntax, <WF> represents any word form; <NB> any sequence of digits. The use of these symbols in no way changes the expressive power of the grammars: these symbols are merely simple abbreviations. For example, in any NooJ grammar we could replace the symbol <D> (*Digit*) with the following regular expression:

(0 | 1 | 2 | 3 | 4 | 5 | 6 | 7 | 8 | 9)

As we will see in Part 3 of this book, NooJ processes annotated texts; annotations are used to associate ALUs or sequences of ALUs from the text with linguistic properties (for example "form of the verb *to bother* in the gerundive" or "Human Noun Phrase"). NooJ can access these annotations and thus linguists can mention them in any grammar, using symbols. There are two types of symbols: lexical symbols and syntactic symbols. Lexical symbols generally represent families of word forms of an ALU (for example all the forms of the verb *to sit*), while syntactic symbols typically represent categories of ALUs defined in dictionaries (for example all the verbs), or sequences of ALUs recognized by a grammar (for example all the noun phrases).

6.7.1. *Lexical symbols*

Once NooJ has annotated all the ALUs in a text, it can access all the information associated with these ALUs, using lexical symbols. For example, the lexical symbol <help> matches in the text all the word forms that were annotated with the lemma *help*. We can combine a lexical symbol with properties using the "+" sign ("has the property") or the "-" sign ("does not have the property"). For example, <help-G> matches all the forms of *to help* except the gerundive form.

It is important to understand that lexical symbols act strictly as abbreviations of regular expressions. For example, we could enter these definitions:

<help> = help | helps | helping | helped
<help+3+s> = helps
<help-G> = help | helps | helped

Inflection is not the only morphological operation that can be "abstracted" thanks to symbols. We saw in section 4.4.2 that it is also necessary to formalize various types of derivation. If, in addition to its conjugation, the derivations of the verb *to help* (*helper*, *helpful*) are formalized, we then get the correspondence:

<help> = help | helps | helping | helped | helper | helpers | helpful

In languages with rich morphology (Turkish for example), a lexical symbol may represent several hundred forms. Lexical symbols then allow us to write in a very compact manner grammars that would be extremely difficult to write in practice.

Lexical symbols typically represent a family of words constructed from an ALU using morphological operations. However, there is nothing to prevent us from going beyond morphology and defining families of spelling variants. Thus the lexical symbol <tsar> could represent all spelling variants, including its feminine and plural forms as well:

<tsar> = tsar | tsars | tsarina | tsarinas | tzar | tzars | tzarina | tzarinas |
csar | csars | csarina | csarinas | czar | czars | czarina | czarinas

We could generalize further the concept of family of variants to the synsets of the WORDNET dictionary. For example, the lexical symbol <acquire> would then represent not only the conjugated forms of the verb *to acquire*, but also its derived forms (e.g. *acquisition*) as well as all inflected and derived forms of its synonyms (e.g. *to win, winning, a winner, to gain, gains*, etc.).

Likewise, one could implement ontologies in this way: for example the symbol <seat> could recognize all its hyponyms, such as *chair*, *armchair*, *rocking chair*, *stool*, *folding chair*, etc.

6.7.2. *Syntactic symbols*

Grammars can also contain symbols that represent categories associated with each ALU or ALU sequence. For example, all the verbs in the NooJ dictionary are associated with the code "V" (for the syntactic category "Verb"): the syntactic symbol <V> thus represents any verbal form. In the same dictionary, nouns are associated with the code "N", and so the syntactic symbol <N> represents all noun forms. Likewise, adjectives are recognized by the syntactic symbol <A>; adverbs by the syntactic symbol <ADV>; determiners by the syntactic symbol <DET>; and pronouns by the syntactic symbol <PRO>.

Just like for lexical symbols, syntactic symbols are not actually hard-coded in NooJ, but are rather defined by the authors of the linguistic resources: anyone could construct a dictionary in which computer terms are associated with the COMPUTER category, medical terms with the MEDICAL category; political terms with the POLITICS category, etc. All these codes could then be instantly used in the form of syntactic symbols (e.g. <POLITICS>) in any NooJ grammar.

Just like lexical symbols, syntactic symbols can be combined with property restrictions using the operators "+" and "-"; for example the symbol <V+3+s> represents all verb forms conjugated in the third person singular.

The regular expression in Figure 6.19:

```
<DET> <N+s> has <V+PP>
```

can be applied to a text to extract all the sequences composed of a determiner (<DET>) followed by a singular noun (<N+s>), the form *has*, and a verb form in the past participle (<V+PP>).

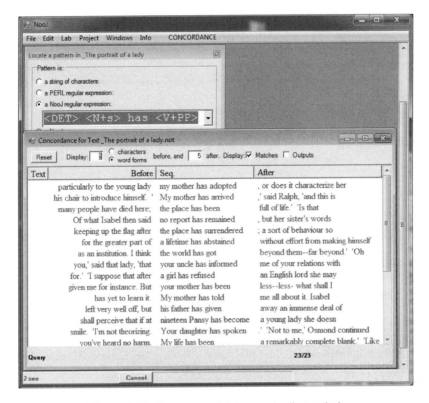

Figure 6.19. *A query containing syntactic symbols*

6.7.3. *Symbols defined by grammars*

It is not only dictionaries that can be used to define lexical or syntactic symbols; grammars can also be used to annotate words or sequences of words. For example, we can construct a grammar that recognizes sequences like "Tuesday, January 3rd, 2015 at 4:20 PM" and then annotate them with the category DATE. After application of this grammar to a text, the <DATE> syntactic symbol will represent all dates and can itself be reused within another grammar which will itself define new categories, and so on. Note that grammars, as opposed to dictionaries, can be used to associate an infinite set of sequences with a certain category (e.g. the DATE grammar in NooJ represents an infinite number of expressions).

In principle, the use of symbols does not increase the expressive power of a grammar; that is, inserting lexical or syntactic symbols into a regular grammar does not make it recognize non-regular languages. Indeed we could theoretically replace the symbol <V> with all the list of verb forms and the symbol <DATE> with the regular grammar that recognizes all dates[7]. In practice, however, it seems difficult to see how we could avoid using symbols that potentially represent hundreds of thousands of ALUs (or even infinite sets in the case of annotations produced by grammars).

The possibility of using complex symbols by combining properties at will, as in the following syntactic symbol:

```
<N-Proper+Human-Politics+Medicine-plural>
```

does not increase the theoretical power of regular grammars, but it considerably reduces the size of the grammars.

6.7.4. *Special operators*

When a parser applies a finite-state transducer to a text, we get the list of matching sequences together with their corresponding outputs. The parser may then interpret these outputs, in particular to verify some constraints.

6.7.4.1. *The operator +EXCLUDE*

If the output produced by the transducer contains the operator +EXCLUDE, then the matching sequence is rejected. This functionality can be used to describe complements of a language in the mathematical sense: we want to exclude a set of exceptions. For example, the following enhanced regular expression:

```
<be> | 's/+EXCLUDE
```

extracts from a text all the forms of the verb *to be* except the sequence "'s". This grammar allows us to avoid extracting numerous false positives from a text, since the sequence "'s" is often used as a genitive marker.

---

7 However, the possibility of applying finite-state automata in a loop would radically increase the power of the machine used, which would then become equivalent to a push-down automaton and would thus be capable of recognizing context-free languages.

6.7.4.2. *The operator +UNAMB*

If the output produced by the transducer contains the operator +UNAMB, NooJ excludes all the other matching sequences in the same position in the text. This feature gives priority to one or more matching sequences over others. For example, the following regular expression:

```
submarine | nuclear submarine/+UNAMB
```

can be used to index all occurrences of the term *submarine*, while when the more complete term *nuclear submarine* is present in the text, only the complete two-word term will be indexed, to the detriment of the subterm *submarine*, although it is also present.

6.7.4.3. *The operator +ONE*

This operator makes sure that a given sub-sequence will occur once (and only once) in each matching sequence. The feature is generally used to process non-ordered sequences of constituents, for example the following sentences:

> *Joe gave an apple to Lea. Joe gave to Lea an apple.*
> *It is to Lea that Joe gave an apple. It is an apple that Joe gave*
> *to Lea.*

In some languages (Hungarian and the Slavic languages for example), the order of constituents in a sentence is free. To recognize all the sentences containing one verb with its nominative subject, one accusative complement, and one dative complement, it would be necessary to construct a regular expression like the one below:

Verb Nominative Accusative Dative | Verb Nominative Dative Accusative |
Verb Accusative Nominative Dative | Verb Accusative Dative Nominative |
Verb Dative Nominative Accusative | Verb Dative Accusative Nominative |
Nominative Verb Accusative Dative | Nominative Verb Dative Accusative |
Accusative Verb Nominative Dative | Accusative Verb Dative Nominative |
Dative Verb Nominative Accusative | Dative Verb Accusative Nominative |
Nominative Accusative Verb Dative | Accusative Nominative Verb Dative |
Nominative Dative Verb Accusative | Dative Nominative Verb Accusative |
Accusative Dative Verb Nominative | Dative Accusative Verb Nominative |
Nominative Accusative Dative Verb | Nominative Dative Accusative Verb |
Accusative Nominative Dative Verb | Accusative Dative Nominative Verb |
Dative Nominative Accusative Verb | Dative Accusative Nominative Verb

The size of the regular expression increases with the number of constituents in the sentence: for a sentence that contains one subject, one verb, and two complements, the grammar already contains 4! (factorial 4), or $4 \times 3 \times 2 \times 1 = 24$ terms. If we add to the sentence a circumstantial complement of location, a time complement, and a complement of manner, the size of the grammar will literally explode: $7! = 5,040$ terms in the grammar. Neither regular expressions nor even other types of generative grammars in the Chomsky-Schützenberger hierarchy are suited to construct grammar for these languages. The operator +ONE is thus used to design regular grammars to describe free-order components, while keeping them compact.

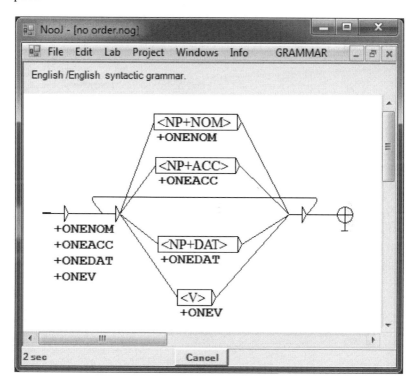

Figure 6.20. *The operator +ONE*

In Figure 6.20, the syntactic symbols <NP+NOM> (Noun Phrase, Nominative), <N+ACC> (Noun Phrase, Accusative), <N+DAT> (Noun Phrase, Dative), and <V> (Verb) correspond to annotations that were produced by a previous parser[8]. The finite-state graph contains a loop enabling the recognition of all sequences of constituents, in any order. The +ONE operators in the output of the transducer are then used to eliminate from the matching sequences those which do not have exactly one and only one constituent <NP+NOM>, one and only one <NP+ACC>, one and only one <NP+DAT>, and one and only one <V>.

6.7.4.4. *The operator +ONCE*

The operator + ONCE is similar to the operator + ONE, but verifies that a constituent appears no more than once (the constituent may not occur). The +ONCE operator is very useful linguistically because there are many words or phrases in natural languages that are optional, but cannot occur more than once in a sentence. For example, both of the sentences below are correct even though they are incomplete:

Joe gave his pen (lacks a dative complement)
Lea gives to charity (lacks an object complement)

On the other hand, both of the sequences below are incorrect: the first contains two direct object complements, while the second contains two dative complements:

* Lea gave it a pen to Joe. *Joe gave a pen to Lea to Ida

This situation is systematic with circumstantial complements, which are all optional by definition and can be placed almost anywhere in a phrase, but which cannot occur more than once in a given sentence, for example:

Yesterday, Lea slept on the floor; Lea yesterday slept on the floor; Lea slept yesterday on the floor; Lea slept on the floor yesterday.

But we cannot have: **Yesterday, Lea slept on the floor yesterday* or, more generally: **This week, Joe slept on the floor last Tuesday.* A simple grammar such as the following makes it possible to recognize all the correct sentences while enforcing that a date complement occurs no more than once:

```
(<E>|<DATE>/+ONCE) Lea (<E>|<DATE>/+ONCE) slept
(<E>|<DATE>/+ONCE) on the floor (<E>|<DATE>/+ONCE).
```

---

8 We will present the Text Annotation Structure in Chapter 10.

6.8. Conclusion

NooJ offers linguists two equivalent variants of regular grammars to formalize regular languages: *regular expressions* and *finite-state graphs*.

NooJ's regular expressions and finite-state graphs can contain lexical and syntactic symbols that function like abbreviations, as well as special operators that act as filters to exclude certain matching sequences. Symbols and special operators considerably reduce the size of the grammars to be built. These "extensions" do not affect the expressive power of the grammars, but rather they greatly facilitate the work of linguistic formalization.

6.9. Exercises

1) Construct the finite-state graph equivalent to the following regular expression:

```
<DET> (very* <A>  |  <E>) <N> (<E>  |  of <DET> (very*
<A>  |  <E>) <N>)
```

2) Construct the regular expression equivalent to the minimal deterministic finite-state graph shown in Figure 6.6. Compare the advantages and disadvantages of regular expressions and finite-state graphs.

3) Complete the finite-state graph in Figure 6.17 so that it will recognize and analyze all the forms of the verbs *to admit*, *to annul*, and *to eat*.

6.10. Internet links

For a mathematical presentation of regular languages, see the Wikipedia article: en.wikipedia.org/wiki/Regular_language.

The algorithm used to construct a deterministic finite-state automaton from a non-deterministic finite-state automaton is presented at:

en.wikipedia.org/wiki/Powerset_construction

The Apple iTunes and Courser courses cited in the *Internet Links* section at the end of Chapter 5 contain a session on regular languages, regular grammars, and finite-state machines.

Wikipedia's pages on LEX and FLEX present these two lexical parsers, which use enhanced regular expressions to describe keywords of programming languages such as Java. Many instruction manuals and course materials for these tools are available on the Internet.

UNIX manuals contain detailed introductions to the tools AWK, GREP, FGREP, and SED, which compile regular expressions into finite-state automata to search for sequences of characters in texts.

I have introduced the finite-state graph notation with INTEX. INTEX was a linguistic platform based on the use of regular grammars; see intex.univ-fcomte.fr.

The tool XFST is presented on the website:

www.cis.upenn.edu/~cis639/docs/xfst.html

The web page web.stanford.edu/~laurik/fsmbook/home.html describes the morphological applications of the XFST tool. Its academic variants HFST and SFST can be downloaded at www.ling.helsinki.fi/kieliteknologia/tutkimus/hfst and code.google.com/p/cistern/wiki/SFST.

7

Context-Free Grammars

Type-2 generative grammars and formalisms such as *Backus-Naur Form* (BNF) [BAC 59], *Generalized Phrase Structure Grammar* (GPSG) [GAZ 85] or *Yet Another Compiler Compiler* (YACC) [JOH 12] introduce the possibility of using auxiliary symbols on the right-hand side of rewriting rules, as in Figure 5.1. Context-free grammars are typically used to formalize programming languages, and to build compilers for them[1].

NooJ context-free grammars consist of sets of named regular expressions, in which names can be inserted. For example, the grammar in Figure 5.1 could be written with NooJ as in Figure 7.1.

Auxiliary symbols correspond in NooJ to regular expression names, introduced by the colon character ":". The left and right members of each rule are separated by the character "=". The right-hand member of each rule is a regular expression; the left-hand member of each rule is its name. Each rule must end with the semi-colon character ";".

---

1 Compilers are pieces of software that translate programs (that is to say texts written in a programming language) into sequences of instructions that can be processed by a computer processor, see [AHO 03].

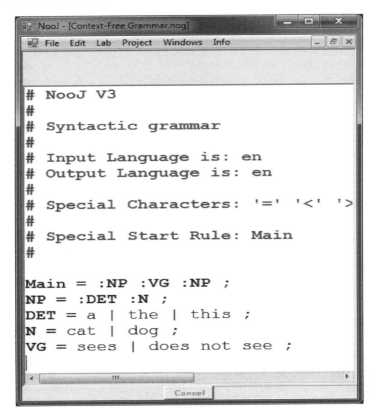

Figure 7.1. *A NooJ context-free grammar*

By using the syntactic symbols <DET> (determiner), <N>(noun) and <V+tr> (transitive verb), it is possible to both simplify the above grammar and generalize it:

> **Main = :NP :VG :NP ;**
>
> NP = <DET><N> ;
> VG = <V+tr+PR> | (does|do) not <V+tr+INF>;

Figure 7.2. *A context-free grammar with syntactic symbols*

In NooJ, context-free grammars can also be represented by sets of Recursive Graphs. Each auxiliary symbol in the context-free grammar thus corresponds to the name of an embedded graph. Here is a Recursive Grammar that corresponds to the context-free grammar presented in Figure 7.3.

This grammar is made up of three graphs. The grammar's entry point is its "Main" graph. The NP, VG and NP nodes are names of embedded graphs (here: the two graphs *NP* and *VG*) and correspond to auxiliary symbols in context-free grammars.

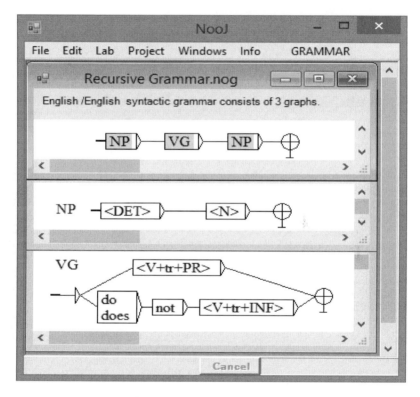

Figure 7.3. *Recursive Graph*

If we further generalize this grammar to account for transitive sentences that accept two complements, noun phrases that contain a modifier on both the left and right sides of the noun, and sentences that contain the auxiliaries *to be* or *to have*, the grammar becomes:

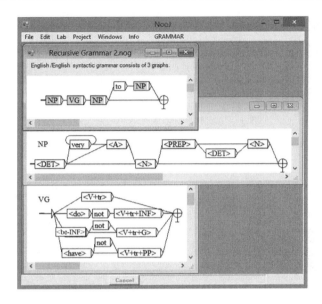

Figure 7.4. *A more general grammar*

The regular expression equivalent to this grammar would be:

```
<DET> (very*<A>|<E>) <N> (<PREP> (<DET>|<E>)
<N>|<E>)(<V+tr> | <do> not <V+tr+INF> | <be>
(not|<E>) <V+G> | <have> (not|<E>) <V+tr+PP>)
<DET> (very*<A>|<E>) <N> (<PREP> (<DET>|<E>)
<N>|<E>)(to <DET> (very*<A>|<E>) <N> (<PREP>
(<DET>|<E>) <N>|<E>)|<E>)
```

Such a grammar would be very difficult to maintain over time, because if we had to make any modifications (for example to improve the description of the noun phrases) it would be necessary to run them through the entire grammar – a time-consuming task... In practice therefore, when it comes to building, accumulating, sharing and maintaining complex grammars it is better to use context-free grammars (or recursive graphs), even if the phenomena to be described could theoretically be described with regular grammars.

7.1. Recursion

Context-free grammars are more powerful than regular expressions, that is to say that they can describe languages that regular expressions cannot describe. The added power of context-free grammars comes from their ability to contain self-referential rules, i.e. rules that are defined more or less directly from themselves: this is called *recursion*. Here is an example of a recursive context-free grammar:

$$\mathsf{S} = \mathsf{a} :\mathsf{S} \; \mathsf{b} \; | \; \mathsf{a} \; \mathsf{b};$$

Figure 7.5. *A recursive context-free grammar*

This grammar contains a single rule named *S*; in the definition of rule *S*, there is a reference to *S*: in other words, the symbol *S* is defined using itself. If we run this grammar, we can produce the sequence "a b" thanks to the second part of the rule:

S → a b

We can also produce the sequence "a a b b", by first using the first part of the rule, and then the second:

S → a :S b → a a b b

By using the first element twice, then the second, the sequence "a a a b b b" is produced:

S → a :S b → a a :S b b → a a a b b b

By using the first element three times, the grammar generates the sequence "a a a a b b b b" in the following way:

S → a :S b → a a :S b b → a a a :S b b b → a a a a b b b b

etc. More generally, this grammar describes the language $a^n \, b^n$ which contains sequences made up of a number n of a, followed by the same number of b. It has been proven[2] that it would be impossible to construct a regular expression that recognizes the same language $a^n \, b^n$.

---

2 Thanks to the pumping lemma – see the link at the end of the chapter – which shows that a regular grammar (or a finite-state machine) can recognize sequences of unlimited length, only if it contains a section that can be repeated an arbitrary number of times, which is not the case for language $a^n \, b^n$.

Context-free grammars are also of interest to linguists, as there are syntactic phenomena that are natural to describe using recursive rules. Three types of recursions can be distinguished: right recursion, left recursion and middle recursion.

7.1.1. *Right recursion*

Consider the following context-free grammar.

The first graph of the grammar in Figure 7.6, named *Sentence*, contains one reference to the graph named **NP1**. The graph **NP1** itself contains a reference to the first graph *Sentence*. Note that the recursive element, *Sentence*, appears to the right of the **NP1** graph. This grammar recognizes the following sentences among others:

> *My cat chases the mouse*
> *The neighbor fears that my cat chases the mouse*
> *Her cousin thinks that the neighbor fears that my cat chases the mouse*
> *Our teacher said that her cousin thinks that the neighbor fears that my cat chases the mouse*
> ...

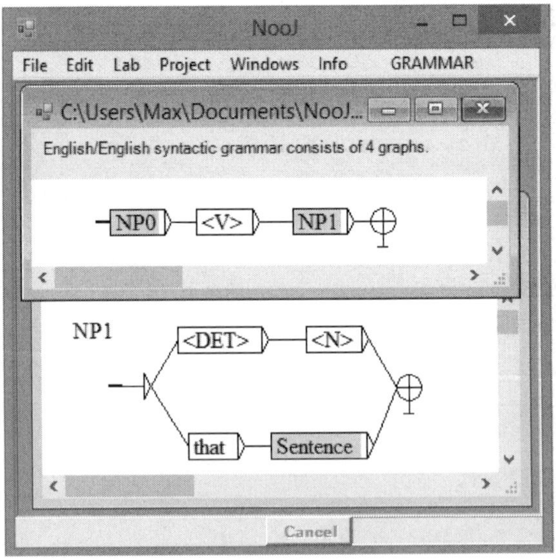

Figure 7.6. *Right recursive grammar*

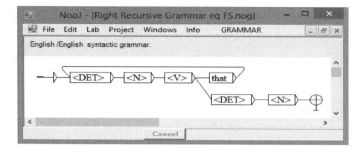

Figure 7.7. *Finite-state graph equivalent to a right-recursive context-free grammar*

It is an important result that context-free grammars that have a right recursion can also be described using regular expressions. For example, the finite-state graph in Figure 7.7 is equivalent to the previous recursive grammar.

The process of removing right recursions from a context-free grammar can be automated[3].

7.1.2. *Left recursion*

Now let us consider the following left-recursive context-free grammar.

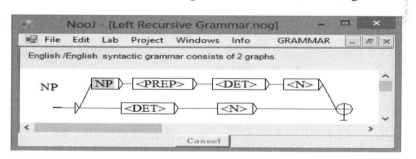

Figure 7.8. *Left recursive grammar*

The graph named **NP** contains a reference to itself, which appears on the left of the graph. This grammar recognizes noun phrases such as:

---

3 Tail call recursions are systematically eliminated by certain functional programming languages, see for instance [STE 77].

The pen
The pen in the box
The pen in the box inside the drawer
The pen in the box inside the drawer under the desk

...

Here too, one can construct a finite-state graph equivalent to this grammar.

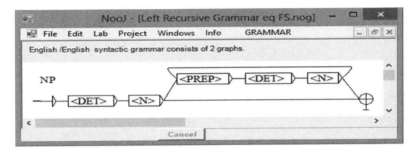

Figure 7.9. *Finite-state graph equivalent to a left-recursive context-free grammar*

The process of removing left recursions from a context-free grammar can be automated [MOO 00].

7.1.3. *Middle recursion*

Figure 7.10 shows a more complex example of recursion, which appears neither on the left or right side of the grammar.

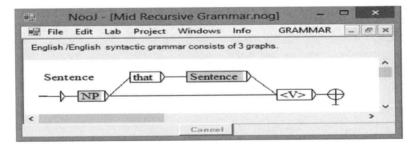

Figure 7.10. *Middle recursion*

The graph named *Sentence* contains a reference to itself. However, this reference is neither on the left or on the right of the graph. This grammar generates sentences such as:

> *The cat sleeps*
> *The cat that Joe got sleeps*
> *? The cat that the neighbor that Joe visited got sleeps*
> ** The cat that the cousin that the neighbor that Joe visited saw got sleeps*
>
> ...

It is thought-provoking to observe that:

– the only examples of embedded sentences that would justify using middle-recursion do not, generally, produce "natural" sentences: for example, beyond two or three embeddings, the previous grammar produces sentences that are not acceptable;

– it is not possible to build regular expressions equivalent to context-free grammars that contain middle-recursions.

As if by chance, "linguistically useful" context-free grammars are those that can be handled by finite-state machines, whereas context-free languages that cannot be handled by finite-state machines are probably not useful linguistically[4]... Does this coincidence tell us anything about how humans process language? In any case, the argument in [CHO 57] on the inadequacy of regular grammars is weakened.

That being said, I would like to remind the reader that even if it turns out that natural languages can be handled solely by finite-state machines, for linguists, this does not detract from the advantage of using context-free grammars to construct, maintain, share and accumulate grammars (see the

---

4 [CHR 92] states that natural languages can be parsed by finite-state machines, whereas [KAR 07] believes that the maximal number of middle embeddings for European languages (English, Finnish, French, German, Latin, Swedish, Danish) is 3. However, if we impose a maximal number of embeddings, then it becomes possible to compute the equivalent finite-state machine. In addition, it must be noted that our example of grammar is linguistically incorrect: the sentence embedded after the relative pronoun *that* is not a complete sentence, because it lacks its requisite direct object (represented itself by the word *that*): for instance, the two sentences "The cat that Joe bought the cat sleeps" and "The cat that Joe snores sleeps" are un-grammatical.

discussion in Figure 7.4). In other words: let us not confuse the nature of languages (which might be processed by finite-state machines) with the nature of grammars that we use to formalize them.

7.2. Parse trees

Generally, applying a grammar to a text produces a binary result: either a sequence of text belongs to the language described by the grammar, or it does not. However, this binary information is often insufficient. For example, if a sentence is structurally ambiguous, it will be recognized in more than one way by a syntactic grammar, and it would be useful to distinguish between the different analyses. For instance, let us consider the grammar given in Figure 7.11.

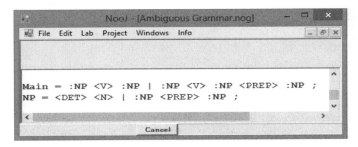

Figure 7.11. *An ambiguous grammar*

This grammar states that a sentence is made up either of a subject, a verb and a direct object (first term of the **Main** rule), or of a subject, a verb, a direct object, a preposition, and an indirect object (second term of the **Main** rule). A noun phrase (rule **NP**) is made up by either a determiner followed by a noun, or a noun phrase followed by a preposition, followed by another noun phrase (the noun complement).

If one applies this grammar to the following sentence:

This man sees a chair from his house

one gets two possible derivations[5]:

---

[5] Left elements of the rule to be applied appear in bold, sequences that have just been produced are underlined.

Main → **NP** <V>**NP**→ This man sees **NP** → This man sees **NP** from **NP**→ This man sees a chair from **NP** → This man sees a chair from his house

or:

Main → **NP** <V>**NP** from **NP**→ This man sees **NP** from **NP** → This man sees a chair from **NP** → This man sees a chair from his house

In the first derivation, the verbal form *sees* has one single direct object: a noun phrase itself made up of a noun followed by a noun complement. A possible paraphrase[6] for this first analysis is: *It is a chair (that was taken) from his house that this man sees.*

In the second derivation, the verbal form *sees* takes two complements: a direct object, and an indirect object introduced by the preposition *from*. A possible paraphrase for this second analysis would be: *It is from his house that this man sees a (non-specific) chair.*

The derivations used to describe these two analyses are not very easy to grasp; there is a more elegant way of illustrating them: *parse trees*. A parse tree is drawn from top to bottom: the *root node* of the tree (usually drawn at the top) is labeled with the starting symbol **Main**. The grammar auxiliary symbols are represented by *branching nodes*. These nodes have *daughter nodes*. Each ALU is represented by a *leaf node*, i.e. a node that has no daughter node.

Figures 7.12 and 7.13 represent the two parse trees produced by the previous grammar for the previous sentence. In Figure 7.12, the **Main** node has three branching nodes: **NP**, *sees* and **NP**. In other words, the sentence contains one direct object complement: *a chair from his house*. The node **NP** on the left (the subject) has two leaf nodes: *this* and *man*. The node **NP** on the right (the direct object complement) has three branching nodes: **NP** (*a chair*), *from* and **NP** (*his house*).

---

6 Chapter 13 shows how to implement sentences' transformations automatically.

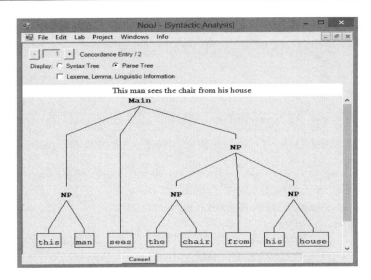

Figure 7.12. *First parse tree for the ambiguous sentence:*
This man sees the chair from his house

In the second parse tree below (Figure 7.13), the **Main** node this time has five branches, among them the subject, the direct objet complement and the indirect objet complement introduced by the preposition *from*.

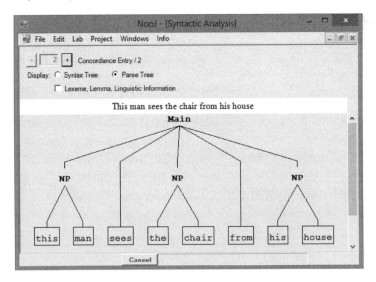

Figure 7.13. *Second derivation for the sentence:*
This man sees the chair from his house

Parse trees are useful for understanding how a text has been parsed by applying to it a given grammar; they constitute an indispensable tool for debugging grammars. In section 12.2.4, we will see the difference between *parse trees* (which reflect the grammar's structure) and *syntax trees* (which represent the structure of the text).

7.3. Conclusion

NooJ offers linguists two equivalent tools for formalizing context-free languages: context-free grammars and recursive graphs. From the perspective of linguistic engineering, these grammars are more compact, natural and maintainable than regular grammars.

It is possible to compile most useful context-free grammars into finite-state machines automatically; the advantage is that finite-state machines can parse texts much more rapidly than context-free parsers. Linguists can therefore benefit from using powerful, compact and elegant context-free grammars (and Recursive Graphs), while not giving up the efficiency of finite-state machines that will parse potentially large texts.

Finally, parse trees allow linguists to visualize how a text has been parsed using a given grammar, and thus constitute a valuable tool for linguists.

7.4. Exercises

1) Construct the prototype for a context-free grammar that describes transitive sentences in which the direct object might contain a sentence introduced by *that*, for example: *Lea tells Joe that Ida is bothering Mary. Joe thinks that Ida likes Mary.*

2) Consider the following generative grammar:

S → N V
S → N V N
N → Joe
N → Lea
N → that S
V → dreams
V → sees

a) Describe the language represented by this grammar informally. Does this grammar recognize un-grammatical sentences?

b) Construct a regular expression (or a finite-state graph) equivalent to this grammar.

7.5. Internet links

GNU BISON [DON 13] and Yacc are syntactic parsers that use context-free grammars (with some additions) to describe the syntax of programming languages such as C or Java. They are typically used to build compilers for these languages, see: www.gnu.org/software/bison.

There are instruction manuals and course materials available on the Internet for both these tools. For example, the following document shows how to build a compiler with LEX and YACC:

epaperpress.com/lex and yacc/download/LexAndYaccTutorial.pdf

The pumping lemma is used to prove that some languages cannot be recognized by finite-state machines, see:

en.wikipedia.org/wiki/Pumping_lemma_for_regular_languages

The courses on Apple iTunes and Coursera cited in the *Internet Links* section at the end of Chapter 5 contain a section on context-free languages and grammars, as well as on push-down automata.

8

Context-Sensitive Grammars

Context-sensitive grammars (i.e. type-1 generative grammars) allow linguists to describe context-sensitive languages, and can be processed by Linear Bounded Automata. The Chomsky-Schützenberger hierarchy shown in Figure 5.3 shows that the set of context-free grammars is included in the set of context-sensitive grammars. Type-1 grammars are generative grammars in which it is possible to specify a context where a given rewriting rule can be activated. Typically, formalisms used in NLP to describe context-sensitive grammars use a unification mechanism to describe these constraints.

The *Lexical Functional Grammar* (LFG) [KAP 82] formalism allows linguists to construct context-sensitive grammars, but in practice LFG parsers would be much too slow to process the large-scale texts typically used by search engines and researchers in Corpus Linguistics. One crucial issue in NLP lies indeed in ensuring that parsers are as efficient as possible; this has led some computational linguists to design formalisms that make a compromise between the expressive power of the grammars, and the efficiency of the parsers that handle them. For example, the formalisms *Combinatory Categorical Grammars* (CCG), *Head Grammars* (HG), *Linear Indexed Grammars* (LIG) and *Tree Adjoining Grammars* (TAG) [JOS 87] do not have as much expressive power as a context-sensitive grammar[1]: they are known as "mildly context-sensitive". Thanks to the limitations of these formalisms, it was possible to construct parsers that are faster than Linear-Bounded Automata, but of course the drawback is that

---

1 [VIJ 94] shows that these formalisms have the same power of expression, i.e. they can describe the same set of languages.

these limitations reduce the grammars' power, which harms the linguistic project of describing *all* linguistic phenomena. I believe that from a purely linguistic point of view, limiting the power of a formalism in the interest of computing efficiency is counter-productive.

8.1. The NooJ approach

The Chomsky-Schützenberger hierarchy is often misinterpreted: the fact that the set of context-free languages is included in the set of context-sensitive languages does not mean that context-free languages are themselves "smaller" than context-sensitive languages.

Indeed, it is important to understand that any given language (whether it is regular, context-free, context-sensitive or even unrestricted) is included in a regular language: for example, the most encompassing of all languages – the language that contains all the sequences that can be constructed from a given vocabulary V, i.e. V* – is itself a regular language. In other words: the Chomsky-Schützenberger hierarchy concerns the inclusion of sets of languages, but says nothing about the inclusion of languages themselves.

| All languages are included in a regular language.

The NooJ approach is based on this fact: a NooJ context-sensitive grammar *Gc* contains two elements:

– a regular or context-free grammar G that defines a superset of the language to be described;

– a set of contextual constraints that exclude some sequences recognized by G, and retain only the ones that belong to the desired context-sensitive language.

In practice, NooJ provides linguists with the power of context-sensitive grammars while still operating with the efficiency provided by push-down automata and finite-state machines[2]. Below are five examples of context-sensitive languages and their implementation in NooJ.

---

2 The context-free grammars used in practice to describe natural languages can often be compiled into finite-state machines; see the discussion on the three types of recursion in the previous chapter.

8.1.1. *The $a^n b^n c^n$ language*

Let us consider the language that contains all the sequences made up of a given number of letters *a*, followed by the same number of letters *b*, followed by the same number of letters *c*: this language thus contains all the words that are written in the form $a^n b^n c^n$ for any value of *n*. Here are some examples of sequences that belong to this language:

"a b c", "a a b b c c", "a a a b b b c c c"

It would be impossible to design a context-free grammar that can produce all these sequences, and only them[3]. Type-1 generative grammars that could formalize this simple language are difficult to understand; Figure 8.1 provides one example.

$$
\begin{aligned}
S &\rightarrow a\,S\,B\,C \\
S &\rightarrow a\,B\,C \\
C\,B &\rightarrow H\,B \\
H\,B &\rightarrow H\,C \\
H\,C &\rightarrow B\,C \\
a\,B &\rightarrow a\,b \\
b\,B &\rightarrow b\,b \\
b\,C &\rightarrow b\,c \\
c\,C &\rightarrow c\,c
\end{aligned}
$$

Figure 8.1. *Context-sensitive grammar for the language $a^n b^n c^n$*

This generative grammar recognizes the language $a^n b^n c^n$. For example, the following sequence:

"a a a b b b c c c"

is generated by this grammar, as the following derivation shows[4]:

---

3 The pumping lemma for context-free languages can be used to prove that this language cannot be described by a context-free grammar.
4 Left members of the rule to be applied appear in bold; sequences that have just been produced are underlined.

S → a **S** B C → a a **S** B C B C → a a a **B** C B C B C → a a a B **H B** C B C →
a a a B **H C** C B C → a a a B B **B CC** B C → a a a B B C **H B** C → a a a B B C **H C** C →
a a a B B **C B** C C → a a a B B **H B** C C → a a a B B **H C** C C → a a **a** B B B C C C →
a a a **b** B B C C C → a a a **b b** B C C C → a a a b b **b** C C C → a a a b b **b c** C C →
a a a b b b **c c** C → a a a b b b c **c c**

The least that can be said is that it is not immediately apparent that this grammar really generates the language $a^nb^nc^n$! The fact that a grammar that is supposed to describe such a simple language is so complex to read is a serious problem for a project that aims for an exhaustive formalization of languages: it is vital to be able to construct grammars that are easy to read so as to be able to test them, modify them, adapt them, share them and accumulate them in large quantities.

With NooJ, this same language is represented by the grammar given in Figure 8.2.

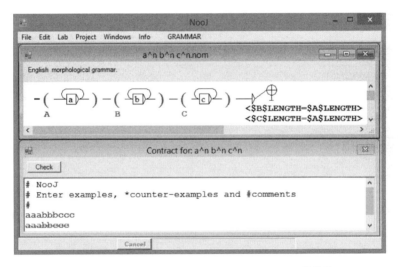

Figure 8.2. *NooJ grammar for the language $a^nb^nc^n$*

This grammar first recognizes all the sequences made up of any number of *a*, followed by any number of *b*, followed by any number of c^5, then verifies that the numbers of *a*, *b* and *c* are equal. Compared to the regular and context-free grammars that we have seen up until now, NooJ's context-sensitive grammars contain two new mechanisms:

---

5 This grammar does not recognize the empty string.

– *variables*[6]: used to store sub-sequences of the matching sequence. The grammar in Figure 8.2 contains three variables \$A, \$B and \$C that store the sub-sequences of *a*, of *b* and of *c*, respectively;

– *constraints*: if the grammar has indeed matched one given sequence of text, then the parser verifies the constraints produced by the grammar. The grammar in Figure 8.2 contains two constraints:

<\$B\$LENGTH=\$A\$LENGTH><\$C\$LENGTH=\$A\$LENGTH>

These two constraints check that the sub-sequences made up of *b's* (stored in variable \$B) and *c's* (stored in variable \$C) have the same length as the sequence made up of *a's* (stored in variable \$A).

NooJ context-sensitive grammars are processed very efficiently: checking that a given sequence of text has the form a*b*c* can be performed by a deterministic finite-state machine (i.e. in linear time), whereas it takes only a constant time to check each contextual constraint. We therefore benefit from the efficiency of finite-state machines and, at the same time, from the power of context-sensitive grammars.

Note that using NooJ, we could construct equally simple grammars to recognize a whole range of similar languages; for example, here is a NooJ grammar that recognizes the language $a^n b^n c^n d^n e^n$.

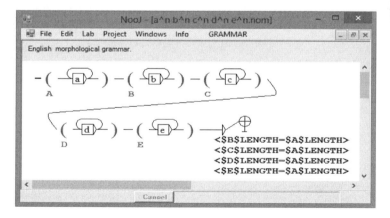

Figure 8.3. *NooJ grammar that recognizes the language* $a^n b^n c^n d^n e^n$

6 NooJ variables are used in a very similar way to the group variables used in the tools EGREP, PERL, PYTHON and SED.

This grammar is really no more complicated than the previous one, whereas a type-1 grammar for this same language would be much more complicated to design. Note that mildly context-sensitive formalisms such as CCG, HG and TAG cannot represent this language.

8.1.2. *The language a^{2^n}*

Here is a second typical language that cannot be described by context-free grammars and requires a context-sensitive grammar: the language that contains all the sequences of a's whose length is a power of 2. For example, this language contains the following sequences:

"aa", "aaaa", "aaaaaa", "aaaaaaaaaaaa",
"aaaaaaaaaaaaaaaaaaaaaaaa"

i.e. this language contains all the words that have length 2, 4, 8, 16, 32, 64, 128, etc. The grammar in Figure 8.3 recognizes this language.

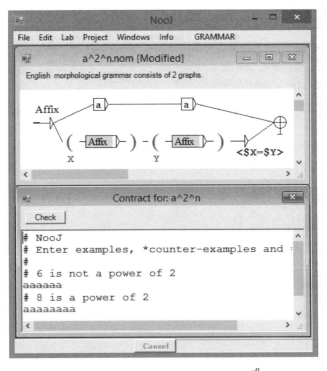

Figure 8.4. *Grammar of language a^{2^n}*

Here too, the parser follows two steps to parse a sequence:

– first, it ignores the constraints, and applies the push-down automaton corresponding to the Recursive Graph to match potential sequences;

– second, it checks recursively that the two sub-sequences in each matching pair are equal, using the constraint <$X=$Y>.

This approach is very efficient: verification that the sequence really has an (aa)* (aa)* form is calculated by a simple push-down automaton; the number of constraints that need to be checked out is less than the length of the matching sequence[7]. Here too, we benefit from the power of context-sensitive grammars and at the same time from the efficiency of push-down automata.

8.1.3. *Handling reduplications*

Now, here are examples that are more linguistically relevant. Consider reduplication. The words *bye bye* and *so so* are examples of reduplications in English; some languages use reduplication to mark a plural (Indonesian), emphasis (Tagalog), or a distributive plural (Japanese, Mandarin, Quechua). For instance, the morphological grammar in Figure 8.5 recognizes reduplications in Quechua words[8].

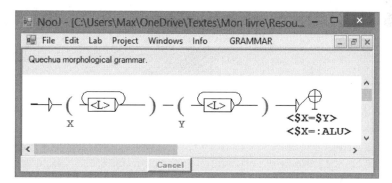

Figure 8.5. *Grammar that recognizes reduplications*

---

7 For a sequence of length n, the number of equality tests corresponds to the number of internal nodes in the binary tree where each leaf would be labeled with a pair "a a", i.e. at worst: $\frac{n}{2}-1$.

8 [DUR 14] presents the morphological grammars for Quechua.

This graph recognizes a sequence of letters (<L>), stored in variable $X, followed by a second sequence of letters, stored in variable $Y. The parser then checks that the two sequences $X and $Y are identical (constraint <$X=$Y>), and that the word stored in $X is indeed an ALU (constraint <$X=:ALU>), i.e. a lexical entry of the Quechua dictionary. This grammar matches the word forms *aqoaqo* [desert] from ALU *aqo* [sand] and *hatunhatun* [huge] from ALU *hatun* [big].

8.1.4. *Grammatical agreements*

There follows an example that shows the advantage for linguists of using context-sensitive grammars, even when the phenomena could just as well be described with regular expressions.

If we wish to construct a grammar that takes account of the agreement inside German noun phrases, between a noun, its determiner and its adjectives, we could construct the finite-state graph in Figure 8.6.

In this grammar, each path contains sequences of words that agree in number, gender and case. For example, the symbol <DET+m+s+nom> recognizes determiners (DET) that are masculine (+m), singular (+s) and nominative (+nom); the symbol <A+f+p+acc> recognizes feminine plural accusative adjectives, and <N+n+s+dat> recognizes neuter singular dative nouns. This grammar thus recognizes sequences such as "der kleine Stift" while rejecting sequences in which some words do not agree, such as "das kleinen Stifte".

This grammar is unsatisfactory for two reasons:

– on the one hand, the same structure is repeated twenty-four times, to take account of all combinations of genders (masculine, feminine or neuter), numbers (singular or plural) and cases (nominative, accusative, dative, genitive). If we refine the description of the noun phrases to include relative clauses, noun complements, noun phrases that contain more than one adjective, etc. the graph will get even larger, and it will then become frankly inconvenient to have to recopy the same structure twenty-four times over…;

– on the other hand, this grammar does not differentiate between sequences that are un-grammatical (e.g. "der Stift kleine") and sequences that are syntactically well formed but which contain a discrepancy in agreement (for example "die kleinen Stift"). However, these two sequences should not be rejected in the same way: the first is not valid for structural reasons, whereas the second has a correct structure, but contains an agreement error[9]...

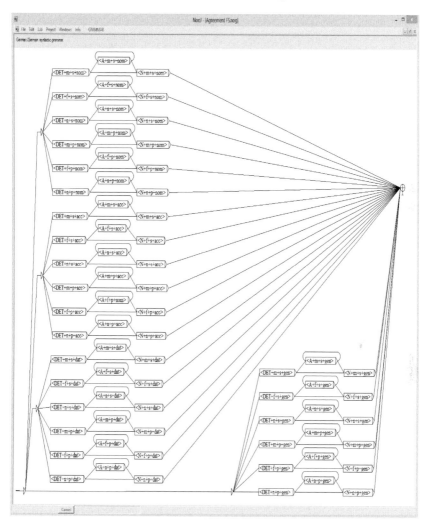

Figure 8.6. *A German finite-state graph to describe agreement in gender, number and case.*

---

9 In French, the plural mark *s* is mostly not pronounced; therefore, a lot of spelling mistakes involve missing *s*'s. It is therefore crucial to design grammars that distinguish well-formed sentences that contain an agreement error (which are frequent, in particular on the WEB) from un-grammatical sequences of texts.

This is why it is preferable to construct the context-sensitive grammar given in Figure 8.7.

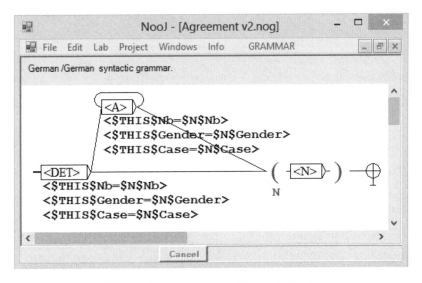

Figure 8.7. *Agreement with constraints`*

This time, we describe a noun phrase's structure only once. We store the head of the noun phrase in variable $N, then we verify each of the constraints:

– each constraint <$THIS$Nb=NNb> checks that the current ALU ($THIS) and the noun ($N) have the same value for the property "Nb" (i.e. same number);

– each constraint <$THIS$Gender=NGender> checks that the current ALU ($THIS) and the noun ($N) have the same value for the property "Gender".

– each constraint <$THIS$Case=NCase> checks that the current ALU ($THIS) and the noun ($N) have the same value for the property "Case".

This grammar is more concise, and easier to maintain than the equivalent finite-state graph. Moreover, an incidental advantage: because this grammar separates the structural description of the noun phrase from the description of the agreements, we can easily construct from this grammar a spell checker that recognizes structurally correct noun phrases, checks all agreements, and then produces an error message when one agreement is not met in a matching noun phrase.

8.1.5. *Lexical constraints in morphological grammars*

Here is a final example that shows the advantage of using context-sensitive grammars, this time at a morphological level.

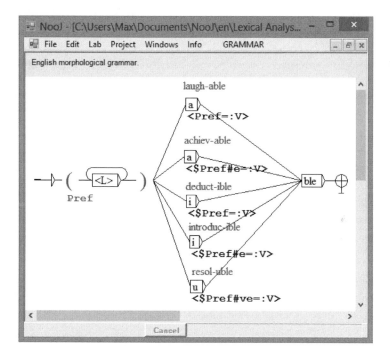

Figure 8.8. *Morphological context-sensitive grammar*

First, the parser recognizes all the word forms made up of any sequence of letters (<L>), followed by the suffix *able, ible* or *uble*, for example: *table, laughable, introducible, resoluble*. In the second step, the parser processes one of the lexical constraints:

<$Pref=:V>, <$Pref#e=:V>, <$Pref#ve=:V>

These constraints ensure that the prefix of the word form (stored in variable $Pref) matches a verb, i.e. constitutes a lexical entry associated with the category "V" in the English dictionary. For example:

– when the grammar recognizes the word form "table", the variable $Pref takes the value "t"; the constraint <$Pref=:V> then becomes <t=:V>. As "t" is not listed as a verb in the dictionary, the constraint is not met; consequently the grammar rejects the word form "table";

– when the grammar recognizes the word form "laughable", the variable $Pref takes the value "laugh"; the constraint <$Pref=:V> then becomes <laugh=:V> which is met since "laugh" is a verb listed as such in the English dictionary;

– when the grammar recognizes the form "achievable", the variable $Pref takes the value "achiev"; the constraint <$Pref#e=:V> then becomes <achieve=:V> which is met since "achieve" really is a verb.

There are a number of similar morphological grammars for parsing word forms with prefixes (e.g. *to rework, to disagree*) or suffixes (e.g. *a worker, a disagreement*). Context-sensitive grammars are particularly well adapted to handling Germanic languages and, more generally, agglutinative languages, for which it is vital to be able to extract each constituent of a compound orthographic form, and impose one or more lexical constraints on it[10].

8.2. NooJ contextual constraints

There are three types of constraint:

1) Equality constraints: to check the identity between two strings, for example:

```
<$X=$Y>, <$NOUN$Nb="p">,
<$DET$Gender=$NOUN$Gender>, <$NP$Dist=$V$NODist>
```

The first constraint checks that the word form stored in variable $X is identical to that stored in variable $Y. The second constraint checks that the property "Nb" of the ALU stored in variable $NOUN has the value "p". The third constraint checks gender agreement between a determiner (stored in

---

10 See section 11.3.4.

variagle $DET) and a noun (stored in variable $NOUN). The last constraint checks that the distribution class of a Noun Phrase stored in (NP Dist) – for example "Hum", "Conc" or "Abst" – is the one expected for the subject of a verb stored in variable $V ($V$N0Dist).

2) Matching constraints: to test that an ALU matches a lexical or syntactic symbol[11], for example:

```
<$X=:N>,  <$Y=:have>,  <$N=:N+Hum-Medic>
```

The first constraint checks that the ALU stored in variable $X is a noun. The second checks that the ALU stored in variable $Y is associated with the lemma "have". The third constraint checks that the ALU stored in variable $N corresponds to a Human noun (+Hum) that does not belong to the set of medical terms (-Medic);

3) Existence constraints: to check that a variable has a defined value. One example of using this constraint is given by the Spanish graph given in Figure 8.9.

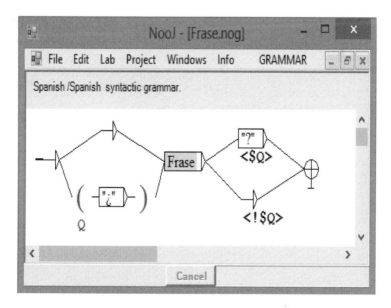

Figure 8.9. *Checking the presence of a question mark*

---

11 Here, we return to the lexical and syntactic symbols described in section 6.7.

This single grammar handles both declarative and interrogative sentences in Spanish: if the sentence (described in the embedded graph *Frase*) is preceded by the character "¿", then the variable $Q is defined, the constraint <$Q> is met, and therefore the right upper path in the graph is activated; if not, it is the lower path that is activated.

Any constraint from the three types can be modified by the negation operator, "!". For example:

– the constraint <!$X=$Y> is satisfied if the strings stored in the variables $X and $Y are not equal;

– the constraint <!$X=:V> is satisfied if the ALU stored in $X is not a verb;

– the constraint <!$Q> is satisfied if the variable $Q has no defined value.

[TRO 13] shows how NooJ constraints can be used to describe French elementary sentences with great precision.

8.3. NooJ variables

NooJ variables have three scopes.

8.3.1. *Variables' scope*

1) the variable $THIS always stores the current linguistic unit (ALU). This variable is very "local", in the sense that several $THIS variables can occur in the same graph while still storing different values. For example, the graph in Figure 8.7 recognizes sequences in which there are any number of adjectives, and checks that each adjective agrees in gender, number and case with the noun. When a given noun phrase matches the grammar, there are more than one resulting $THIS variables, each having a value independent from each other;

2) NooJ variables are "local" by default, in the sense that NooJ seeks their value either in the graph that refers to them, or in its embedded graphs. For example, we can imagine that the *NP* graph in Figure 8.7 would itself be used in a higher level graph such as in Figure 7.4. In the latter graph, each of

the *NP* nodes refers to the same graph, but the values of $N used in each *NP* are independent from one another, which makes it possible to check agreement inside each noun phrase with no interference.

3) NooJ also allows linguists to use global variables, that is to say variables that are garanteed to have only one value, regardless of their location in the grammar's structure. To indicate that a variable is global, the prefix "@" is used in front of its name, for example @Subject. The value of a global variable can be defined at any level of imbrication in the complete grammar (including in a higher level) without fear that its value will become inaccessible, or hidden by a higher level graph.

We will see in Chapter 13 that global variables are typically used to perform semantic analyses. Global variables are also useful to parameterize NooJ grammars. For example, a generic grammar could be constructed to recognize all transitive sentences; in this grammar the main verb would then be refered to by a global variable, say @Verb. It would then be possible to set the @Verb variable, for example to the ALU *to see*, and then to apply the instanciated grammar to a corpus of texts. In that case, applying the grammar would extract all the transitive structures from a text in which the main verb is *to see*[12].

8.3.2. *Computing a variable's value*

By default, a variable refers to a linguistic unit (ALU) rather than to a given word form; it can therefore have several forms. For example a $Predicate variable which would have the following ALU as its value:

```
<donate,V+FLX=ATE+DRV=OR>
```

could just as well be used to produce the verb form *donating* as the noun form *donor*. We will see in Chapter 13 that this feature allows linguists to design transformations very simply, for example to compute the transformation *He is donating his blood* → *He is a blood donor* just by performing simple morphological operations such as $V_N (to nominalize the ALU stored in variable $V).

---

12 This is the operation carried out in section 4.4.6. when the different meanings of the French verb *abriter* were identified by instanciating the main verb in the generic grammars *T* and *P*.

To retrieve the ALU of the $THIS variable, NooJ's parser just checks the TAS at the current position in the matching sequence of text. To compute the value of a local variable, NooJ's parser explores the trace produced while matching the current sequence, first to the left of the variable reference, then to its right. Global variables' values are stored in a table that is external to the parser.

One can set a variable to a different value than its matching text sequence. For example, in the following graph, the $Answer variable takes the value "YES" or "NO", depending on the answer given. However, for instance, the variable's value will be set to "YES" whether the actual matching expression was "I agree", "right", "certainly" or "ok". In the same way, this variable will be set to "NO" whether the actual matching answer was "no", "I disagree", "certainly not", etc.

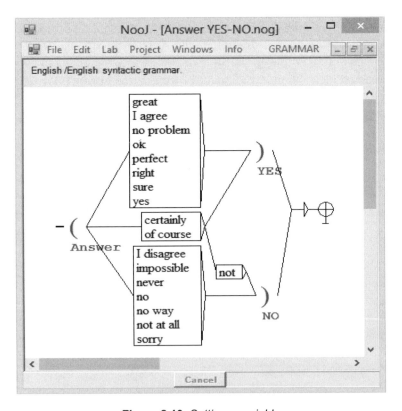

Figure 8.10. *Setting a variable*

8.3.3. *Inheriting a variable's value*

The contents of a variable can be transferred to another variable, and so a variable can be made to inherit a value computed in a lower level graph: for example, in the grammar in Figure 8.11, the $NPH variable (Noun Phrase Head) is set to the content of the $N variable ("noun"), which is itself defined inside the first noun phrase (NP) graph.

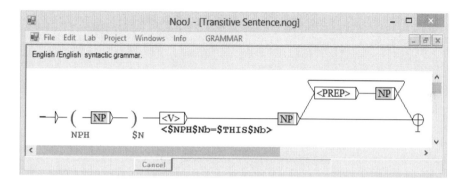

Figure 8.11. *Inheritance: $N →$NPH*

In other words, the value of the $N variable (which stores the head of the noun phrase) is copied to the $NPH variable. At the sentence level, the constraint <TGNNb=$THIS$Nb> checks that the verb agrees in number with its subject.

8.4. Conclusion

NooJ offers linguists the possibility of adding *contextual constraints* to context-free grammars – indeed even to regular expressions – that operate on variables. These constraints enable the value of some variables to be tested, as well as lexical, syntactic or semantic properties to be checked, and allow linguists to design grammars that take into account grammatical or distributional agreements. This mechanism allows linguists to construct context-sensitive grammars.

NooJ's parser works in two steps: in the first step, constraints are not taken into account; consequently, the parser matches all the correct sequences of text, as well as a number of extra "bad" ones. This stage can be carried out by a push-down automaton, or even, often, by a finite-state automaton. At the second stage, NooJ checks the contextual constraints and eliminates the matching sequences that do not satisfy them. This two-step approach allows linguists to separate the description of the sentences' syntactic structure, from the description of grammatical or distributional agreement or, more generally, of compatibility between ALUs.

8.5. Exercises

1) Consider the vocabulary {*are*, *brave*, *brother*, *is*, *my*, *sisters*}. Design a context-sensitive grammar that describes all the sentences that can be constructed using this vocabulary, taking agreements into account.

2) Construct the regular expression (or finite-state graph) equivalent to the context-sensitive grammar above.

8.6. Internet links

The following Wikipedia entries present the context-sensitive languages, generative type-1 grammars as well as linear bounded automata:

en.wikipedia.org/wiki/Context-sensitive_language

en.wikipedia.org/wiki/Context-sensitive_grammar

en.wikipedia.org/wiki/Linear_bounded_automaton

The pumping lemma for context-free languages is explained on the site:

en.wikipedia.org/wiki/Pumping_lemma_for_context-free_languages

The courses on Apple iTunes and Coursera listed in the section *Internet links* at the end of Chapter 5 contain a section on context-sensitive languages and grammars as well as on linear-bounded automata.

The formalism *Lexical Functional Grammar* (LFG) allows linguists to construct context-sensitive grammars, see the following sites for more details:

www.essex.ac.uk/linguistics/external/lfg

nlp.ioperm.org/lfg-parser.html

www.xlfg.org.

The formalisms CCG, HG, LIG and TAG allow linguists to construct mildly context-sensitive grammars, see the Internet links at the end of the first chapter.

9

Unrestricted Grammars

In the discussion on the *Chomsky-Schützenberger hierarchy* in section 5.3, we saw that unrestricted grammars (or "type-0" grammars) can describe any recursively enumerable language.

In linguistics, unrestricted grammars are the most general grammars[1]: they contain rules such as $\alpha A \beta \rightarrow \gamma$, where A is an auxiliary symbol and α, β and γ are sequences of any number of terminal and auxiliary symbols. Figure 9.1 shows an example of a unrestricted grammar.

$$S \rightarrow \textbf{SING NPVNP}$$
$$S \rightarrow \textbf{PLUR NPVNP}$$
$$\textbf{SING NPV} \rightarrow \text{this } \textbf{SING NOUNSING V}$$
$$\textbf{PLUR NPV} \rightarrow \text{these } \textbf{PLUR NOUNPLUR V}$$
$$\textbf{SING V} \rightarrow \text{see}$$
$$\textbf{PLUR V} \rightarrow \text{sees}$$
$$\textbf{NP} \rightarrow \textbf{SING NOUN}$$
$$\textbf{NP} \rightarrow \textbf{PLUR NOUN}$$
$$\textbf{SING NOUN} \rightarrow \text{cat}$$
$$\textbf{PLUR NOUN} \rightarrow \text{dogs}$$

Figure 9.1. *Unrestricted grammar*

Unrestricted grammars can be written with NooJ with the help of finite-state transducers that recognize the γ sequences, and produce the

---

1 There are languages that are not recursively enumerable, but these languages are exotic mathematical constructs that have no clear linguistic application, see the Internet link at the end of Chapter 5.

corresponding αAβ sequences. For example, the grammar in Figure 9.1 is written with NooJ as shown in Figure 9.2.

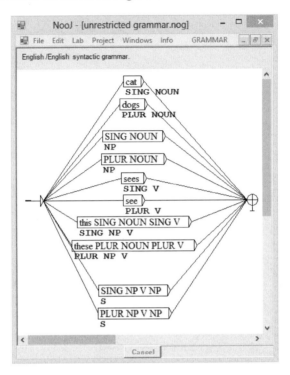

Figure 9.2. *NooJ unrestricted grammar*

This graph can be applied to a text in a loop, i.e. to perform substitutions until the final text "S' is produced, or until no more new substitutions can be carried out.

In the general case, it is not possible to place a limit on the maximal number of substitutions that a grammar will produce, and it is impossible to determine in advance if this process will even stop; see [TUR 37]. Concretely, when NooJ applies grammars in sequence, it imposes the sequence to have a limited length, typically ten grammars at most, which limits its power, but makes it manageable. In other words, NooJ does not have the full power of a Turing Machine, even though it can be used to write unrestricted grammars. In Chapter 13 we will see applications for unrestricted grammars in building NLP applications such as NLP automatic paraphrase production, semantic analysis and automatic translation.

9.1. Linguistic adequacy

Remember that the linguistic project described in this book does not aim at handling rhetorical phenomena such as litotes, metaphors or metonyms, computing reference to pronouns, solving anaphors, describing poetic language, resolving semantic ambiguities, locating plays on words, and even less making extra-linguistic judgements to draw out inferences or check a statement's validity: therefore one must be careful not to use these phenomena to justify the need for unrestricted grammars or powerful formalisms such as *Head-Driven Phrase Structure Grammar* (HPSG) [POL 94].

However there are a few syntactic phenomena that are not easily described with context-sensitive grammars, for example sentences that contain the adverb *respectively* such as the following one:

> *Joe, Lea, Jean and Rufus are respectively*
> *my son, my teacher, my wife and my dog.*

In order for this type of sentence to be grammatical, the number of its subjects must be equal to the number of the corresponding attributes; moreover, we need to link each attribute to its corresponding subject: *Joe is my son, Lea is my teacher, Jean is my wife* and *Rufus is my dog*.

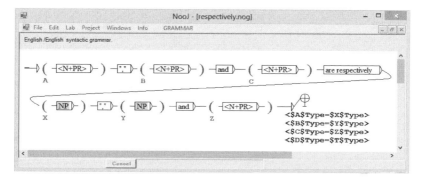

Figure 9.3. *Respectively*

In the general case, it is not possible to construct a context-sensitive grammar that computes these links, whatever the number of subject/attribute pairs. However, it is possible to construct a context-sensitive grammar that handles this type of sentence if we accept a limit on the maximal number of subject/attribute pairs. For example, the context-sensitive grammar in Figure 9.3 recognizes sentences that contain 4 subject/attribute pairs, and checks that each subject in of the same type as its corresponding attribute:

<\$A\$ Type=\$X\$ Type> checks that the first name *Joe* has the same type (e.g. Human, Masculine) as the first attribute *my son*;

<\$B\$ Type=\$Y\$ Type> checks that the second name *Lea* has the same type (Human) as its attribute *my teacher*;

<\$C\$Type=\$Z\$Type> checks that the third name *Jean* has the same type (e.g. Human, Feminine) as its attribute *my wife*;

<\$D\$ Type=\$T\$ Type> checks that the last name *Rufus* has the same type (Animal) as its attribute *my dog*.

It is interesting to note that sentences using *respectively* become somewhat perplexing, if not incomprehensible, if there are more than four or five pairs, which in itself justifies the argument that context-sensitive grammars might be sufficiently powerful to describe natural languages. Moreover, checking constraints between subjects and their attributes in sentences with the adverb *respectively* involves performing extra-linguistic computation, just like solving anaphors or retrieving the referent to a pronoun. For example, the name *Rufus* is often a dog's name, but can also be a name for a person: to check that Rufus is a dog, we would need to know more about the "real world" Rufus; the name *Jean* is feminine in the United States or England, but masculine in France: how can we check that *Jean* and *wife* are compatible, if we don't know anything about Jean?

It therefore makes sense in the framework of our strictly linguistic project not to attempt to check subject/attributes links. And if we do remove this type of verification, then it becomes possible to design a context-sensitive grammar that checks only that the number of subjects equals the number of attributes[2].

---

2 We could use a constraint such as <\$BEFORE\$LENGTH=\$AFTER\$LENGTH>, on the model of the grammar in Figure 8.3.

9.2. Conclusion

I would not venture to state that *no* linguistic phenomenon that comes into play in *any* language absolutely justifies the need for unrestricted grammars, considering that there are around 9,000 languages[3], and to this day no one has produced a complete formalized description for even one language... However, it can reasonably be assumed that regular expressions, context-free grammars and context-sensitive grammars are sufficient to formalize almost all typographical, orthographical, morphological, syntactic and semantic linguistic phenomena.

Although an actual need to use unrestricted grammars to describe strictly linguistic phenomena remains to be demonstrated, we can find interesting applications for them in NLP, in particular to compute transformational analyses or to produce paraphrases automatically. We will discuss these applications in Chapter 13.

9.3. Exercise

Using the model of the grammar in Figure 9.2, construct an unrestricted grammar that recognizes all the sentences that can be built with the vocabulary {*Joe, Lea, sees, loves*}, and then modify the grammar so that, for each recognized sentence, it produces the corresponding sentence in which *Joe* and *Lea* have been replaced by pronouns, for example:

> Joe sees Lea → He sees Lea.
> Lea sees Joe → Lea sees him.

9.4. Internet links

The course on Apple iTunes listed in the *Internet links* section at the end of Chapter 5 contains a section on unrestricted grammars and Turing machines.

---

3 The ISO code 639-3 currently lists 8,648 languages and dialects, but this list is incomplete; for example, it does not contain Québécois or Acadian, and confuses the Alsatian dialect with Swiss German.

There are several sites that allow users to program Turing machines, for example: zanotti.univ-tln.fr/turing/turing.php.

Alan Turing's paper that describes Turing machines, introduces the *Entscheidungsproblem* and discusses the halting problem:

www.thocp.net/biographies/papers/turing_oncomputablenumbers_1936.pdf

The halting problem is also explained on the Wikipedia page:

en.wikipedia.org/wiki/Halting_problem

The site for the formalism Head-Driven Phrase Structure Grammar (HPSG) contains numerous resources: hpsg.stanford.edu.

Several HPSG parsers are available, among them the TRALE software that can be used to construct HPSG grammars and is available on the site:

milca.sfs.uni-tuebingen.de/A4/Course/trale.

PART 3

Automatic Linguistic Parsing

In the first part of this book, we focused on the base elements of languages: the characters that make up their alphabet, and the Atomic Linguistic Units (ALU) which make up their vocabulary. In the second part, we were given formal tools (i.e. grammars) with which we can formalize how linguistic units combine.

Once we have built a grammar that formalizes a certain linguistic phenomenon, we can run a parser that automatically applies this grammar to any text: the third part of this book therefore focuses on the use of linguistic resources (dictionaries and grammars) for the automatic parsing of texts. Linguistic resources are by definition neutral descriptions: I will show some applications that use dictionaries and grammars to *generate* (rather than parse) word forms, phrases or sentences: these applications are referred to as *automatic generation applications*.

Chapter 10 introduces the *text annotation structure* (TAS), which stores the results of the analyses produced by the different linguistic parsers at any level (from the orthographical up to the semantic levels). This structure is indispensable, as many linguistic phenomena are in fact interconnected; for example, computing the noun *admirer* from the verb to *admire* is both a lexical problem (only certain verbs can be nominalized), a morphological problem (add the suffix *-er*) as well as a syntactic problem that involves restructuring sentences (e.g. *Joe admires Lea → Joe is a Lea's admirer*).

In Chapter 11, I present the first stage of any linguistic analysis: the *lexical analysis*, which consists of computing the ALUs in a text from the sequences of characters that make up the text-file. This stage includes orthographical analysis (to recognize word forms), text segmentation (to recognize words and sentences), several types of morphological analysis (to link word forms to their corresponding lemma) and consulting dictionaries (to get the properties of the corresponding ALUs).

Chapter 12 is dedicated to *syntactic analysis*. I first present *local syntactic analysis* which mainly consists of identifying simple sequences of ALUs. This stage allows NooJ to identify multiword terms, certain "interesting" sequences of grammatical words, semantic units such as named entities, and to disambiguate certain words, based on their context.

The annotations stored in the TAS can be used to represent the structure of each sentence, thus performing *structural syntactic analysis*. The TAS can then be visualized by a *syntax tree*, and I will show how this tree is different from the *parse tree* that we saw in section 7.2, which reflects the structure of the grammar. Syntax trees have a nice application: their construction allows NooJ to resolve most lexical ambiguities, merely by deleting from the TAS all the ALUs that are not present in them. I will show how the TAS can also be used to construct other possible representations of the sentence, in particular *dependency trees*, with minimal modifications to the underlying grammars.

In Chapter 13, I examine *Transformational Analysis*, which aims to produce elementary sentences (or "predicates") expressed by a complex sentence, or conversely to compute complex sentences from one or several elementary sentences. I will show that there is no such thing as a "transformational grammar" that would exist independently from other levels of the linguistic description, that is to say that transformational analysis can and must be carried out using only structural syntactic grammars. Transformational analysis is very similar to semantic analysis, and I will discuss how it could be used to implement some sophisticated NLP applications such as Question Answering or Machine Translation.

Text Annotation Structure

10.1. Parsing a text

All NooJ grammars (regular, context-free, context-sensitive or unrestricted grammars) can produce outputs associated with the text sequences that they recognize. Generally, these outputs themselves belong to the language recognized by these grammars; for example the form *tsar* which is produced by the grammar in Figure 6.15 is recognized itself by the same grammar, and the term *bank card* produced by the grammar in Figure 6.16 is itself recognized by this grammar.

However, the output produced by a grammar may also *not* belong to the language described by the grammar. For example, Figure 6.18 shows a graph that recognizes certain expressions in English and produces a corresponding translation in French. Similarly, the graph in Figure 6.17 recognizes word forms that belong to the English language, whereas the sequences produced by the grammar, such as "INF" or "PR+3+s", are codes that represent linguistic information such as "Infinitive" or "Present, 3rd person, singular" and belong to a metalanguage.

For NooJ, *parsing a text* means linking each matching sequence to some linguistic information; this information can be written in the form of sequences of codes such as, for example, "NP+Hum" for "Noun Phrase, Human" or "V+tr" for "Verb, Transitive". In other words, NooJ parses a text by applying grammars to it; the grammars produce sequences of codes that represent the linguistic properties of the matching sequences and constitute the *analysis* of the text.

What should we do with the resulting analyses? They might be typically displayed as the ending results to linguists, or they can feed a NLP application, for instance to construct an index or a terminology database, etc. However, if the resulting analyses need to be reused by another linguistic parser at a higher linguistic level, then it is necessary to give the later parser access both to the original text itself, and also to the analyses produced by the previous parsers.

10.2. Annotations

One way of combining a text with its analyses is to annotate it, that is to say, to associate sequences in the text with *annotations*. An annotation is a link between a text sequence and some corresponding piece of information. An annotation is defined by the following three pieces of data:

– the location of the text sequence to be described;

– the length of the text sequence;

– a series of codes that represents the information associated with the text sequence.

Nothing prevents several annotations from sharing the same location, and even the same length (for example in ambiguous cases). For instance, the following text:

> *hot dog*

could be linked to three annotations:

– start=1, length =7: <FOOD>;

– start=1, length =3: <ADJ>;

– start=5, length =3: <ANIMAL>.

These three annotations can account for two analyses: *FOOD* (as in *I just ate a hot dog*) or *ANIMAL* (as in *That poor dog is really hot*). Parsers used in NLP usually represent texts annotated using the XML format, that literally merges the text and its analyses. XML uses tags like angle-shaped brackets to write each analysis "around" the corresponding sequence of text. For example, the previously analyzed text could be represented by the following XML text:

```
<FOOD><ADJ> hot </ADJ><ANIMAL> dog </ANIMAL></FOOD>
```

The entire sequence is thus annotated "FOOD", whereas the form *hot* is annotated "ADJ" and the form *dog* is annotated "ANIMAL". This type of annotation is often used to represent texts, in particular by the TEI[1].

10.2.1. *Limits of XML/TEI representation*

Merging the analyses and the text itself with the help of XML tags poses three significant problems[2]:

– it is not possible to annotate sequences that overlap; for example, it is impossible to use a single XML tag (e.g. <TERM>) twice to annotate both the terms *big screen* and *screen star* in the following text:

big screen star = movie star vs *a screen star who/which is big*

This is a crippling limitation for syntactic analysis as there are often ambiguities over the span of certain noun phrases, which often results in multiple concurrent syntactic analyses;

– it is not possible to insert annotations inside agglutinated or contracted forms without modifying the initial text; for example it is not possible to keep the contracted form *cannot* in the text as it is, and at the same time annotate it with two annotations: one for *can* (<VERB>) and one for *not* (<ADVERB>). This is a serious limitation for Germanic languages, and more generally for all languages that accept some agglutinations;

– it is not possible to annotate discontinuous sequences using a single XML tag; for example, it is not possible to annotate the phrasal verb *to call*

---

1 The *Text Encoding Initiative* constitutes the *de facto* standard in Corpus Linguistics and in the social sciences; its directives describe how to use XML tags to annotate texts. See www.tei-c.org.
2 The XML file format is largely independent of the TEI standard. In particular, the SOAP format based on XML enables any data structure to be described, including NooJ Text Annotations Structures (TAS).

back (and only the phrasal verb) using a single XML tag in the text *Lea called her friend back.*

10.3. *Text annotation structure (TAS)*

NooJ stores annotations in a specific structure, separated from the text: the text annotation structure (TAS) [SIL 06][3]. The texts annotated by NooJ, unlike tagged texts, can represent all types of ALU: affixes, simple words, multiword units and discontinuous expressions [SIL 07]. NooJ annotations are not subject to the same constraints as XML tags: NooJ can represent ambiguous annotations (as in Figure 10.1), annotations that overlap (Figure 10.2), annotations within a word form (Figure 10.3), and even annotations associated with discontinuous expressions (Figure 10.4).

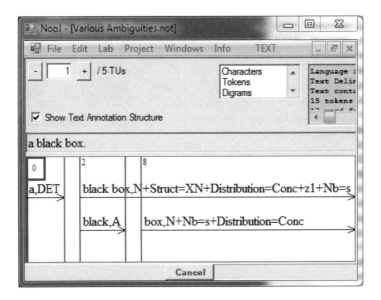

Figure 10.1. *Annotations for the ambiguous sequence "black box"*

---

3 NooJ can import any XML document and integrate the XML annotations into the TAS, and conversely it is also possible to export the TAS to create an XML document, but certain NooJ annotations will then be lost, if they cannot be represented in the form of XML tags.

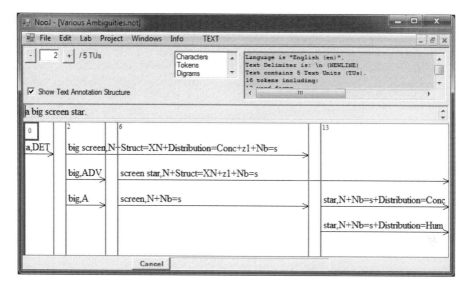

Figure 10.2. *The two terms "big screen" and "screen star" overlap*

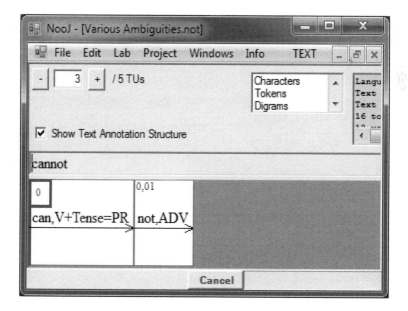

Figure 10.3. *Annotating the contracted form "cannot"*

Figure 10.4. *Annotating the phrasal verb "call back"*

More importantly, the TAS can represent unresolved ambiguities, which enables all potential, or hypothetical, analyses to be retained temporarily, with the expectation that a later, more sophisticated analysis (e.g. produced by a syntactic or semantic parser) will be able to remove the incorrect annotations from the TAS [SIL 09].

Figure 10.5 for example shows a text annotated by NooJ right after its lexical analysis, and before its syntactic analysis: the TAS describes an unresolved ambiguity for the form *on*: either a particle as in *Joe gets on well with Lea*, or a preposition as in *Joe gets on the bus*, as well as for the form *well* (interjection, noun, adjective or adverb). It will fall to a later syntactic or even to a semantic parser to resolve these ambiguities, i.e. to remove from the TAS the four incorrect annotations <on, PREP>, <well, INTJ>, <well, N> and <well, A>.

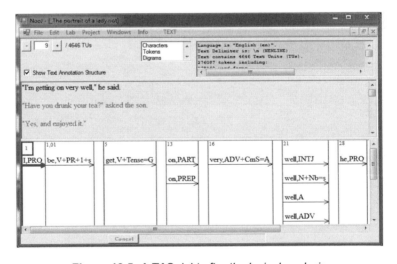

Figure 10.5. *A TAS right after the lexical analysis*

Keeping the TAS and the original text separated has at least two advantages:

– the text to be parsed is never modified; consequently, adding an annotation to it never changes the location of a text unit relative to one another; the text's index remains unchanged, whether it has been annotated or not, whether it was already lemmatized or not, whether it contains structural syntactic information or not;

– linguists can develop linguistic resources (dictionaries and grammars) without worrying about possible clashes that might occur between these resources and some annotations that were added previously to a text. Grammars can therefore be applied independently from each other, even in parallel (simultaneously) or in cascade (one after the other) [SIL 08].

Beyond these technical advantages, the possibility of incrementally adding annotations in a TAS by applying elementary linguistic resources (small, specific dictionaries and local grammars) "in cascade", allows linguists to simplify all parsers. All parsers then behave basically the same way, whatever their level of analysis from orthography to semantics[4]: a parser always takes a text and its TAS as its inputs, and then adds annotations to the TAS and/or deletes annotations from it. The linguistic data represented in the TAS always has the same nature (set of annotations), and is accessible to any parser that needs it.

10.4. Exercise

The goal of this exercise is to compute and display the Text Annotation Structure for the text: *Joe saw this red tape*. To do this: build a dictionary that contains all the ALUs that may occur in this sentence (there are at least 10 potential ALUs). Then, build the inflectional grammar that links the text's word forms to their corresponding lexical entries (for example *saw → see*). Finally, compile the dictionary and the grammar, and then apply them to the text to display the final TAS.

---

4 Actually, NooJ handles two types of annotation: annotations that represent ALUs, and annotations that represent the structure of syntactic units (for example noun phrases) or semantic units (for example predicates), see [SIL 07].

10.5. Internet links

For a presentation of XML, see the Wikipedia page:

en.wikipedia.org/wiki/Extensible_Markup_Language

The site: en.html.net/tutorials/html contains several tutorials on XML. The consortium *Text Encoding Initiative* has the portal:

www.tei-c.org/index.xml

11

Lexical Analysis

Lexical analysis aims to identify all the text's atomic linguistic units (ALUs), starting from the sequences of characters that make up the file that represents the text.

The first mention of lexical analysis for natural languages can be found in [SIL 87]. [SIL 93] introduced the software INTEX, the first automatic lexical parser capable of handling orthographic, morphological and lexical ambiguity (including between simple and compound words), for a large coverage of vocabulary. [KAR 97] describes the XFST tool, often used in industry to construct automatic lexical parsers.

An automatic lexical parser should solve problems linked to breaking texts down into a series of word forms (*tokenization*), associating these word forms with their corresponding lexical entry (*lemmatization*) and annotating multiword units and discontinuous expressions. Note that the result of a lexical analysis is mostly ambiguous; removing all lexical ambiguities from the results produced by a lexical parser will be the objective of further syntactic or semantic analyses.

11.1. Tokenization

At the lowest level, analyzing a text involves identifying the word forms in a computer file which is made up of sequences of codes. Whatever the encoding system used to represent characters (e.g. ASCII or Unicode) or the file format used to represent the text structure (e.g. DOC or HTML), we must in the first place separate its textual content from its formatting data (e.g. italics, bold), its structural data (e.g. titles and headers) or other data that can appear in the texts (e.g. images). The files' purely textual content can then be seen as a strict sequence of alphabetic (that is to say *letters*) and non-alphabetic (that is to say *delimiters*) characters.

Each language creates particular difficulties: for example the lack of spaces in Chinese texts, the lack of vowels in Arabic texts, punctuation used inside words in Armenian, systematic ligatures in devanāgarī, etc. Even for languages that use the Latin alphabet, typographic rules vary from one language to another: for example, German uses capital letters at the beginning of nouns, English uses an apostrophe for the possessive, Italian uses the apostrophe as an accent, French uses the apostrophe for elisions. In English, the comma is used to separate thousands in numbers and a period is used in decimal numbers, but the reverse is true in French, etc. It is therefore necessary to build a tokenizer specific to each language.

To recognize word forms from a text-file automatically, we must solve three levels of problems:

– recognizing letters, which involves replacing missing accents, diacritics, and vowels, handling foreign letters and potential transliterations as well as ligatures, and homogenizing orthographic variants;

– handling ambiguous delimiter characters: for example, the apostrophe/quotation mark, dash/hyphen and period/dot ambiguities in English;

– linking different word variants together.

For English, reference works such as *The Chicago Manual of Style* and *The Oxford Style Guide* list the typographical rules used by professional editors and publishers, however, many texts available for analysis (including on the Internet) are not always edited by professional editors.

11.1.1. *Letter recognition*

Remember that it is necessary to unify characters that have several possible UNICODE codes (see section 2.4.4.2). Some languages provide a great deal of alphabetic variation. For instance, in traditional Chinese, over a thousand characters have one or more variants: a word containing three letters therefore has a dozen potential orthographic variants[1].

In some Semitic languages (for example in Arabic and Hebrew), vowels are only occasionally written in texts; the missing ones must therefore be computed. Dictionaries contain lexical entries with vowels, and are represented by finite-state transducers[2]. An adaptation of the transducers' lookup algorithm allows NooJ to re-establish the missing vowels[3]. When the dictionary returns several lexical entries for a given word form, it has produced an orthographic ambiguity.

> Word Form with no vowel: حسب(hsb)
> حَسَبَ(hasaba) = *to compute*
> حَسُبَ(hasuba) = *he is noble*
> حَسِبَ(hasiba) = *he believed*

Figure 11.1. *Ambiguity triggered by the lack of vowels[4]*

In English, there is a similar, but very limited phenomenon: the accents on letters in foreign words are often omitted, for example: *cafe* instead of *café* and *voila* instead of *voilà*. In French, words written in capitals are often written without accents; for example the word form *ELEVE* can represent an instance of the word form *élevé* [high] or the word form *élève* [student].

The Latin alphabet is present even in texts written in languages that use other alphabets. For example, in the text in Figure 11.2, written in Hebrew, there are technical terms (for example *LCD, ACTIVE CONTROL*) or units of measurement (for example *Hz, cd/m^2*) written in the Latin alphabet[5].

---

1 A equivalence table for more than 1,000 Chinese characters is included in the Chinese module for NooJ, see [LIN 08].
2 See Chapter 6.
3 During the transducer lookup, vowels and diacritics are treated as empty strings. The transducer is therefore non-determinist and applying it to an Arabic vowel-less word form returns all the corresponding lexical entries with their vowels.
4 Personal communication from Héla Fehri (University of Sfax). [MES 08a] shows the architecture of an analyzer that carries out automatic lexical analysis of Arabic texts by combining orthographic and morphologic analyses.
5 My thanks to Yaakov Bentolila (Univ. Ben Gourion), Dusko Vitas (Univ. of Belgrade) and Vincent Bénet (INALCO, Paris) for these examples of alphabetic variation.

יש לנו את המחיר הכי זול בישראל,פראייר מי שלא קונה!!!
טלוויזיה 42" LCD – רזולוציית מסך FULL H.D -1920 X 1080p.
קליטת אותות וידאו 1080p) בתדרים 24 Hz -60Hz)

PIXEL PLUS H.D -.טכנולוגיה ייחודית להכפלת הרזולוציה לקבלת תמונה חדה
ACTIVE CONTROL -בקרה ושיפור של איכות התמונה בכל רגע על פי איכות
השידור.
LIGHT SENSOR -בקרה של התמונה על פי תאורה בחדר
AUTO FORMAT -התאמה אוטומטית של פורמט התמונה לפורמט השידור ללא
עיוותים.
יחס קונטרסט דינמי : 1:30000
בהירות 500 cd/m²
זמן תגובה: 5 msec
2 רמקולים מובנים בהספק כולל 30 W RMS

Figure 11.2. *Hebrew and Latin alphabets together in same text*

In the Russian text in the following figure, there is the name of the banker *Warren Buffett* written in Cyrillic characters, then the name of his company *Berkshire Hathaway* written in Latin characters.

«Я на самом деле ношу дорогие костюмы, просто на мне они выглядят дешево», – любит говорить о себе известный американский финансист Уоррен Баффет. Сегодня дешево выглядят акции инвестиционной компании Баффета Berkshire Hathaway.

Figure 11.3. *Itogi Weekly no. 40, October 3rd 2011*

Korean, Japanese and Vietnamese texts often contain Chinese characters. So, in Japanese, the *hiragana* alphabet exists side by side with (Chinese) *kanji* characters, often within the same word: typically, the root of verbs is written in kanji, and their suffix in hiragana.

In modern Greek texts, foreign proper terms or names are not always typed correctly by authors who forget to change their keyboard mode: it is frequent to find the acronyms such as "NATO" written in Greek letters *N* (nu), *A* (alpha), *T* (tau) and *O* (omicron) instead of Latin letters. The same problem exists for texts written in Cyrillic, where some Cyrillic letters are visually indistinguishable from Latin letters.

Other confusions can occur between graphically similar letters, some systematically. For example, in Egyptian texts, confusion between the *alif* and the *hamza* letters is very common[6].

A more systematic orthographic variation concerns foreign letters present in foreign proper names or terms. For example, in English texts, some accents are often omitted (e.g. *angstrom* instead of *ångström*), whereas other letters are transliterated (e.g. "ss" in place of the German letter "ß" and "ue" in place of "ü"). Professional journalists usually use the ISO norm to transliterate foreign alphabets, for example: ISO-233 for Arabic, ISO 7098 for Chinese, ISO/TR 11941 for Korean, ISO 9 for Cyrillic, ISO 3602 for Japanese, ISO 259-2 for Hebrew etc. But of course, texts found on the Internet are not always written by professional editors so we find numerous variants that must be retranscribed, for example with the help of grammars such as those in Figure 11.4.

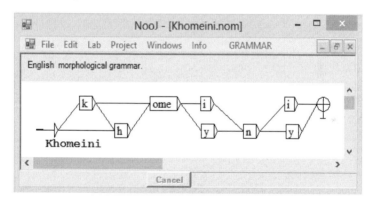

Figure 11.4. *Transliteration variants*

11.1.2. *Apostrophe/quote*

The apostrophe (Unicode U+27 code)[7] is neither a letter nor a punctuation mark; it is used:

– inside a multiword unit: Ma'am, o'clock, O'Connors, y'all;

– as an abbreviation sign for shortened forms, often in poems or songs: *'twas, 'cause, 'course*;

---

6 Personal communication from Slim Mesfar.
7 The apostrophe is also often represented by the character U+E28099.

– as a single quotation mark, instead of an opening and closing quotation mark, e.g. *the 'donor'*. The opening quotation mark must appear at the beginning of a word; the closing quotation mark must appear at the end of a word;

– as the genitive marker "'s" or alone when the previous word ends in "s": *a Levi's store, at McDonald's, Chris' house*;

– to represent some foreign letters: *Shi'ism, Roch'Hodech*;

– to represent the minute, or the unit of an angle or time: *an angle of 10.35'*;

– the verb forms *be, could, have, must, need, shall, should* and *will* can be contracted, as in Figure 11.5.

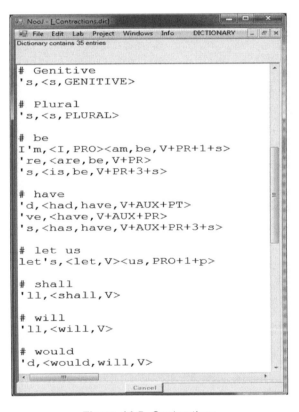

Figure 11.5. *Contractions*

Some sequences are therefore ambiguous, for example:

's→ <s,GENITIVE>   *Lea's nice car*
's→ <s,PLURAL>   *The word* abbey *has two b's*
's→ <has,have,V+AUX+PR+3+s>   *Joe's eaten all his spinach*
's→ <is,be,V+PR+3+s>   *Ida's pretty rich*

– the negating adverb *not* can also be contracted, as can be seen in Figure 11.6.

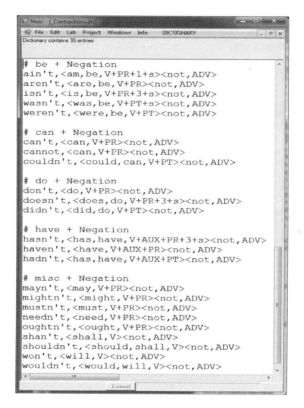

Figure 11.6. *Contractions of "not"*

11.1.3. *Dash/hyphen*

The dash (U+2D) can appear:

– as a punctuation mark, instead of the en-dash (U+2013), or the em-dash (U+2014) (it is then doubled);

– instead of the hyphen (U+2010), inside a word form cut off at the end of a line. Generally, hyphens are placed automatically by programs that prepare documents for print and therefore have a specific code that can easily be removed, but if the text was obtained from an Optical Character Recognition (OCR) software, it is necessary to implement a procedure to distinguish the dash from the hyphen;

– in many multiword units or proper names, *well-being*, *Claude Lévi-Strauss*. The dash often alternates with a space or a concatenation; we saw in section 4.4.3 that NooJ electronic dictionaries contain the two special characters "_" and "=" for handling the systematic alternation between dash, space and concatenation.

– after a hundred prefixes, for example in Figure 11.7;

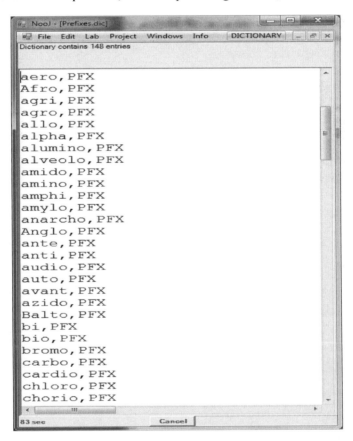

Figure 11.7. *Prefixes*

– in numbers written entirely in letters, e.g. *forty-two thousand five hundred thirty-six dollars and ninety-nine cents*. Numbers must be recognized and annotated by a specific grammar. The following figure shows an extract from the grammar that recognizes numeric determiners written in letters, for example, *seventy-three, thirty thousand and three hundred and forty-four, fourteen hundred*, etc;

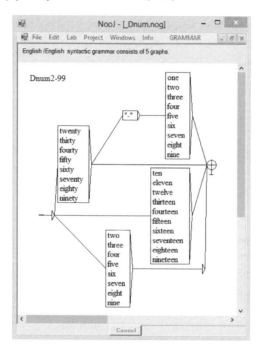

Figure 11.8. *Numerical determinants*

– in adjectival expressions, e.g. a *fifty-pound salmon*, a *French-born singer*;

– as a conjunction:

An interface between a human and a machine = a human-machine interface.

The years between 2010 and 2020 = the years 2010–2020

– to represent the mathematical subtraction operator or the negative sign.

11.1.4. *Dot/period/point ambiguity*

The full stop character has the same code (UTF 2E), whether it represents an abbreviation mark, a decimal point or the period (indicating the end of a sentence). Most often, the function "end of sentence" can be recognized when this character is followed by a word in capitals, but not always.

When an abbreviation occurs at the end of a sentence the dot is not doubled. It is therefore necessary to explicitly add the sentence delimiter.

A parser that has access to abbreviation dictionaries will be able to distinguish the following simple cases:

1) *Apples, bananas, cherries, etc. are all types of fruit.*

Since "etc." is a standard abbreviation, and it is not followed here by a word in capitals, it is therefore an abbreviation mark.

2) *Apples and bananas are types of fruit. Cherries are too.*

"fruit." is not a standard abbreviation, and the next word is in capitals, therefore it marks the end of a sentence.

But capitals are used not only to mark the beginning of a sentence: proper names always start with capitals. Ambiguity between *word-abbreviation* (before the dot) and *proper name-word* (after the dot) combine to make it nearly impossible to identify the end of sentences on a strictly orthographic level, without further analyzing the text. Consider the following cases:

3) *Joe C. Smith told me that.*

4) *It has plenty of vitamin C. Smith told me that.*

In (3), "C." corresponds to an abbreviated middle name; in (4), the dot represents the end of a sentence.

The ambiguity between words and abbreviations is systematic for the 26 letters of the alphabet written in capitals when they appear at the end of a sentence, for example, A = musical key, B = Chemical element Boron, C = Roman Numeral 100, etc.

Any letter can be used in a mathematical context (e.g. *factorize variable X*), which creates systematic ambiguities each time a single capital letter is followed by a dot/period.

Consequently, the algorithm for recognizing the end of sentences should be able to produce ambiguous results: ambiguity can only be resolved by later analyses (syntactic or semantic)[8].

Finally, note that some sentences can be embedded, such as this one: (*A sentence between two parentheses or quotes is written inside another one*), or this one:

> *This is a citation.*

which complicates sentence representation. However, in the context of building NLP applications, it is sensible to build lexical parsers such as those described by [SIL 87] and produce results that are satisfactory when parsing regular texts, such as news articles, or fairly structured technical documents.

Abbreviations and acronyms that are written without the abbreviation mark can be processed as simple words or proper names and listed in a specific dictionary. Here is a list of standard abbreviations and acronyms that carry abbreviation marks, and thus interfere with analyzing the full stop character.

> *A.S.A.P. (As Soon As Possible), A.D. (Anno Domini), a.m. (ante meridian), B.A. (Bachelor of Arts), B.C. (Before Christ), B.C.E. (Before Common Era), B.S. (Bachelor of Sciences), B.Y.O.B. (Bring Your Own Bottle), C.E. (Common Era), cf. (confer), chap. (chapter), D.I.Y. (Do It Yourself), Dr. (Doctor), ed. (editor), E.T.A. (Estimated Time of Arrival), et al. (et alii), etc. (et cætera), e.g. (exempli gratia), fig. (figure), ibid. (ibidem), id. (idem), i.e. (id est), Inc. (Incorporated), Jr. (Junior), Ltd. (Limited), M.D. (Medicinae Doctor), m.o. (modus operandi), Mr. (Mister), n.b. (nota bene), p. (page), p.m. (post meridian), Prof. (Professor), P.S. (Post Scriptum), R.S.V.P.*

---

8 This is what NooJ does, for example to tokenize a Chinese text.

(Répondez s'il vous plait), Sr. (Senior), St. (Saint, Street), vol. (volume), vs. (versus).

We can add to this list the following abbreviations:

Jan. Feb. Mar. Apr. Jun. Jul. Aug. Sep. Oct. Nov. Dec. L.A., N.Y.C., S.F., U.S., U.S.A., U.S.S.R., Washington D.C.

common abbreviated honorary, military and religious titles:

Capt. (Captain), Col. (Colonel), Comdr. (Commander), Cpl. (Corporal), Gen. (General), Gov. (Governor), Hon. (Honorable), Lt. (Lieutenant), Msgr. (Monsignor)

as well as abbreviations of nouns for measuring length (in.), surface (sq. ft.), volume (gal.), mass (lb.), money (U.S. $), temperature (°F), pressure (psi), power (kW), food (tbsp.), etc. When building an NLP application for processing technical or scientific texts in a particular domain (chemistry, finance, medicine, physics, etc.), we list all the abbreviations from that domain in a dictionary.

11.2. Word forms

The aim of lexical analysis is to identify the ALUs that occur in the text. Once we have processed (i.e. recognized, calculated and unified) the alphabetic characters and delimiters, we can then process the sequences of letters, that is to say, the word forms.

11.2.1. *Space and punctuation*

For languages that do not separate words by a space, such as Chinese, the system's dictionaries are consulted character by character. In these languages, there is no real difference between simple words and multiword units: the ALUs are identified by applying the dictionary to every sequence of characters and all the corresponding matches produce lexical solutions. Generally, a Chinese sentence will therefore be broken down in several different ways (see Figure 11.9): it will be the role of syntactic or semantic analyses to delete useless annotations and retain only the correct ones.

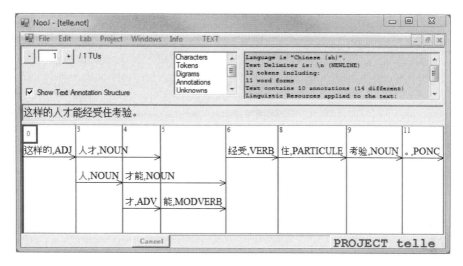

Figure 11.9. *Multiple solutions for breaking down a Chinese text*

For writing systems that use spaces, a simple rule for alternating forms/separators is used to break the text down into forms, but there are some exceptions. We saw that in English, analyzing the dash/hyphen, apostrophe/quotation and period/dot characters requires building linguistic resources.

In Armenian, intonation signs are written inside word forms; we therefore need to extract them. We use a grammar such as that in Figure 11.10 to analyze the word forms that contain these signs.

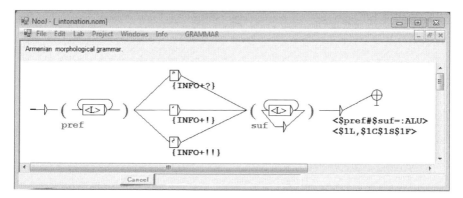

Figure 11.10. *Intonation in Armenian*

In this grammar, the <L> symbol represents any letter; the variables $pref and $suf contain sequences of letters to the left and right of the intonation sign: the paruyk (which corresponds to the question mark), the yerkar (exclamation) and the šešt (injunction or contrast) [DON 07]. The sequence $pref#$suf contains the initial word form whose intonation sign was removed. The lexical constraint:

```
<$pref#$suf=:ALU>
```

checks that this form corresponds to an element of Armenian vocabulary (i.e. ALU). If this constraint is verified, the lexical parser produces an annotation that corresponds to the analysis of the reconstructed form: $1L refers to its lemma, $1C to its category, $1S to its syntactic-semantic properties and $1F to its morphological properties. Finally, a "+?", "+!" or "+!!" feature is added to the annotation to indicate the type of intonation that was recognized.

11.2.2. Numbers

The ten digits occur in texts to represent quantities, dates or zip codes, within email addresses or Internet sites. They are also used to number titles, chapters, sections, examples and figures, etc. For example, the grammar in Figure 11.11 recognizes US telephone numbers.

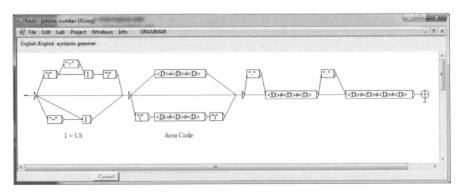

Figure 11.11. *Recognizing US Phone Numbers*

In this graph, <D> represents any digit:

<D> = 0 | 1 | 2 | 3 | 4 | 5 | 6 | 7 | 8 | 9

The special character "#" represents a forbidden space. For example, in the telephone number "(+1) 304-555-0199", no space can be inserted between the three "5" digits.

Numbers can be prefixed by a sign and can be followed by an exponent, for example in engineering and scientific notations: -1.23×10^{-3}. But if we need to analyze scientific or technical texts that contain mathematical or numerical expressions, it will be necessary to design grammars capable of handling mathematical expressions and containing at least the following special characters[9]:

$$= \neq \approx + - \pm \times : / \div \sqrt{} <> \leq \geq ()\{\}[]$$
$$\tfrac{1}{2} \tfrac{1}{3} \tfrac{2}{3} \tfrac{1}{4} \tfrac{3}{4} \tfrac{1}{5} \tfrac{2}{5} \tfrac{3}{5} \tfrac{4}{5} \tfrac{1}{6} \tfrac{5}{6} \tfrac{1}{8} \tfrac{3}{8} \tfrac{5}{8} \tfrac{7}{8}$$

A Roman numeral is a sequence defined by the alphabet {c, d, i, l, m, v, x}. Roman numerals appear entirely in lower case, such as *xiv*, or entirely in upper case, such as *XIV*, but upper and lower cases cannot generally be mixed, except for ordinal numbers, such as *the XXth century*. Roman numerals can be described by the following grammar.

Unit = i | ii | iii | iiii| iv | v | vi | vii | viii | ix ;
Ten = x | xx | xxx | xl | l | lx | lxx | lxxx | xc ;
Hundred = c | cc | ccc | cd | d | dc | dcc | dccc | cm ;
Thousand = m | mm | mmm | mmmm ;
Main = (:**Thousand** | <E>) (:**Hundred** | <E>) (:**Ten** | <E>) (:**Unit** | <E>) ;

Figure 11.12. *Roman numerals*

When numbers represent ordinal adjectives, they can be followed by the suffix "st", "rd" or "th". For example, we can find:

> *It happened during the XIIth century*
> *From the IIIrd century BCE up to the IInd century CE*

---

9 Mathematical expressions can be recognized by a Context-Free Grammar.

Roman numerals therefore interfere with lexical analysis, since they are indistinguishable from regular word forms, for example "CM" (= 900 or *centimeter*) or "IV" (= 4 or *intravenous*). Integrating and applying the grammar of Roman Numerals together with regular dictionaries enables word/Roman numeral ambiguities to be represented. Further syntactic or semantic analyses will have to resolve these lexical ambiguities, taking into account the words' syntactic or semantic context.

11.2.3. *Words in upper case*

Most European languages use a double upper/lower case system[10]. Upper case letters are typically used to mark proper names or the beginning of sentences. To identify the ALUs from word forms, it is therefore often necessary to rewrite words that contain one or several capital letters in lower case. A lexical parser therefore handles three types of word forms, depending on their case:

– words written entirely in lower case, for example: "*table*". To recognize these words, we simply consult the dictionary. If we do not find the word in the dictionary, then the word is considered incorrect (we can then run an automatic spelling corrector);

– words whose first letter is upper case: for example: "*When*", "*Joe*", or in which all the letters are upper case: "*INTRODUCTION*", "*IBM*". To identify these words, we generally need to consult two dictionaries: a dictionary of common words (since all common words may appear in upper case letters, at the start of a sentence or in a title) and a dictionary of proper names;

– more general word forms: "*McCarthy*", "*RedOw*", "*kW*", "*dnaC*", etc. These proper names and acronyms should be listed in a specific dictionary.

---

10 Some languages only have one alphabet; some languages have two alphabets but they do not overlap (e.g. squared and cursive alphabet in Hebrew); some languages have more than two alphabets that overlap, sometimes even within forms (for example Japanese). Remember that most languages also use the Latin alphabet, at least occasionally, to denote certain proper names (for example *USA*), names of products (for example *iphone*) or technical terms (for example *kph*).

In the scope of our strictly linguistic project, it is not feasible to build an exhaustive dictionary of proper names: it would be immense since it would have to contain all the first and family names in the United States, Britain and the world, all the street names, names of towns, regions and countries, all the names of societies, organizations, acronyms, brands and products, etc. Actually, it would have to be infinite since any author might invent names of people or places in a novel (for example *Zygtone-Trumard* is a city on planet Mars). And the resulting database would still be of limited benefit, since in the following sentence:

X went to Y to buy the latest model of Z's phones

anyone can guess that X is the name of a person, Y a place name and Z a brand name. In other words, when we have a sufficiently complete description of a language, we will be able to recognize proper names, without having to list them all.

However, when building NLP applications specific to a certain domain/market, we need to get access to exhaustive lists of proper names, for example to enable a spell checker to correct the incorrect form "Masachussets". The classic approach [MCI 81] then consists of building dictionaries of proper names adapted to the texts to be analyzed: if we are analyzing newspapers, we will insert the names of countries and political figures into the dictionaries, if analyzing economic reports, we insert the names of businesses and companies into them, etc.

Finally, note that there are many ambiguities between proper names, acronyms and common words, for example *Seal* (a British singer), *a navy SEAL* (a special force) and *a seal* (a marine mammal). This type of ambiguity is systematic for languages that do not have upper case letters (for example Arabic, Chinese, Korean, Hebrew, Japanese). Here too, a structure such as the TAS enables lexical ambiguities to be temporarily stored, pending a more sophisticated analysis to resolve them.

11.3. Morphological analyses

Morphological analyses aim at linking word forms to the lexical entries that represent the corresponding vocabulary elements (ALUs).

11.3.1. *Inflectional morphology*

Inflectional morphology describes conjugating verbs, putting nouns and adjectives into the plural (and the dual in Arabic), making adjectives feminine or neuter (for example in German), and declining nouns and adjectives (nominative, accusative, dative and genitive for example). A language's inflectional morphology is described by a set of paradigms; each inflectional paradigm corresponds to a regular or context-free grammar that describes how to generate all the forms for a given lexical entry. For example, the paradigm TABLE is defined by the grammar in Figure 11.13.

TABLE = <E>/s | s/p;

Figure 11.13. *Paradigm TABLE*

This grammar describes two suffixes, each producing an output that represents linguistic properties. So, if we apply this grammar to the lexical entry *pen*:

– the suffix <E> (empty string) added to the lexical entry generates the same form, that is to say *pen*; for this form the grammar produces the property "s" (=singular);

– the suffix "s" added to the lexical entry generates the form *pens*; for this form, the grammar produces the property "p" (=plural).

The information produced by inflectional grammars is represented by codes. For example, here are some inflectional codes from the English module for NooJ:

Code	Meaning	Code	Meaning
G	Gerund	3	3rd Person
INF	Infinitive	f	feminine
PP	Past Participle	p	plural
PR	Present	s	singular
PT	Preterite	m	masculine

Figure 11.14. *Inflection codes used in the English NooJ module*

We can use the paradigm **TABLE** to describe inflection fora large number of words: in fact all of the nouns that take "s" in the plural (more than 30,000 simple nouns), for example:

```
abandon,N+FLX=TABLE
abbey,N+FLX=TABLE+Conc
abbot,N+FLX=TABLE+Hum
abbreviation,N+FLX=TABLE
abdication,N+FLX=TABLE
abdicator,N+FLX=TABLE+Hum
...
```

The paradigm **TABLE** can also be used to inflect tens of thousands of compound nouns, for example:

educational system → educational systems

Below (Figure 11.15) is another productive paradigm.

HELP = <E>/INF | <E>/PR | s/PR+3+s | ing/G | ed/PT | ed/PP ;

Figure 11.15. *Paradigm HELP*

The grammar **HELP** enables nearly 5,000 verbs to be conjugated, for example:

```
abandon,V+FLX=HELP
abduct,V+FLX=HELP
abort,V+FLX=HELP
absorb,V+FLX=HELP
abstain,V+FLX=HELP
accustom,V+FLX=HELP
act,V+FLX=HELP
adopt,V+FLX=HELP
afford,V+FLX=HELP
aim,V+FLX=HELP
...
```

Note that this grammar produces some ambiguous forms: for example the form *acted* will be linked to the code +PT (Preterite) and also to the code +PP (Past Participle).

The grammars we just saw are fairly simple because they produce forms using the lexical entry as the root; in other words, it is enough to add a suffix to the lexical entry to obtain any of its inflected forms. Generally, however, the situation is more complex. For example, to obtain the form *knew* from the lexical entry *to know*, we need to remove the last two letters of the lexical entry and then add the suffix "ew".

To delete the last letters, we use the "Backspace" special character: *deleting* the last letter of a word is performed by *adding* the "Backspace" character to the suffix. Note that from a computer point of view, there is little difference between regular alphabetic keys such as "e", and control keys such as "Backspace". For example, the grammar **KNOW** used to conjugate the verbs *to blow, to grow, to know, to throw*, etc. is:

KNOW = <E>/INF | <E>/PR | s/PR+3+s | <B2>ew/PT | n/PP ;

Figure 11.16. *Paradigm for KNOW*

In this grammar, the suffix "<B2> ew" can be understood the following way: press the Backspace key twice, then add "e" and then "w". From the initial lexical entry *blow*, the grammar produces the form *blew*. This form is then linked to the code +PT (Preterite).<B> is one of several morphological operators available. Here is the list of NooJ morphological operators for English.

<B> Delete the current character
<C> Change the case of the current character
<D> Duplicate the current character
<L> Move the cursor left
<R> Move to the right
<S> Delete the character after the cursor
<N> Move the cursor to the beginning of the next word[11]
<P> Move the cursor to the end of the previous word

Figure 11.17. *Morphological operators*

---

11 Some word processors (such as MS-Word) use the command Control-Arrow to the right to move the cursor to the beginning of the following word and the command Control-Arrow to the left to move the cursor to the beginning of the previous word.

The operators <N> (Next word) and <P> (Previous word) move the cursor from word to word, regardless of each word's length. So to write the term *work in progress* in the plural, we could apply the following grammar:

NX = <E>/s | <P2>s/p;

Figure 11.18. *Paradigm for works in progress*

<P2> moves the cursor to the end of the previous word, twice: therefore the command "<P2>s" positions the cursor at the end of the word "work", and then adds a "s" to it, to produce the resulting inflected form *works in progress*. This inflected form is then linked to property "p" (plural).

In many cases, a multiword unit's constituents must agree in gender and number, and for some languages case as well. For example, when we inflect the English noun *woman writer*, we should produce the following two forms:

   woman writer, women writers

but not these forms:

   *women writer, *woman writers

By default, NooJ checks the agreement of all the compound noun's components when it applies an inflectional grammar. So the following paradigm:

NN= :TABLE <P> :MAN;

Figure 11.19. *Paradigm NN*

simply reuses the paradigm **TABLE** to inflect *writer* and the paradigm **MAN** to inflect *woman*. NooJ then filters out the inflected forms that produce both features "s" and "p", which are described in the system as incompatible.

But agreement does not always have to be imposed, as in the following four forms:

> *proof of purchase, proofs of purchase, proof of purchases, proofs of purchases*

where the two constituents *proof* and *purchase* do not have to agree in number.

The operators above enable linguists to lower the number of paradigms considerably. NooJ provides the possibility of adding new operators that are specific to each language. Here are some examples of operators developed specifically for languages other than English:

– in Spanish: the operator <Á> adds an accent to the current vowel *a, e, i, o* or *u*. For example, from *ampliar*, the suffix"<B><Á>is" produces the form *ampliáis*;

– in Hebrew: the operators <B>, <L> and <R> take account of the presence of the soft daguesh[12] in some consonants. If a consonant contains a daguesh, these operators will process the consonant and the daguesh as one single character;

– the operator <D> is used to double letters. For example *b →bb*. However, some Hungarian consonants are written with two or three letters; when they are doubled, the Hungarian orthographic convention is to double only the first letter, for example *sz→ssz*;

– in Quechua: the operator <Q> can duplicate an entire word. For example, applied to the lexical entry *sacha* [a tree], the suffix "<Q>" produces the form *sachasacha* [a forest].

11.3.2. *Derivational morphology*

Derivational morphology describes the links between all the forms that an ALU can take, in any syntactic category; for example, from the verb *to*

---

12 It is a diacritic sign represented by a dot, which is written at the center of a consonant to modify its pronunciation. For example, ב is pronounced "vet" whereas בּ is pronounce "bet". From a linguistic point of view, the consonant thus formed constitutes an indivisible letter: it is therefore necessary for morphological operators to treat it as a whole.

drink, we can create the nouns *a drink, a drinker,* as well as the adjective *drinkable.*

Derived forms must be treated as occurrences of the same ALU, that is to say from a unique vocabulary element, represented by a single lexical entry. Derivation is not a purely academic problem: it is crucial for many NLP applications. For example, if we enter the request "good actor" into a search engine, it will not find "Her acting was good" if there is no link between *acting* and *actor*. Derivation is also important for translation systems. It is often the case that a noun in one language must be translated by an adjective in another language, or a verb in one language by a noun, etc. for example, the following French/English translations involve changing categories:

> *Il a raison* [*he has reason] ↔ *He is right*
> *Elle déjeune* [*she lunches] ↔ *She is having lunch*
> *Il est culotté* [* he is underpanted] ↔ *He has nerve*

For English, to my knowledge, only the NomBank family dictionaries include derivation links.

In a NooJ dictionary, derivation is described with the help of the property +DRV. For example, consider the following lexical entry:

```
act,V+FLX=HELP+DRV=NOP:TABLE+DRV=OR:TABLE+DRV=AING:
NOP+DRV=NING:NOP
```

This entry represents that *to act* is conjugated on the model of HELP and has four derivations: +DRV=NOP:TABLE (the derived form *an act* is itself inflected based on the model of TABLE), +DRV=OR:TABLE (the derived form *an actor* is also inflected on the model of TABLE), +DRV=NING:NOP (the derived noun *acting* which has no inflection) and +DRV=AING:NOP (for the derived adjective *acting*).

The main derivations are:

A → N	*red → redness*
A → V	*black → to blacken*
A → ADV	*quick → quickly*

N → V	*a table → to table*
N → A	*an artist → artistic*
N → ADV	*an artist → artistically*
V → N	*to organize → an organization*
V → A	*to love → lovable*
V → ADV	*to love → lovably*

With NooJ, derivations are formalized in the same way as inflections. For example, to formalize the derivation *to organize → organization*, the following grammar would be used:

ATION = <B>ation/N

This grammar produces the form *organization* from the lexical entry *organize*, then associates the resulting form with the category "Noun" (code N). Note that the resulting noun form *an organization* itself has an inflection: it uses the inflectional paradigm **TABLE** (takes an "s" in the plural).

When the derived form has exactly the same inflection as the base form, then the inflectional paradigm can be left out. For example, the prefixes *re-* or *dis-* do not modify the inflection of verbs:

```
mount,V+FLX=HELP+DRV=RE+DRV=DIS
```

To *remount* and *to dismount* are conjugated in exactly the same way as *to mount*, so it is not necessary to write the inflectional paradigm of the derived verb explicitly.

11.3.3. *Lexical morphology*

Lexical morphology deals with families of derived words. For example, in French, the words *France, français* [French], *franciser* [to Frenchify], *francisation* [Frenchification], *francophonie* [French-speaking communities], *francophile*, etc. are all based on the noun *France*. This family of words can be represented with the help of the following graph.

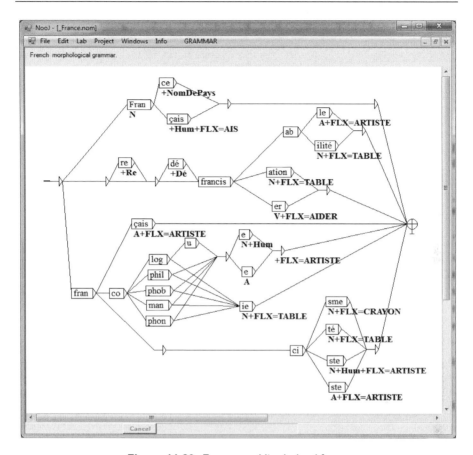

Figure 11.20. *France and its derived forms*

This grammar associates each of the derived forms with an inflection code (for example +FLX=CRAYON), which allows NooJ to recognize all the corresponding inflected forms.

Some forms are recognized several times (that is to say, following several paths on the graph), and thus produce several different analyses. For example, the form *francophone* [Francophone] is analyzed either as a human noun (N+Hum), or as an adjective (A).

This grammar is equivalent to a dictionary that lists the same forms; actually the NooJ command "GRAMMAR > Generate Language" automatically builds the equivalent dictionary.

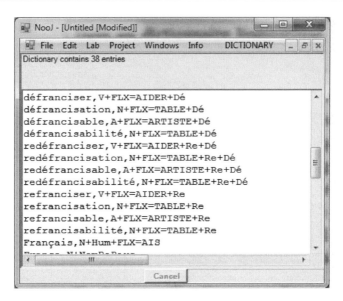

Figure 11.21. *Dictionary produced automatically from a morphological grammar*

Some prefixes or suffixes can be applied productively to sizable groups of ALUs. For example, many verbs take the prefix *over-*, as in *overact*, *overbook*, *overcharge*, *overdevelop*, *overeat*, *overflow*, etc. Rather than doubling the size of the dictionary by listing all the verbs and their correspondents with the prefix *over-* separately, it is much simpler and more economical to put in place a productive morphological Context-Sensitive Grammar as follows:

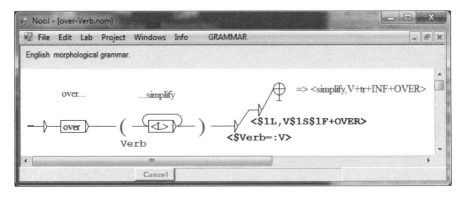

Figure 11.22. *A productive morphological rule*

The symbol <L> represents any letter. In a first step, this grammar recognizes all the word forms that start with the prefix *over*, for example *overture* and *overeat*. In a second step, the constraint <$Verb=:V> checks that the sequence after the prefix really is a verbal form: NooJ then eliminates *overture* since *ture* is not listed as a verb, whereas it retains *overeat* since *eat* is a verbal form. The resulting analysis <$1L,V$1S$1F+OVER> associates the analyzed form (*overeat*) with the lemma (*eat*), as well as the syntactic-semantic (+Transitive+Food) and inflectional information (+INF) associated with the ALU recognized by the constraint (*to eat*).

11.3.4. *Agglutinations*

Some typical examples of languages known as "agglutinative" are Finnish, Hungarian and Turkish. I use the term agglutination more generally to describe   all cases of sequences of several ALUs written in a single orthographic form, without spaces. Agglutination is the exact opposite of composition: an agglutinated form must be analyzed as a sequence of ALUs, whereas a multiword unit must *not* be analyzed. I do not distinguish agglutination from contraction (e.g. *cannot* in English); however, contracted forms are usually very rare and can easily be listed in a small dictionary, whereas agglutination is productive and concerns thousands of combinations that it is not desirable (or indeed possible) to list.

For example in Semitic languages, it is possible to agglutinate several grammatical words to the noun that follows them: the sequence "and in the house", for example, is written as a single form in Hebrew: ובבית ‏: ‏ו [and] + ב [in the] + בית+ [house]. In Arabic, the same sequence of four ALUs is also written as a single contracted form " وببيته", without spaces.

Romance languages also have several productive agglutinations. In Spanish, for example, pronouns complementing the verb are attached to its right. For example, in the sentence:

Se niega a regalármelo [He refuses to offer it to me]

the form "*regalármelo*" should be analyzed as a sequence of three ALUs "regalar" [offer] + "me" [me] + "lo" [it]. Morphological grammars such as that in Figure 11.23 are used to parse the agglutinated forms[13]. When the graph is applied to the form "regalármelo", it matches and its prefix "regal" is then stored in variable $Verb. The constraint <$Verb#ar=:V+INF> becomes <regalar=:V+INF>, NooJ then checks that the form *regalar* really corresponds to an infinitive verbal form (V+INF).

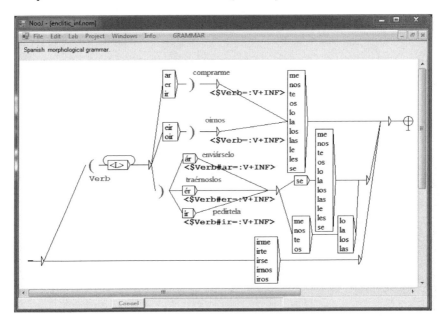

Figure 11.23. *Description of Spanish clitics (infinitive form)*

This grammar can be improved by adding constraints on the complements allowed for each verb: for example the grammar should not recognize the sequence "sleep it to me" since *to sleep* is an intransitive verb.

In Germanic languages, agglutination is used to build very long word forms[14]; for example the following German form:

---

13 This graph is part of the NooJ Spanish module NooJ and was built by Sandrine Fuentes from Autonome University in Barcelona.
14 Note the terminology: these forms are sometimes called Compound Nouns. In our framework, however, compound nouns are multiword units and therefore non-analyzable ALUs, whereas agglutinated forms are made up of several ALUs that must be broken down in order to be analyzed.

Donaudampfschiffahrtsgesellschaftskapitän

is made up of four ALUs: *Captain*, *Company*, *Steamer* and *Danube*. A lexical parser should aim at producing the sequence of ALUs from this agglutinated form.

For example, the grammar in Figure 11.24 analyses German word forms made up of two ALUs: a first ALU stored in variable $pre, a possible "s", and a second ALU stored in variable $noun. The constraints then check that the variable $pre contains a verb, an adjective or a noun and that the variable $noun contains a noun. The resulting lexical analysis is the sequence of the two ALUs.

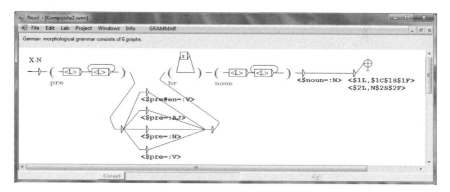

Figure 11.24. *Agglutination in German*[15]

11.4. Multiword unit recognition

Remember that multiword units are atomic linguistic units (ALU) that meet the following definition:

| A *multiword unit* is an ALU that contains letters and delimiters.

Inside multiword units, the most frequent delimiter is the space, but many multiword units contain a dash, some an apostrophe, and many technical terms or names of organizations or products contain digits or other delimiters:

---

15 This graph is part of the German NooJ module built by Ralph Mueller, University of Frieburg (Switzerland).

as soon as possible, well-prepared, McDonald's, the .NET framework, OSX 11, B2B, open 24/7, AT&T

Most multiword units are compound nouns. If we take the standard vocabulary of one language, and add all of the specialized vocabularies in the arts, sciences and technical domains, there are millions of multiword units.

Multiword units are typically recognized by consulting a dictionary such as DELAC. Remember that in general, recognition of a multiword unit by a lexical parser only means that this ALU *potentially* occurs in the text: for example if the sequence *egg roll* is found in a text, it does not mean that this culinary specialty is actually present in the text. For example the sentence: *I saw the egg roll off the counter*, must be analyzed word for word. A lexical parser simply presents all potential lexical hypotheses (by adding them to the TAS): a syntactic or semantic parser will then resolve ambiguities (by deleting annotations from the TAS).

Generally, multiword units and technical terms are described in dictionaries. But it can be better sometimes to regroup terms in grammars. For example, the grammar in Figure 11.25 contains a group of more than 2,500 potential terms dealing with types of insurance. A dictionary displayed in alphabetical order would be less easy to maintain.

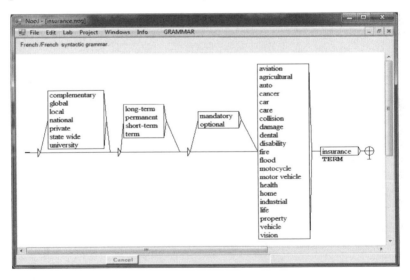

Figure 11.25. *A family of terms*

In practice, software applications that automatically index terms in technical texts (for example *Medline* in the field of medicine) use several hundred local grammars of this type.

11.5. Recognizing expressions

Remember that expressions make up the fourth type of ALU:

> An *expression* is an ALU written as a potentially discontinuous sequence of word forms.

The essential difference between multiword units and expressions is that multiword units do not accept any insertion between constituents[16]:

> *a delicious sweet potato,* * *a sweet delicious potato*
> *a cooked sweet potato,* *a sweet cooked potato*

whereas expressions accept insertions:

> *the more ... the more ...* =: *the more* he speaks *the more* they laugh
> *to ask ... out* =: *Joe asked* Ida *out*
> *to have ... dinner* =: *Lea had* a really nice *dinner*
> *to take ... into account* =: *Joe took* this problem *into account*

As opposed to recognizing simple words and multiword units, automatic recognition of expressions in texts poses different problems since it is necessary to identify the different constituents of an expression when they occur in a sentence, as well as to assemble them and represent the whole expression using a single annotation in TAS.

Among expressions, there are idiomatic or metaphorical expressions (e.g. *to kick the bucket*), technical expressions (e.g. *to draw blood*), phrasal verbs (e.g. *to act out*) as well as light verb/predicative noun combinations (e.g. *to make a decision*). The construction of a dictionary of English expressions will be necessary[17].

---

16 It is always possible to insert a word or clause in a multiword unit, for example *a bad, really dark dream.* We do not treat these stylistic constructs.

17 There are relatively complete dictionaries of expressions in lexicon-grammar format for a dozen languages, see [LEC 98].

As for multiword units, we seek to recognize all occurrences of an expression: if the lexical parser is not able to identify an expression in a sentence, further analyses of the sentence are doomed to failure. "Silence" is not preferable to "noise". As for multiword units, the lexical parser will provide *many* lexical hypotheses, all of which are stored in the TAS temporarily, and some of which are eliminated by later syntactic or semantic analyses.

11.5.1. *Characteristic constituent*

Generally, an expression can occur in different ways; to be able to identify all its occurrences, it is vital to characterize it with an invariant that will "activate" the lexical parser. This invariant is a characteristic constituent of the expression and so constitutes the lexical entry which will represent the ALU.

Sometimes, several constituents can be considered. For example, two possible lexical entries can be envisaged for the expression "to take something into account". Either the expression is accessed via the lexical entry *to take*:

```
take,V+EXP="to take something into account"
```

Or the expression uses the noun *account* as a lexical entry:

```
account,N+EXP="to take something into account"
```

These two solutions are equivalent, and linguists will make their choice depending on methodological considerations. But in many cases, the characteristic constituent can only be one constituent. For example, if we decided to describe the expression *to have lunch* using the following lexical entry *have*:

```
have,V+EXP="have lunch"
```

then this expression would not be put forward by the lexical parser when the verb *to have* does not occur, for example in the following sentences:

Joe and Lea's lunch was really good.
Let's get lunch.

However, the expression *to have lunch* is really present in these two sentences since they can be paraphrased respectively as:

Joe and Lea's lunch was really good = *Joe and Lea had a lunch; it was really good.*
Let's get lunch = *Let's go and have lunch.*

Therefore, it is better to characterize this expression using its characteristic constituent *lunch*:

```
lunch,N+EXP="have lunch"
```

In this case, the lexical parser can focus on this expression each time the word *lunch* occurs in a text.

Conversely, we must be careful not to activate the lexical parser too many times for no good reason. For example, for the phrasal verb *to blow up*, it would be unwise to choose the particle *up* as its characteristic constituent:

```
up,PART+EXP="blow up"
```

because in this case, the lexical parser would have to validate or invalidate the presence of the expression *to blow up* each time the word form *up* occurred in the text! But this particle is very frequent, and occurs in nearly 700 phrasal verbs [MAC 10]:

ask up, bring up, catch up, dress up, eat up, fill up, give up...

Of course, the expression *to blow up* would then be invalidated each time *to blow* does not occur in the context of the particle *up*, but in the end, activating thousands of occurrences of phrasal verbs, to later eliminate all of them is much too costly an operation in terms of data computation.

11.5.2. *Varying the characteristic constituent*

In the previous examples, the characteristic constituents *account* and *lunch* are invariable (necessarily singular), which makes them easier to recognize in texts, but this is not always the case. The verbs *to take* (in *to take into account*) and *to blow* (in *to blow up*) can be conjugated in texts, for example:

Joe should have <u>taken</u> the fact that it already <u>blew up</u> <u>into account</u> when he made the decision to go ahead.

It is therefore necessary to formalize inflection in the dictionary, for example:

```
take,V+FLX=TAKE+EXP="take into account"
```

Some expressions take lexical variants, for example:

to lose one's (marbles | mind | sanity | senses | wits)

Each variant can be described in a dictionary by linking them all to the same ALU:

```
marbles,N+EXP="lose one's mind"
mind,N+EXP="lose one's mind"
reason,N+EXP="lose one's mind"
sanity,N+EXP="lose one's mind"
senses,N+EXP="lose one's mind"
wits,N+EXP="lose one's mind"
```

11.5.3. *Varying the light verb*

Generally, *light verb/predicative noun* combinations take aspectual or modal variants[18]:

to be hungry =:
   The late meeting made Ida hungry. Ida was getting hungry.

to have some courage =:
   That event gave him the courage to speak his mind
   Joe (found | lost) the courage to tell Ida the truth

To parse these examples, a syntactic parser needs to have access to the individual expressions *to be hungry* and *to have courage* even if the respective verbs *to be* and *to have* do not occur in the text. To do so, the characteristic constituent is reduced to a word: *hungry* and *courage*. These

---

18 Concerning the distinction between *compound verbs, support verbs* and *operators*, see [GRO 81].

expressions are therefore treated in the same way as simple words: just as the lexical parser systematically associates different uses of the simple word *run* to the word form *run* without being able to choose between them (*to run a test* vs *to run in the woods*), it will add the expression *to have courage* to the TAS each time the word form *courage* occurs. It will be left to the syntactic or even to the semantic analyses to validate or invalidate the presence of each expression.

11.5.4. *Resolving ambiguity*

By entering the characteristic constituent for each expression in the dictionary we can ensure that the lexical parser will recognize all the expressions that occur in the text. But this approach is very costly since it involves producing tens of lexical hypotheses that will then be invalidated: there are in fact tens of expressions in which characteristic constituents, such as *account, courage, mind*, etc. are very frequent. Take for example the word *mind*; this word is the characteristic constituent of over twenty expressions[19]:

> *be of one mind, be in one's right mind, be of a different mind, be of sound mind, be on someone's mind, be out of one's (right |*
> *<E>) mind, bear in mind, change one's mind, close one's mind to, come to mind, keep in mind, don't mind if I do, give someone a piece of one's mind, have a mind to, have something in mind, have a mind of one's own, mind one's own business, mind one's Ps & Qs, mind the gap, mind the store, open one's mind to, pay something no mind, put something out of one's mind, spring to mind*

But we do not want the lexical parser to produce all these potential lexical hypotheses for each occurrence of the word form *mind* in texts. Moreover, this word form is relatively frequent in texts, which carries the risk of dramatically increasing the size of the TAS.

Generally, it is not possible to decide with absolute certainty if an expression is really present in a sentence without at least carrying out a syntactic analysis of the sentence. For example, only a syntactic analysis of the following sentence:

---

19 Examples taken from the *Merriam Webster Dictionary*.

Keep in mind the store is closed after 6PM.

enables us to eliminate the expression *mind the store* by checking that *mind* is not a verb in this sentence, and therefore *the store* is not its complement. Nevertheless, in practice, it is possible to eliminate a large number of expressions simply by checking their context. For example, in the previous sentence, it would be useless to produce the lexical hypotheses *be of one mind, be of a different mind, bear in mind* since the respective constituents *one, different, bear* are not present in the sentence.

To filter as many useless lexical hypotheses as possible, we use two pieces of information:

– we add data on the context for each expression to the dictionary, for example:

```
mind,V+FLX=HELP+EXP="mind the gap"+NP1="the gap"
```

– we add a constraint in a grammar to check that the property described in the dictionary (above: +NP1) corresponds to the context of the characteristic constituent (here: *mind*), (Figure 11.26).

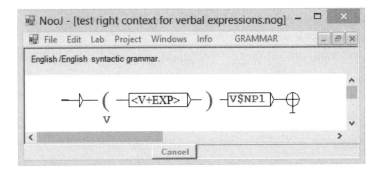

Figure 11.26. *Checking context for the characteristic constituent*

This grammar is read in the following fashion: the characteristic constituent (here: *mind*), which corresponds to the lexical entry and is matched by the symbol <V+EXP>, is stored in variable $V. In this case VNP1 takes its value in the property "+NP1", that is to say the string *the gap*. The grammar checks that the expression's complement (*the gap*) really is present in the context of the verb (*mind*). A single grammar such as this one can be used in conjunction with a dictionary which has several hundred expressions with the structure *Verb + Frozen Complement*. It will allow the lexical parser to reject the similar expressions *bear in mind, keep in mind, come to mind, spring to mind* and *mind the gap* in the sentence *Keep in mind the store is closed after 6PM*, but it will not be able to reject the expression *mind the store*.

In practice, a very large number of expressions (more than 95%) can be rejected with very superficial checks on the context of the characteristic constituent.

While staying within the bounds of lexical analysis, it is possible to construct slightly more sophisticated grammars; for example, in the previous grammar, we could add a description of the possessive determinant for the expressions that contain *one's*:

mind ones' own business =: *mind (my|your|his|her|our|your|their) own business*

```
mind,V+EXP="mind one's own business"+DPoss0+N1="own
business".
```

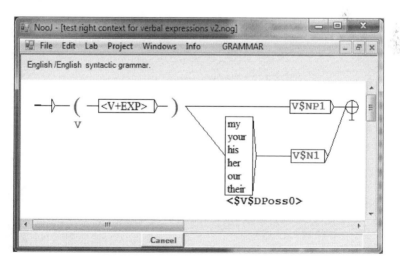

Figure 11.27. *Checking context, v2*

The constraint <VDPoss0> checks that the verb expects a possessive determinant; if this constraint is validated, then the bottom path on the graph is activated and the grammar seeks a sequence that begins with one of the possessive determinants (for example *your*), followed by the value +N1 of the lexical entry (here: *own business*).

Expressions such as *on someone's mind* would be more complicated to handle, since *someone* can represent any human non phrase, for example:

on someone's mind =: *It was definitely on my neighbor's cousins' minds*
open one's mind =: *Joe opened his student's mind*

There is no question of being able to recognize human noun phrases when we are still at the earlier stage of lexical analysis: we will therefore content ourselves with checking that the genitive marker or a possessive determinant occurs in a context fairly close to the expression's characteristic constituent. The lexical entry will therefore be:

```
open,V+FLX=HELP+EXP="open one's mind"+G1="<mind>"
```

and the corresponding grammar will therefore become that shown in Figure 11.28.

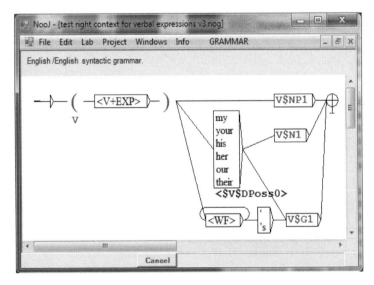

Figure 11.28. *Checking context, v3*

The loop above <WF> enables any sequence of word forms to be recognized; the expression *open one's mind* will be recognized in both the following examples:

> *Joe opened all his students' minds; Lea opened her friend's mind.*

The grammar shown above is very useful for eliminating numerous useless lexical hypotheses and so reducing the size of the TAS dramatically and consequently easing the work of the syntactic parser. But it does not enable *all* the incorrectly recognized expressions to be rejected, as it is not possible to circumvent the syntactic and semantic analyses necessary to validate the presence of each expression in the sentence definitively. For example, the previous grammar does not prevent the expression *open one's mind* from being listed wrongly in the TAS for the sentence:

> *Lea opened the door and Joe's mind brightened up.*

But once again, the lexical parser's role is to produce all lexical hypotheses with a recall of 100%: it will fall to the syntactic and semantic parsers to delete all the superfluous annotations.

11.5.5. *Annotating expressions*

The dictionaries and grammars presented above enable all expressions to be recognized in a text. The expressions recognized must now be listed in the TAS [SIL 08][20].

When an expression occurs in the text without interruption, such as for example the expression *open one's mind* in the sentence:

> *Lea opened his mind*

then there is no difficulty annotating it: an annotation similar to those used to represent multiword units is produced, such as in Figures 10.1 or

---

20 NooJ contains the only lexical analyzer capable of annotating discontinuous lexemes; NooJ syntactic and semantic analyzers handle discontinuous annotations just like other annotations.

10.2. But when an expression is discontinuous in the text, it is necessary to produce and manage a discontinuous annotation in the TAS.

NooJ represents a discontinuous annotation as a suite of piecemeal annotations, linked to one another by the key word XREF. For example, the grammar below recognizes a set of more than 1,200 phrasal verbs (<V+PV>) listed by [MAC 12] and produces an annotation for each phrasal verb even if the phrasal verb and the particle are separated (bottom of the graph).

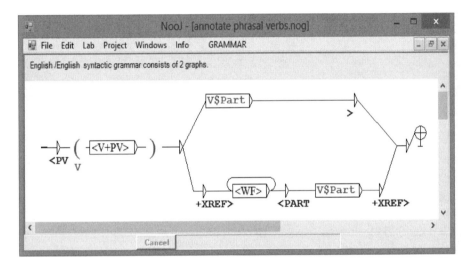

Figure 11.29. *Annotate phrasal verbs*

This grammar produces an annotation <PV> for the sequence *Lea turned off the lights*, thanks to the upper path. If we analyze the sentence *Joe turned the lights off*, the grammar annotates the word form *turned* as <PV+XREF> and the word form *off* as <PART+XREF>: these two annotations are then collated to make only one in the TAS, as seen in figure below[21].

---

21 The annotation shown in Figure 11.30 is actually produced by the grammar Phrasal_Verbs.nog included in the English NooJ module. It is richer than that produced by the grammar in Figure 11.29.

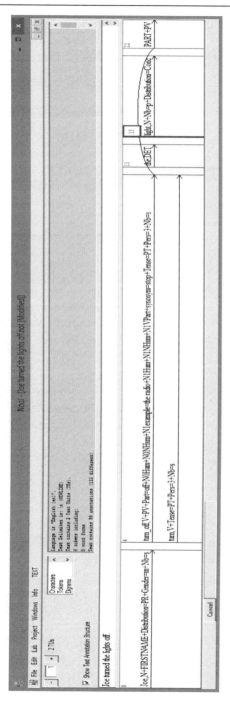

Figure 11.30. *Discontinuous annotation in the TAS*

Linking a dictionary of characteristic constituents with a grammar that formalizes each expression's context, in order to add annotations in the TAS is simple to implement and makes the lexical parser very efficient.

11.6. Conclusion

The first stage of linguistic analysis consists of identifying all the text's atomic linguistic units (ALUs) and storing them as annotations in the TAS. This stage, called lexical analysis, is itself complex to implement; moreover, the phenomena used to describe ALUs differ depending on the individual language's writing system and morphology.

The first stage of lexical analysis consists of grouping letters and delimiters in order to identify a text's word forms. To do this, it is necessary to resolve problems linked to encoding, which can be multiple for some letters (for example compound letters and ligatures) – from the ambiguity of some characters (in English: apostrophe/quote, dash/hyphen and period/abbreviation mark) to ambiguities produced by absent data that have to be replaced, as in the lack of spaces in Chinese, the lack of vowels in Arabic, the lack of accents in English, etc.

Then, an orthographic parser is used to link each word form to its orthographic variants, and parsers capable of processing inflectional, derivational and agglutinative morphology compute the lexical entry corresponding to the word form. Note that at this stage, multiword units (that are necessarily listed in the electronic dictionary) are processed exactly like simple words.

Recognizing expressions is more complicated as they cannot be recognized by a simple dictionary lookup. Because they might be discontinuous, it is necessary to enter their characteristic constituent in the dictionary, and then to describe – even very crudely – a "minimal" contextual constraint that will be used to reject impossible expressions (e.g. we do not want the lexical parser to recognize the phrasal verb *to turn off* if the particle *off* does not even occur in the sentence).

It is important to remember that from the perspective of lexical analysis, "recognizing" an ALU in a text does not necessarily mean that this element really occurs in the text: the lexical parser is required to recognize all potential ALUs (100% recall), and consequently recognizes too many, i.e.

after lexical analysis, the TAS will temporarily contain numerous ambiguities (represented by parallel annotations) which will have to be resolved later. We will see how to resolve most ambiguities by taking account of syntactic or semantic constraints in the following chapters.

11.7. Exercise

Using NooJ: enter the following text: *John's running out of control* in a NooJ not text-file. Build a NooJ .dic dictionary file that contains all the ALUs that may occur in this text. The TAS must represent all the ambiguities between common words and proper names, between simple words, multiword units, and phrasal verbs. Construct an inflectional .nof grammar to describe the conjugation of the verb *to run*. Compile the dictionary, then parse the text using the command TEXT > Linguistic Analysis. How many annotations are listed in the TAS?

Syntactic Analysis

A language's syntax describes how its vocabulary elements (ALUs) can be combined in texts, to make up phrases or sentences. *Local grammars* can be distinguished from *structural grammars*.

12.1. Local grammars

Local grammars describe relatively limited sequences of ALUs, for example numerical expressions, addresses, dates, sequences of grammatical words, word agreement within a noun phrase, etc. Recognizing these sequences does not require recognizing the entire sentence; typically, a local grammar represents expressions or constructions consisting of just a few words that contain "interesting" information.

12.1.1. *Named entities*

When texts are analyzed, many expressions that resemble ALUs but which cannot be listed in a dictionary can be found.

For instance, from a syntactic or semantic perspective, there is no real difference between the word "yesterday" and the sequence "the day before yesterday": both are instances of an adverb of date. But if we want to treat the sequence "the day before yesterday", then there is no reason not to treat "three days before yesterday", "seven days after tomorrow", and why not "five days ago", "on Monday, June 3rd", "on the twenty-seventh of May", "last summer", "three years ago", etc. All these sequences will be described by a local grammar.

Other examples of named entities are:

– expressions of numerical quantity: "$*12.99 per pound*", "*10°F below zero*";

– time durations: "*from 9AM to 5PM*";

– addresses: "123, 45th St., NYC, 10045 NY"

Internet and email addresses: www.nooj4nlp.net, j_p.smith@yahoo.com

– telephone numbers: "*+1-212-123-4567*";

– person or place names: "Mr. George P. Smith, Jr.", "Everglades National Park";

– names of companies and organizations and their acronyms: "Florida Power & Light Company" (FPL), "United States Department of Transportation" (DOT), "doctors without borders" (MSF);

– names of jobs, titles or functions: "Aeronautical project engineer", "Chief Dispatcher", "Secretary of Education";

– etc.[1]

These sequences can typically be described with regular grammars or finite-state graphs. For example, the grammar in Figure 12.1 recognizes common email addresses: it recognizes any sequence made up of orthographic forms (<WF>), numbers (<NB>) or certain characters (for example "#" or "."), followed by the character "@", followed by the name of a domain, itself made up of word forms, numbers, dashes or dots[2].

---

1 BBN Technologies puts forward 29 types of named entities, see [BRU 02].
2 To be valid, email addresses should follow protocol RFC6531 of the Internet Engineering Task Force (IETF): in particular, they can contain special characters, such as the email address given as an example by [WIK 13]: "very.,:;<>[]\".VERY.\"very@\\   "very\". unusual"@[IPv6:2001:db8:1ff::a0b:dbd0].

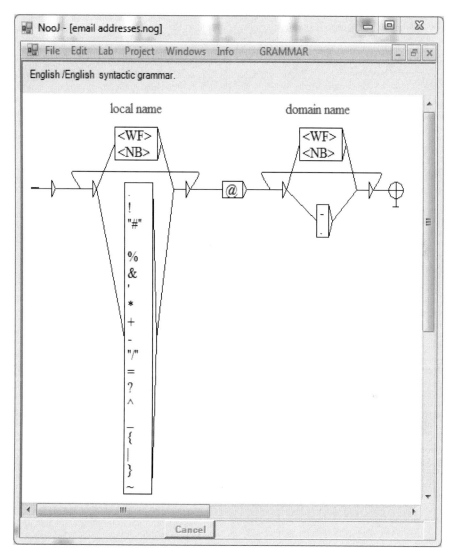

Figure 12.1. *A local grammar for common email addresses*

Grammars used to recognize expressions of date are more complex. The graph in Figure 12.2, entitled "on the 3rd of June", recognizes sequences such as *on Tuesday, the 31st of January, 2014.*

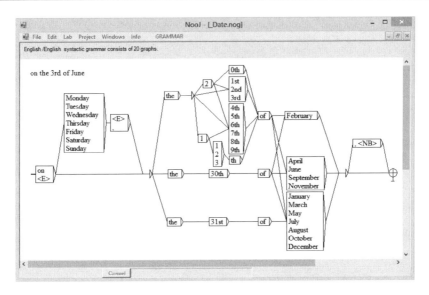

Figure 12.2. *Graph "on the 3rd of June"*

The graph in Figure 12.3, "at seven o'clock", recognizes sequences such as *at a quarter past five in the morning*.

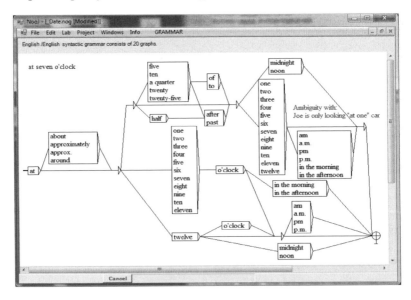

Figure 12.3. *Graph "at seven o'clock"*

The two previous graphs are used in a grammar whose main graph is given in Figure 12.4.

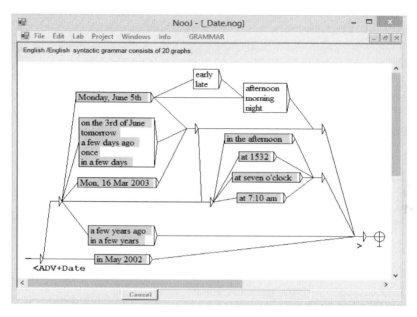

Figure 12.4. *Date grammar*

The Date grammar contains 20 embedded graphs and recognizes complex expressions such as *Tuesday, February the 3rd at exactly half past three in the afternoon*. The sequences recognized are then annotated as adverbs of date (annotation <ADV+Date>), as seen in the following figure.

Figure 12.5. *A syntactic annotation in TAS*

This annotation, once inserted into the TAS, can be used in queries, such as <PRO><V><ADV+Date>, to locate sequences such as *He came three weeks ago*, as well as in more complex grammars. By applying local grammars in cascade, more and more named entities can be annotated, which allows us to carry out sophisticated analyses, such as applying the query: <N+Company><HIRE><N+Person><ADV+Date> to locate sequences such as *General Electric hired John W. Smith last Monday*.

Information extraction software typically will use tens of local grammars of this type.

12.1.2. *Grammatical word sequences*

Local grammars are very useful for describing sequences of words that, although not frozen, have a very restricted syntax. For example in French, preverbal particles are used in a very rigid order:

Joe le lui a donné [Joe gave it to her]
Joe lui en a donné [Joe gave her some]
* *Joe lui le a donné* [Joe gave her it]

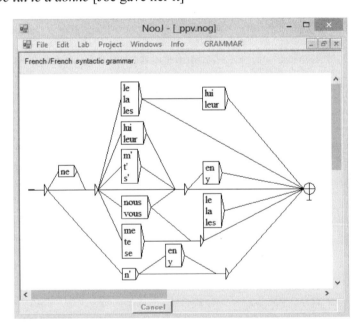

Figure 12.6. *Grammar of preverbal particles in French*

This grammar describes the group of well-formed sequences for preverbal particles in French, as in *Joe ne nous en donne pas* [Joe does not give some to us] or *Lea le lui rendra* [Lea will give it back to her].

12.1.3. *Automatically identifying ambiguity*

In general, local grammars such as those we have seen up to now are used to add annotations to the TAS. But it is also useful to delete annotations that we know to be superfluous or incorrect: so one important use of local grammars is automatic disambiguation. For example, *a priori*, the word *this* can be a pronoun (as in *Joe saw this*) or a demonstrative determiner (*This pen is broken*). Consequently, after lexical analysis, the TAS contains both of these ALUs each time the word form *this* occurs, in the form of parallel annotations. This systematic ambiguity can often be detected with the aid of a grammar such as that in the following figure.

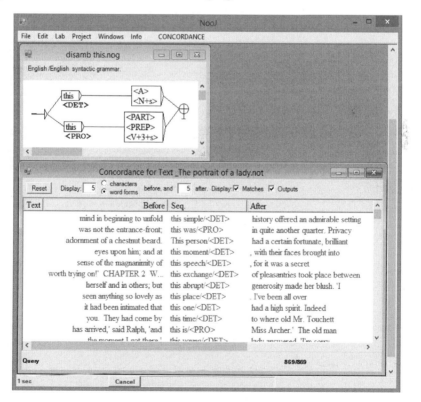

Figure 12.7. *Detecting ambiguities in the word form "this"*

This grammar produces "filters" used to delete all incompatible annotations from the TAS: the <DET>filter deletes all annotations in the TAS that are not compatible with the symbol <DET>, while the <PRO>filter deletes all annotations incompatible with the symbol <PRO> in the TAS.

This local grammar is not perfect: it was able to resolve ambiguity in 869 occurrences in the text *The Portrait Of A Lady*, although the text contains 1,036 occurrences of the word form *this*, so 84% of occurrences were disambiguated. Here are two occurrences that were not disambiguated:

> *... Isabel thought this rather sharp; ...*
> *... ; this rather meagre synthesis exhausted the facts ...*

In the first example, *this* is a pronoun; in the second example, *this* is a determiner. These are the problems that POS Taggers encounter (see our discussion in section 1.5.2): it is impossible to resolve all ambiguities reliably without carrying out a total syntactic (or even semantic) analysis of the sentence. The advantage of local grammars over the statistical methods is that they do not have to resolve all ambiguities: they can leave the difficult cases in the TAS.

In practice, when parsing large texts, a set of twenty local grammars built around the most frequent ambiguous words in a language, such as:

> *to (PART or PREP), her (DET or PRO), that (ADV, CONJ, DET or PRO), in (A, PART or PREP), as (CONJ or PREP), for (CONJ or PREP), but (CONJ or PREP), his (DET or PRO), on (A, PART or PREP), this (ADV, DET or PRO), if (CONJ or N), what (DET, INTJ or PRO), so (ADV or CONJ), one (DET, N or PRO), 's (be, have or GENITIVE), there (ADV, INTJ or PRO), which (DET or PRO), no (DET, INTJ or N)*

allows the TAS's size to be reduced by a factor of 5, introducing a negligible number of errors (less than 0.1%)[3].

---

3 An example of an error can be found in the sequence: *"No, I've not had time. I've seen the girl but this once"*, said the Countess. As the word *once* was not described as a noun in the dictionary, the grammar has wrongly produced the analysis *this* = PRO. To correct this error, *once* = N should be added to the dictionary. Note that Henry James' novel *The Portrait Of A Lady*, used for this test, dates from 1880, whereas NooJ's dictionary is supposed to describe contemporary English.

12.2. Structural grammars

Structural grammars describe sentence structure: how the ALUs link to create larger constituents – Noun Phrases, Verb Groups, Relative Clauses – which in turn combine to construct the sentence. A structural syntactic parser usually displays the result of its analysis in the form of a *syntax tree*[4], different from the *parse tree* that we saw in Chapter 7. For example, we can display the structure of the phrase *Joe thinks Lea cannot see Ida* using a tree like the one in Figure 12.8.

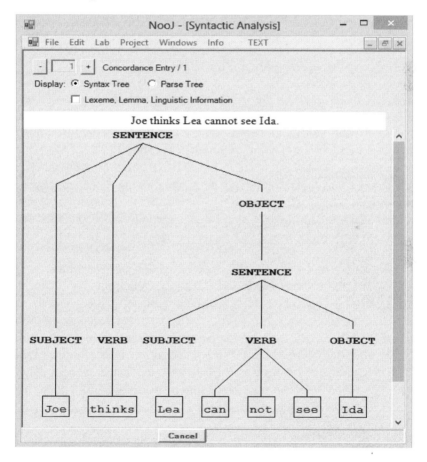

Figure 12.8. *A syntax tree*

In this figure, the syntax tree is shown from top to bottom:

– the root of the tree is the node at the top labeled SENTENCE;

– the trees' leaves are at the bottom and represent the sentence's ALUs;

– the SENTENCE is broken down into three constituents: a SUBJECT (*Joe*) followed by a verbal group VERB (*thinks*) and an OBJECT;

– this OBJECT is itself made up of a SENTENCE;

– this last SENTENCE is itself made up of a SUBJECT (*Lea*), a VERB (*cannot see*) and an OBJECT (*Ida*).

12.2.1. *Complex atomic linguistic units*

We saw in Chapter 11 that a lexical parser should handle all types of linguistic units: affixes and agglutinated words, simple words, multiword units and discontinuous expressions. These four types of linguistic units are represented in a unified fashion, by annotations stored in the TAS, which is itself handled by NooJ's syntactic parser [SIL 10]. Representing all types of ALU in a unified way – including contracted or agglutinated forms and discontinuous expressions – enables linguists to construct syntactic grammars that are considerably simplified, since they no longer need to take into account the various forms that each type of ALU can take.

For example, the form *cannot* is the contraction of the verb *can* and the adverb *not*: these two ALUs are actually represented in the TAS. Consequently the sequence *cannot* will be processed by the syntactic parser exactly like the sequence *can not*, i.e. it will match the sequence of symbols <V><ADV>. Figure 12.8 above shows that the contracted form *cannot* is actually processed as two ALUs (*can* and *not*). Thus, in the grammar SENTENCE, we have simply described the fact that a verbal group can contain the modal verb *can* possibly followed by an adverb, without having to add exceptions for any contracted forms.

Similarly, a syntactic parser should also be able to handle discontinuous expressions. For example, the following figure visualizes the tree built for the text *Joe turned the lights off*, whose TAS we saw in Figure 11.30. The expression is highlighted on the syntax tree, without interfering with the sentence's syntactic structure[5].

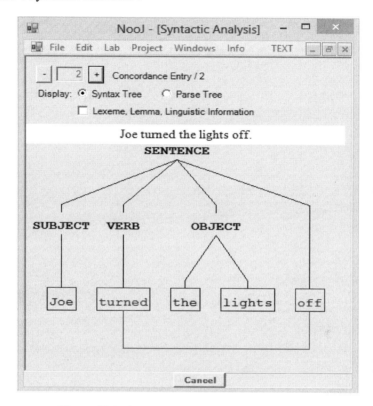

Figure 12.9. *Structure of a sentence that contains a discontinuous expression*

More generally, as the syntactic parser has access to the TAS, there is no longer a need to handle agglutinated forms, multiword units or expressions separately in the grammar, since all the ALUs can now be processed in a unified fashion. While this simplification is useful for English and Romance languages, where there are few contractions, it is indispensable for agglutinative languages, where morphemes that may belong to different phrases, are agglutinated systematically inside word forms.

---

5 [VIE 10] shows the problems linked to parsing sentences that contain discontinuous expressions in Italian.

12.2.2. *Structured annotations*

NooJ syntactic grammars are typically used to annotate sequences of words that make up units of meaning or entities (for example "The President of the European Central Bank", "Monday, June 3rd at 15:45"). But they can also be used to annotate syntactic units [SIL 10]. The annotations thus created therefore represent sentence structure.

NooJ context-free and context-sensitive grammars can also produce annotations themselves: this time, we will use these annotations to represent information on sentence structure. For example, consider the following grammar that recognizes simple transitive sentences[6].

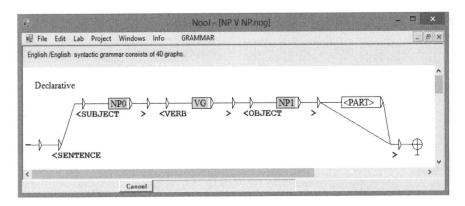

Figure 12.10. *A grammar produces structured annotations*

This grammar annotates the matching transitive sentences with the annotation <SENTENCE>; at the same time, it annotates the subject of the matching sentence with the annotation <SUBJECT>, its verbal group with the annotation <VERB> and the direct object complement with the annotation <OBJECT>.

Graphs NP0, NP1 and VG as well as their descendants can themselves produce annotations. If we apply this grammar to the sentence *Joe thinks Lea cannot see Ida*, we obtain the TAS shown in Figure 12.11.

---

6 This grammar has been used to produce the analyses in Figures 12.8 and 12.9.

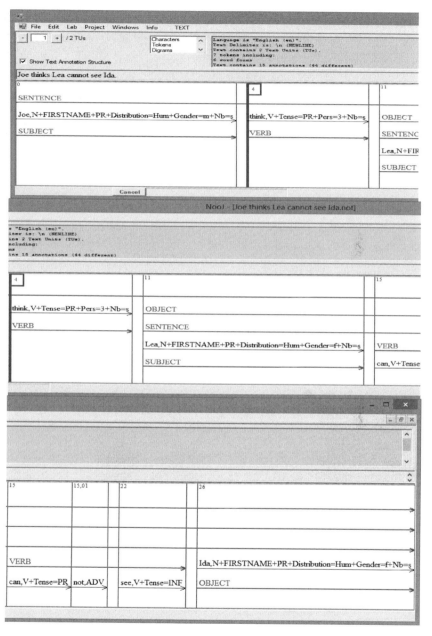

Figure 12.11. *A structured group of syntactic annotations*

The TAS contains two SENTENCE annotations: one for *Joe thinks Lea cannot see Ida*, and the other for *Lea cannot see Ida*. Similarly, we find two SUBJECT annotations (*Joe* and *Lea*), two VERB annotations (*thinks* and *cannot see*) and two OBJECT annotations: *Lea cannot see Ida*, and *Ida*.

In the TAS, syntactic annotations (displayed in green in NooJ) differ from lexical annotations:

– lexical annotations listed in parallel represent ambiguities. These annotations are concurrent, since they cannot co-exist;

– syntactic annotations correspond to levels of analysis that correspond to different levels of constituents in an expression, phrase or sentence. In the previous TAS for example, the annotation <SENTENCE> coexists with the three annotations <SUBJECT>, <VERB> and <OBJECT>, as well as with the annotation <SENTENCE> for the embedded sentence. These parallel annotations are all valid simultaneously: they represent different structural levels.

The previous TAS it not very legible: in practice, it is preferable to visualize it in the form of a syntax tree such as that in Figure 12.8.

12.2.3. *Ambiguities*

Lexical ambiguities of course have an effect on syntactic parsing; most multiword units and expressions are ambiguous, so each different lexical analysis may produce a different syntax tree. For example, for the following sentence:

He switched the computers on Monday

there are two possible analyses that correspond to the presence of the verb *to switch*, or to the verbal phrase *to switch on*:

= *On Monday, he swapped the computers*, or
= *Monday, he switched on the computers*

as shown in Figure 12.12.

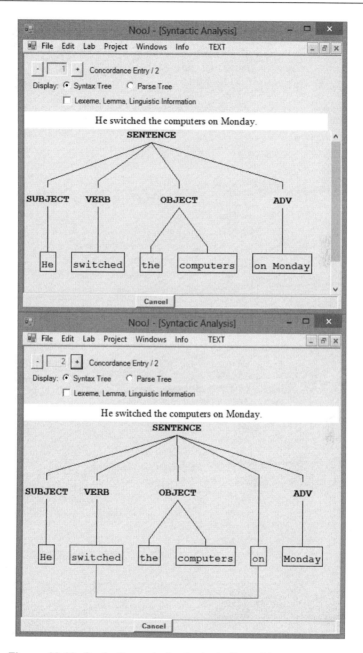

Figure 12.12. *Syntactic analysis of a lexically ambiguous sentence*

There are also cases of purely syntactic ambiguity for sentences that have the same lexical material, as we saw in Chapter 7 for the sentence *This man sees the chair from his house*. In this case, several syntax trees are built concurrently, as shown in Figure 12.13.

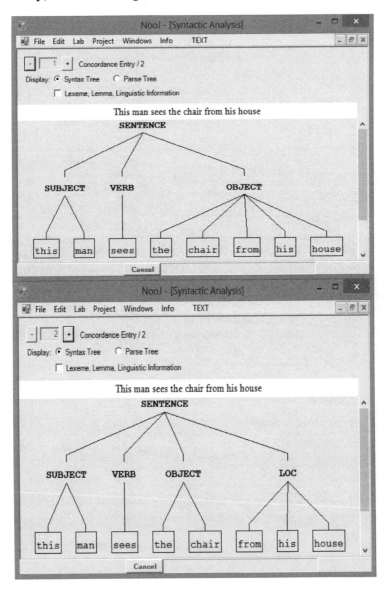

Figure 12.13. *Analyzing a structurally ambiguous sentence*

12.2.4. *Syntax trees vs parse trees*

Be careful[7] not to confuse these syntax trees with the parse trees that we saw in Figures 7.12 and 7.13. Syntax trees are designed to represent sentence structure, whereas parse trees represent the structure of the grammar visited during parsing.

Remember that parse trees represent derivation chains that are constructed when parsing a sentence and exploring its grammar, and are therefore particularly useful for "debugging" a grammar. This is why many syntactic parsers used in NLP offer these parse trees as results of syntactic analysis; by doing this, these pieces of software equate sentence structure and grammar structure.

The problem then is that each time the grammar is modified, the resulting parse tree given for the same sentence is also modified. For example, if we remove NP recursions from the grammar on Figure 7.11[8], we get:

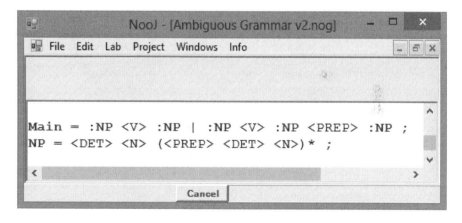

Figure 12.14. *Simplified grammar*

---

7 This confusion occurs a lot in the domain of NLP.

8 When compiling a grammar, it is possible to automatically delete some recursions, make it deterministic and optimize the use of NooJ lexical symbols. The resulting grammar is equivalent to the original grammar, but can be applied to the text much more quickly, often by a finite-state machine, in linear time.

we then obtain the new parse tree:

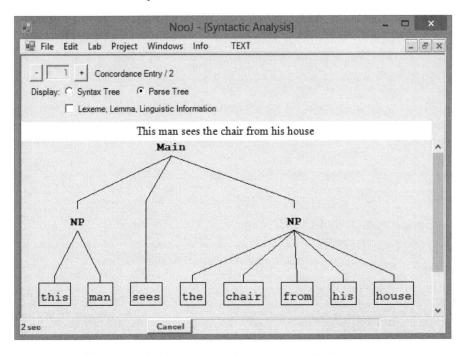

Figure 12.15. *Another parse tree for a simplified grammar*

Compare this new tree with that in Figure 7.12: the two parse trees are different, even though the two grammars are equivalent and the sentence is unchanged.

Typically, when building large-scale grammars for a substantial portion of a language, it will be necessary to organize them, independently from the structure of the sentences to be analyzed. For example, the grammar in Figure 12.10, which is still a simple grammar, contains 40 graphs[9]: there are in fact several types of transitive sentences (declarative, interrogative, nominal), several types of Noun Phrases (subject, object), several types of proper names (person, place), several types of verbal groups (verbs

---

9 [SIL 03b] describes a grammar that recognizes determiners for French: definite (e.g. *cette* [this]), adverbial (e.g. *beaucoup de* [a lot of]), adjectival (e.g. *certaines* [some]), as well as those that use pre-determiners (e.g. *toutes les* [all the]) and nouns (e.g. *la majoritéde* [the majority of]). This grammar contains more than 130 graphs, but can be compiled to form a finite-state grammar (i.e. into an enormous single graph).

conjugated in simple or compound tenses, with auxiliary, aspectual and/or modal verbs), several types of determiners (definite, indefinite, nominal, adverbial), etc. As a consequence, the parse tree showing the analysis of the sentence *Joe thinks that Lea cannot see Ida* is rather lengthy (Figure 12.16).

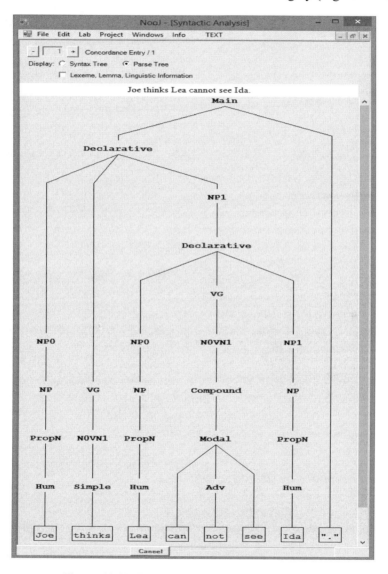

Figure 12.16. *Parse tree for a structured grammar*

This parse tree represents the structure of the (very structured) grammar but not the structure of the sentence (which is a simple transitive sentence). Compare this parse tree with the syntax tree in Figure 12.8.

When a grammar is worked on, each time it is modified (to refine it, for example), its structure may change, and so its parse trees will also change.

For example, if we decide to refine the formalization of determiners, we will typically replace a single initial DET graph with several embedded graphs: DDef (e.g. *the*), DDem (e.g. *this*), DNoun (e.g. *the majority of*), DAdv (e.g. *a lot of*), as well as a DPred graph for the pre-determiners (e.g. *all*) etc.

Similarly, if we adapt the grammar (e.g. the date grammar) for a specific NLP application (for example, extracting dates from official requests for proposals in civil engineering), we will need to restructure it, by separating informal dates such as *three months after my birthday* from formal dates such as *three months after the acceptation of this estimate*.

Finally, grammars are optimized by NooJ without the author of the grammar even noticing: for example, NooJ may optimize graphs (for instance to make them deterministic), replace some lexical symbols with the corresponding word forms, handle orthographic variants, remove left and right recursions, make the grammar more compact, etc.

For all these reasons, it is better that the sentence structure produced by the grammar is independent of the grammar's own structure: the syntactic structure of a text is produced by structured annotations that are produced by grammars, independently from their own structure.

12.2.5. *Dependency grammar and tree*

A variant of the grammar shown in Figure 12.10 has the same structure, but produces different structured annotations: this time, rather than annotating the sentence's constituents (such as SUBJECT, VERB or OBJECT), I have annotated the semantic predicates: both verbs as well as both nouns. Two samples from the new grammar are shown in the following figure:

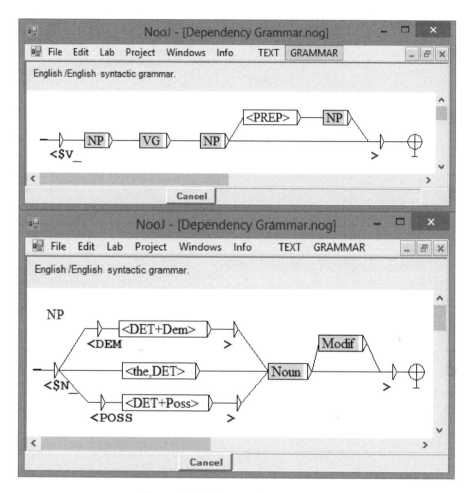

Figure 12.17. *Dependency grammar*

In this grammar, $V is defined in the VG graph and takes the value of the main verb of the current proposition; $V_ produces its lemma. Similarly, $N is defined in the NP graph and takes the value of the main noun in the current noun phrase; $N_ produces its lcmma. When applying this grammar to the sentence *This man sees the chair from his house,* we obtain two syntax trees, including the one shown in Figure 12.18.

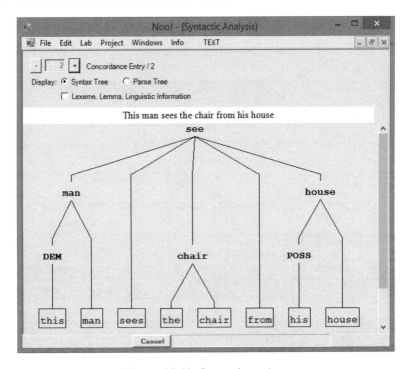

Figure 12.18. *Dependency tree*

This tree, which is called a *dependency tree* [MEL 87], is different from both the *syntax tree* and the *parse tree*. In the dependency tree, the tree's nodes represent predicates or their semantic arguments. The dependency tree thus represents the following logical formula:

```
see ( man (DEM), chair, house (POSS) )
```

Some NLP applications use this type of logical formula to represent sentence meaning, and then feed "knowledge bases" with the predicates in order to extract facts, perform logical computations (e.g. inferences), etc. Exporting the TAS to XML format produces a semantically annotated text, typically used by NLP information extraction applications:

```
<see><man><DEM> this </DEM> man </man> sees <chair>
the chair </chair> from <house><POSS> his </POSS>
house </house></see>.
```

12.2.6. *Resolving ambiguity transparently*

Until now, the only method we have seen for automatically resolving ambiguities in texts involved applying local grammars in order to identify the contexts in which some grammatical words were used, then producing "filters" in order to delete incorrect annotations from the TAS. Even if local grammars are easy to develop and can be used very effectively – they are represented by finite-state transducers – in most cases, they cannot solve all the lexical ambiguities in every sentence.

However, a complete syntactic analysis of the sentence enables most lexical ambiguities within it to be resolved[10]. To see this, it is enough to point out that the leaves of the syntax tree are in fact ALUs, as shown in the Figure 12.19[11].

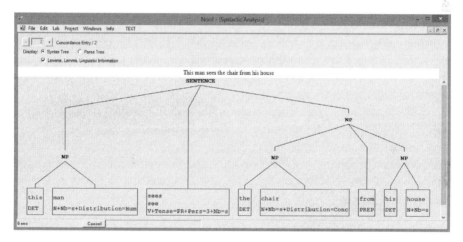

Figure 12.19. *ALUs in the syntax tree*

When a sentence is linked to a single syntax tree, we infer that this sentence is not ambiguous, and therefore we can eliminate from the TAS all the ALUs that are not present in the tree: the sentence is then automatically disambiguated.

---

10 A syntactic parser eliminates all lexical hypotheses that are not used by the grammar. Of course, some lexical ambiguities might remain, which will be resolved by semantic analysis, and there might still be some ambiguities that can only be solved by extra-linguistic calculations, as we saw in section 1.4.

11 In NooJ, check the option "Display Lexeme, Lemma, Linguistic Information".

12.3. Conclusion

In NooJ, syntactic analysis consists of annotating sequences of ALUs, described by grammars. NooJ's syntactic parser takes account of all types of ALU (affixes, simple words, multiword units and potentially discontinuous expressions) since it works on the TAS rather than on sequences of word forms. This enables it to handle all ALUs, and simplifies the writing of syntactic grammars considerably.

Grammars can be local, that is to say that they only concern relatively simple ALU sequences; these grammars are typically used to annotate entities such as names of companies, expressions of measurement, dates, places, etc. and can also be used to resolve ambiguity in grammatical words as well as words that appear in their immediate context.

The annotations produced by syntactic grammars can also represent information on structure, such as for example NP or VG; these annotations are stored in the TAS, and then be displayed as a syntax tree. The syntactic structure represented by the syntax tree is independent of the grammar's organization: *syntax trees* are thus distinguished from *parse trees*. This distinction is crucial for wide-ranging linguistic description projects that necessarily require accumulating a large number of grammars whose structure will be unstable. Parse trees are very sensitive to linguistic resource management problems, whereas syntax trees, represented by structured annotations in the TAS, can be carefully designed by linguists based on theoretical arguments, involving transformational or semantic analysis.

Controlling the structure produced by the grammar enables linguists to include all kinds of information in it; in particular, there is no fundamental distinction between a constituent grammar and a dependency grammar: a single syntactic grammar may be used to produce both a *syntax tree* and a *dependency tree*.

Finally, when a syntactic parser produces a single syntax tree for a given sentence, it can at the same time delete all the unused lexical annotations in the TAS. So ultimately there are two mechanisms for resolving lexical ambiguities: a mechanism based on local grammars that enables relatively small but common sequences to be handled efficiently, and another, more powerful mechanism based on a full syntactic analysis of the sentences, that enables more complex cases of ambiguity to be resolved.

12.4. Exercises

Construct a local grammar (file .nog) to detect ambiguities in the forms *this* and *these*. Apply this grammar to the text *Portrait of a Lady* and using the concordance, check to see if the grammar has made any errors. Then delete the incorrect annotations in the TAS (Concordance > Add/Remove Annotations): how many annotations have been removed?

Build a dictionary (file .dic) and a syntactic grammar (file .nog) to compute the two syntax trees for the sentence *Joe saw the boy with the telescope*.

12.5. Internet links

The grammar that describes valid email addresses is shown on the site: en.wikipedia.org/wiki/Email_address; the grammar that represents valid Internet addresses is shown on the site: en.wikipedia.org/wiki/URI_scheme# Generic_syntax.

With the help of lists taken from several web sites, specialized dictionaries can be built rapidly and used by local grammars for extracting named entities:

– names of jobs, see for example: www.careerplanner.com/DOTindex. cfm

– of place, see: en.wikipedia.org/wiki/Lists_of_places#General_lists_of_ places

– of first names, see: www.genealogyroadtrip.com/census/male_names_ 1.htm and www.genealogyroadtrip.com/census/female_first_names_1.htm

– names of units of measurement, see: www.convert-me.com/en/unitlist. html

Parse trees are presented inWikipedia, but there they are often confused with syntax trees: en.wikipedia.org/wiki/Parse_tree. Dependency trees are presented on the page: en.wikipedia.org/wiki/Dependency_grammar.

Transformational Analysis

Transformational grammar focuses on relationships between sentences that share the same lexical material[1], for example: how to link a sentence to its negative or passive forms, or how to combine several sentences to build a complex sentence [HAR 70][2]. Each pair of the following sentences is associated with a *transformation*; for example a [Passive] transformation could link the following two sentences:

[Passive] *Joe loves Lea = Lea is loved by Joe*

Similarly, a [Negation] transformation could link the following two sentences:

[Negation] *Joe loves Lea = Joe does not love Lea*

Transformations can also link a complex sentence to several simple sentences, for example:

[Coordination] *Lea loves Joe, Joe loves Ida = Lea loves Joe and Joe loves Ida*

After [HAR 70], transformations are bidirectional relationships, represented by the symbol "=" in the previous examples.

---

1 In the transformational grammar proposed here – as opposed to the transformational grammars introduced by [CHO 57] – transformations link pairs of "surface" sentences, rather than abstract structured representations. Variation of grammatical words and morphemes is allowed.
2 We saw some examples of transformational rules in section 3.4.3.

Building a complete transformational grammar for a language is an exciting project and some linguists, in particular Maurice Gross, have spent their entire professional lives on it, see [GRO 68, GRO 77, GRO 86][3]. A formalized transformational grammar should be usable by two computer programs:

– an automatic generation program capable of producing all the transformed sentences from a given sentence. For example, Figure 13.1 shows an extract of around 400,000 declarative sentences produced automatically from the sentence *Joe loves Lea*.

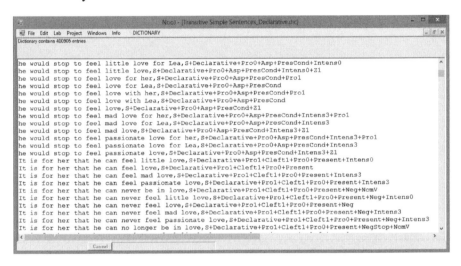

Figure 13.1. *The sentence Joe loves Lea is transformed automatically*

Among the sentences produced, there are sentences in which the verb is conjugated in various tenses and modes (e.g. *Joe loved Lea*), passive sentences (e.g. *Lea is loved by Joe*), sentences that involve left dislocation (e.g. *It is Lea that Joe loves*), negation (e.g. *Joe never loved Lea*), adverbs of intensity (e.g. *Joe loves Lea passionately*), aspectual verbs (e.g. *Joe stopped loving Lea*), or modal verbs (e.g. *Joe might love Lea*), and sentences with pronouns (e.g. *Joe loves her*), nominalized forms (e.g. *Joe is in love with Lea*), etc. Many transformations can be applied to a given sentence, as in:

It is Lea that he will no longer love passionately

---

3 For a comprehensive bibliography of works on transformational grammar by Maurice Gross's team, see [LEC 98].

which explains the large number of sentences produced;

– an automatic transformational analysis program capable of associating any sentence with the transformations that link it to the initial elementary sentence, which is generally the simplest sentence (in the active, without negation, without aspect, without modality, etc.). For example, the previous sentence has been automatically associated with the following sequence of features:

```
+Declarative+Cleft1+Pro0+Future+NegStop+Intens3
```

Each of these features represents a transformation:

[Declarative]: a declarative sentence is built. Note that in addition to declarative sentences, nominal sentences can be constructed (e.g. *Joe's love for Lea*) as well as interrogative sentences (e.g. *Who is in love with Lea?*).

[Cleft1] *He will no longer love Lea passionately → It is Lea that he will no longer love passionately*. The object is extracted. Other extractions are possible: [Cleft0] builds *It is he who no longer loves Lea passionately* whereas [Cleft Pred] produces *It is love that he feels for Lea*.

[Pro0] Joe will no longer love Lea passionately → *He will no longer love Lea passionately*. The sentence's subject is turned into a pronoun; [Pro1] turns the object into a pronoun, e.g. *Joe will no longer lover her passionately*.

[Future] *Joe does no longer love Lea passionately → Joe will no longer love Lea passionately*. The verb is conjugated in the future tense. All other tenses are possible, e.g. *Joe did no longer love Lea, Joe does no longer love Lea, Joe has no longer loved Lea*.

[NegStop] *Joe loves Lea passionately → Joe does no longer love Lea passionately*. The aspectual negation *no longer* is applied. Other negations are possible (e.g. *Joe's never loved Lea passionately, Joe feels no love for Lea*) as well as other aspects (e.g. *Joe started to love Lea, Joe keeps being in love with Lea*).

[Intens3] *Joe loves Lea → Joe loves Lea passionately*. The adverb of intensity *passionately* is applied. Other adverbs of intensity are possible (e.g. *Joe loves Lea very much*); intensity can also be expressed by an adjective (e.g. *Joe feels little love for Lea*). The sentence can contain one intensifier at most (which is handled by the grammar feature +ONCE): sentences such as *Joe madly loves Lea very much* are therefore neither recognized nor produced by the grammar.

13.1. Implementing transformations

When texts are parsed automatically, we would like to be able to transform the matching sentences, for instance to make paraphrases of them, to link a question to its answer, etc. Let us consider the two following sentences:

Joe eats an apple = An apple is eaten by Joe

The operation that consists of computing the right sentence from the left one is *passivization*. When the left sentence is computed from the right, this is called a *transformational analysis*[4]. Following the model of unrestricted grammars seen in Chapter 9, it is possible to build a grammar that automatically replaces each sequence recognized in the text (here for example: *Joe eats an apple*) with the corresponding transformed sequence (here: *An apple is eaten by Joe*). One example of such a grammar is shown in the following figure.

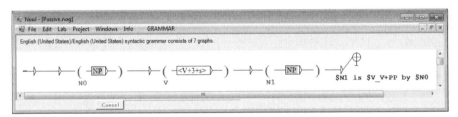

Figure 13.2. *Passive*

If we apply this grammar to the sentence *Joe eats an apple*, NooJ stores the word *Joe* in variable $N0, the word *eats* invariable $V and the sequence *an apple* in variable $N1. The morphological operation $V_V+PP produces

---

4 The idea of transformation generalizes the idea of the paraphrase since it accepts sentences that share the same semantic material which are not necessarily synonymous, for example: Joe sleeps ↔ Joe does not sleep.

the participle form of $V, that is to say *eaten*, and the sequence produced by the grammar "$N0 is $V_V+PP by $N1" therefore takes the following value:

an apple is eaten by Joe

This grammar constitutes therefore a directed *transformation operation*, unlike the transformations presented at the beginning of this chapter which were bidirectional. I will therefore use the symbol "→" to distinguish transformation operations from bidirectional transformation relations (marked with the symbol "=").

The following grammar in Figure 13.3 implements the operation [Neg]→: from the sentence *Joe eats an apple*, it produces the sentence *Joe does not eat an apple*.

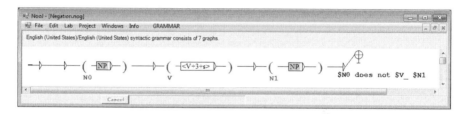

Figure 13.3. *Negation*

Figure 13.4 is an example of an operation that takes agreement constraints into account.

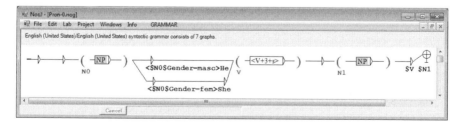

Figure 13.4. *Making the subject into a pronoun*

This grammar contains two constraints on the subject's gender[5]: the <SGender="m"> constraint is validated if the subject is masculine, whereas the <SGender="f"> constraint is validated if it is feminine. In the first instance, the upper path is activated, and the grammar produces the pronoun "He"; in the second instance, it is the lower path that is activated, and the grammar then produces the pronoun "She". This grammar therefore makes the subject into a pronoun:

> *Joe eats an apple → He eats an apple*

> *Lea eats an apple → She eats an apple*

By combining the use of constraints (to define the subject, verb and complement types) with inflection or derivation operations, we can build grammars capable of producing relatively sophisticated transformed sentences. For example:

> *Joe loves apples → Joe is an apple lover*

> *Joe loves apples → Joe's love for apples*

If $V has the value *loves*, the $V_N+Hum+s operation will produce the form *lover* whereas the $V_N+Abs+soperationwill produce the form *love*. For both of these operations to be available, it is of course necessary for the verb *to love* to be linked to the two derivations *lover* and *love*. Remember that this is done in the dictionary, that includes derivational paradigms +DRV:

```
love,V+tr+FLX=LOVE+DRV=ER:TABLE+DRV=E:TABLE
```

The derivational paradigm ER:TABLE produces the two forms *lover*, *lovers* whereas the E:TABLE paradigm produces the two forms *love*, *loves*.

An exhaustive formalized description of the transformations of a language would have to contain hundreds of elementary transformations, as the following figure shows us:

---

5 It would be necessary to add two tests on number, so that sentences containing a plural subject can be handled: *These people eat a sandwich →They eat a sandwich.*

[Pron0ms]	Joe eats an apple = He eats an apple
[Pron0fs]	Lea eats an apple = She eats an apple
[Pron0n]	The rat eats an apple = It eats an apple
[Pron0Part]	Some bread fell = Some fell
[Pron0p]	Joe and Lea eat an apple = They eat an apple
[Pron1m]	Joe sees Paul = Joe sees him
[Pron1f]	Joe sees Lea = Joe sees her
[Pron1n]	Joe eats an apple = Joe eats it
[Pron1Part]	Joe eats some bread = Joe eats some
[Pron1p]	Joe eats two apples = Joe eats them
[Pron2m]	Joe gives an apple to Paul = Joe gives him an apple
[Pron2m']	Joe gives an apple to Paul = Joe gives an apple to him
...	
[N1Z]	Joe eats an apple = Joe eats
[N2Z]	Joe gives an apple to someone = Joe gives an apple
...	
[PresProg]	Joe eats an apple = Joe is eating an apple
[PastProg]	Joe eats an apple = Joe was eating an apple
[FutProg]	Joe eats an apple = Joe will be eating an apple
[PresPerf]	Joe eats an apple = Joe has eaten an apple
[PastPerf]	Joe eats an apple = Joe had eaten an apple
[FutPerf]	Joe eats an apple = Joe will have eaten an apple
[Preterit]	Joe eats an apple = Joe ate an apple
[Future]	Joe eats an apple = Joe will eat an apple
[PresCond]	Joe eats an apple = Joe would eat an apple
[PastCond]	Joe eats an apple = Joe would have eaten an apple
[NearFuture]	Joe eats an apple = Joe is going to eat an apple
[NearPast]	Joe eats an apple = Joe has just eaten an apple
...	
[Passive]	Joe eats an apple = An apple is eaten by Joe
[PassiveZ]	Joe eats an apple = An apple is eaten
...	
[Neg]	Joe eats an apple = Joe does not eat an apple
[Neg-no]	Joe eats an apple = Joe eats no apple
[Neg-AspCont]	Joe eats apples = Joe never eats apples
[Neg-AspStop]	Joe eats an apple = Joe no longer eats an apple
...	
[Cleft0]	Joe eats an apple = It is Joe who eats an apple
[Cleft1]	Joe eats an apple = It is an apple that Joe eats
[Cleft2]	Joe gives an apple to Lea = It is to Lea that Joe gives an apple
[CleftAdv]	Joe ate an apple yesterday = It is yesterday that Joe ate an apple
...	
[Intens0]	Joe works = Joe works a little
[Intens1]	Joe loves Lea = Joe loves Lea very much
[Intens2]	Joe loves Lea = Joe loves Lea passionately
...	

[Adv0]	Joe ate an apple yesterday = Yesterday, Joe ate an apple
[Adv1]	Joe ate an apple quickly = Joe quickly ate an apple
…	
[Nom0]	Joe loves apples = Joe is an apple lover
[Nom1]	Joe loves Lea = Lea is the love of Joe
[NomV]	Joe loves Lea = Joes feels love for Lea
	…
[Vable]	One can love this cat = This cat is lovable
[Aly]	Joe drinks in a quick way = Joe drinks quickly
…	
[ASPstart]	Joe eats the apple = Joe starts to eat the apple
[ASPcontinue]	Joe eats the apple = Joe continues eating the apple
[ASPfinish]	Joe eats the apple = Joe finishes eating the apple
…	
[MODcan]	Joe eats an apple = Joe can eat an apple
[MODmight]	Joe eats an apple = Joe might eat an apple
[MODmust]	Joe eats an apple = Joe must eat an apple
[MODneed]	Joe eats an apple = Joe needs to eat an apple
…	
[OPmake]	Lea makes + Joe eats an apple = Lea makes Joe eat an apple
[OPfind]	Lea finds + Joe eats an apple = Lea finds Joe eating an apple
…	
[COORD]	Lea sleeps + Joe eats an apple = Lea sleeps and Joe eats an apple
[COORDN0]	Lea sleeps + Lea eats an apple = Lea sleeps and eats an apple
[COORDN1]	Lea sees Joe + Lea sees Ida = Lea sees Joe and Ida
[COORDbut]	Lea sleeps + Joe eats an apple = Lea sleeps but Joe eats an apple
…	
[REL0]	A boy sleeps + The boy eats = The boy who sleeps eats
[REL1]	Lea sees a boy + The boy eats = The boy Lea sees eats
[REL2]	Lea gave an apple to the boy + The boy eats = The boy Lea gave an apple to eats
…	
[SUBwhen]	Lea sleeps + Joe eats = Lea sleeps when Joe eats
[SUBwhere]	Lea sleeps + Joe eats = Lea sleeps where Joe eats
…	
[Quest0Hum]	Joe eats an apple = Who eats an apple?
[Quest0nHum]	Driving bothers Joe = What bothers Joe?
[Quest1Hum]	Joe sees Lea = Whom does Joe see?
[Quest1Hum']	Joe sees Lea = Who does Joe see?
[Quest1nHum]	Joe eats an apple = What does Joe eat?
[Quest2toHum]	Joe gives an apple to Lea = To whom does Joe give an apple?
[QuestHow]	Joe gives an apple to Lea = How did Joe give an apple to Lea?
[QuestWhen]	Joe gives an apple to Lea = When did Joe give an apple to Lea?
…	

Figure 13.5. *A few elementary transformations*

Moreover, each transformation corresponds to two reverse operations. For example, the [Neg] transformation in fact corresponds to the following two operations:

> *Joe eats an apple* **[Neg]**→ *Joe does not eat an apple*
> *Joe does not eat an apple* **[Neg-inv]**→ *Joe eats an apple*

Figure 13.6 shows the transformational [Passive-inv] operation being implemented; note that this graph is different from the graph in Figure 13.2.

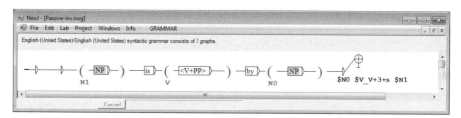

Figure 13.6. *The operation [Passive-inv]*

Unfortunately, completing the list of transformations from Figure 13.5 to formalize all the elementary transformations (as well as their opposite) would not be sufficient to describe all the sentences in a language since numerous sentences are produced by combining several transformations. The idea behind transformational grammar – at least, as developed by [HAR 70] – is to use sequences of transformations. For example, to produce the sentence *It is not the apple that he does not want to eat* from the sentence *Joe eats the apple*, we would apply several transformational operations in sequence as seen in Figure 13.7.

> *Joe eats the apple* **[OPwant]**→
> *Joe wants to eat the apple* **[Neg]**→
> *Joe does not want to eat the apple* **[Pro0]**→
> *He does not want to eat the apple* **[Cleft1]** →
> *It is the apple that he does not want to eat* **[Neg]**→
> *It is not the apple that he does not want to eat*

Figure 13.7. *A transformation chain*

The mechanism for applying transformations in sequence corresponds exactly to the way Turing machines work (already discussed in Chapter 9), which are capable of modifying and re-parsing a text in a loop. But to be able to apply the sequence of transformations seen in Figure 13.7, we must redesign each transformational operation in such a way that it can be applied not only to elementary sentences, but also to any sentence that has already been transformed. For example, the [Neg]→operation is applied twice: once to modify the sentence *Joe wants to eat the apple*, and again to modify the already transformed sentence *It is the apple that he does not want to eat*. We can easily see that the grammar that implements the full [Neg]→ operation (capable of processing any sentence) will be much more complicated to build than Figure 13.3 suggests.

13.2. Theoretical problems

Although it is used by most contemporary linguists, this model of transformations in sequence poses at least four problems[6]: the order in which the transformations are applied, equivalence between different transformational sequences, the necessity of constructing intermediary, a grammatical stages, and the number of individual transformations to be built.

13.2.1. *Equivalence of transformation sequences*

Let us consider the following two transformational sequences:

(1a) *Joe saw the car* **[Pro0][Neg][Cleft0]** → *It is he who did not see the car*

(1b) *Joe saw the car* **[Neg][Pro0][Cleft0]** → *It is he who did not see the car*

These two different sequences produce the same sentence. Let us now consider the following two sequences:

(2a) *Joe saw the car* **[Cleft0][Neg]** → *It is not Joe who saw the car*

(2b) *Joe saw the car* **[Neg][Cleft0]** → *It is Joe who did not see the car*

The latter two sequences do not produce the same sentence. In other words: sometimes the order of the transformations is important, and

---

6 [SIL 11] describes other theoretical and methodological problems linked to designing a group of transformation chains.

sometimes not... A formalization of a language should at least enable us to predict if two different sequences of transformations produce the same result or not, and conversely if two different analyses for a given sentence are equivalent or not. I do not see how to formalize equivalence between sequences of transformations, unless of course we list all the possible sequences, and compare them one by one, which is impossible since the number of potential sequences of transformations is infinite.

13.2.2. *Ambiguities in transformed sentences*

We saw how the sentence *It is he who did not see the car* can be produced by two different sequences of transformations: (1a) and (1b). But this sentence just has one single meaning: it is not ambiguous, neither syntactically, nor semantically. Let us now compare the two following sequences of transformations:

(3a) *Joe loves Lea + Joe loves Ida too* [CoordV]→ *Joe loves Lea, and Ida too*

(3b) *Joe loves Lea + Ida loves Lea too* [CoordVN1]→ *Joe loves Lea, and Ida does too* [doZ]→ *Joe loves Lea, and Ida too*

Here, the same sentence *Joe loves Lea, and Ida too* is produced by two different sequences of transformations; it is therefore ambiguous. We are therefore looking at two different cases: sometimes, a given sentence produced by two sequences of transformations should be handled as ambiguous, and sometimes not.

Here too, a transformational model should allow us to explain why two sequences of transformations sometimes produce an ambiguous, and at other times a non-ambiguous result. Conversely, if a sentence is associated with two different analyses it is vital to know if the two analyses are equivalent (as in examples 1a-1b above), or if they correspond to two different meanings (as in examples 3a-3b).

I do not see how it is possible to distinguish *a priori* different but equivalent sequences of transformations from different but non-equivalent sequences of transformations, unless again we list them all, and compare every one of them, which is impossible since the number of sequences of transformations in infinite.

13.2.3. *Theoretical sentences*

Let us consider the following sequence of transformations:

> *We drink this potion* [MODcan]→ *We can drink this potion* [Passive]→ *This potion can be drunk* [Vable]→ *This potion is drinkable*

It is natural to analyze the adjectival ending *–able* using the very productive (i.e. general) sequence of the three elementary transformations [MODcan], [Passive] and [Vable]. But this sequence of transformations will produce many intermediary a grammatical sequences, for example:

> *We bear Joe* [MODcan]→ *We can bear Joe* [Passive]→ **Joe can be borne* [Vable]→ *Joe is bearable*

What should be done with the intermediary sentence **Joe can be borne*? I see two solutions:

– either we describe it as a theoretical sentence, which allows the sequence of transformations to be used. But having the language's generative grammar[7] recognize theoretical sentences will pose many problems, particularly with generation (when we do not wish to produce these sentences) and these theoretical sentences will create many artificial ambiguities with actual sentences. For instance, analyzing the sentence *Joe can be borne* might trigger a totally different and irrelevant interpretation, like in *a mosquito-borne disease*.

– or we construct a direct transformation, e.g.:

> [MODcanPassiveVable] *One can bear Joe = Joe is bearable.*

But this approach will massively increase the number of direct transformations, since for each exception[8], we will need to construct a direct complex transformation that is equivalent to each sequence of transformations. The very idea of constructing direct transformations goes against the sequence of transformations approach, since they are redundant:

---

7 By generative grammar, I mean the grammar (type 0, 1, 2 or 3) that recognizes (or produces) all the sentences in a language, possibly by producing information on structure, see Chapter 12.

8 It can reasonably be predicted that all the transformations will have exceptions.

each time a direct transformation is built, the equivalent sequence of transformations is made useless.

13.2.4. *The number of transformations to be implemented*

Generally, a transformation developed to be applied to an elementary sentence cannot necessarily be applied to sentences that have already been transformed. For example, let us return to the elementary [Passive]→ operation in Figure 13.2 which produces the sentence *Lea is loved by Joe* from the sentence *Joe loves Lea*. If we apply this operation to the already transformed sentence *He loves Lea*, an incorrect sentence is produced:

He loves Lea [Passive]→ * *Lea is loved by he*

To obtain the following correct result:

He loves Lea [Passive]→ *Lea is loved by him*

it is therefore necessary for the [Passive]→ grammar to take account of sentences in which the subject is *he*, that is to say sentences transformed beforehand by the [Pro0]→ operation.

Similarly, if we apply the same [Passive]→ operation to a negative sentence, the word form *does* must be deleted and negation attached to the verb *to be*:

Joe does not love Lea [Passive]→ *Lea is not loved by Joe*

The [Passive]→operation should therefore take account of potential negations in the sentences to be analyzed. It will also have to allow for sentences in which the verb is conjugated in a compound tense:

Joe has loved Lea [Passive]→ *Lea has been loved by Joe*

as well as cases where the main verb is combined with one or several operation (e.g. find), modal (must) or aspectual verbs (stop) e.g.:

Joe might have loved Lea [Passive]→ *Lea might have been loved by Joe* and cases where sentences have been restructured, etc.

How do we evaluate the complexity of such a system? Note that supplementing the [Passive]→ grammar so that it can recognize all the sentences that can be written in the passive is equivalent to building a group of specific grammars for each type of sentence already transformed: a group of specialized operations would then be constructed: a [Passive_simple]→ operation to put simple sentences into the passive, a [Passive_Pro0]→ operation to place sentences in which the subject has been changed into a pronoun into the passive, a [Passive_Neg]→ operation to put negative sentences into the passive etc.

Some of the sentences already transformed are incompatible with the [Passive]→ operation. For example, a sentence that is already passive cannot be put into the passive, a sentence with an impersonal construction cannot be put into the passive (*It rained lots of droplets* → **Lots of droplets were rained*), an inverted sentence cannot be put into the passive (*There come the students* → **The students are come by there*), nor a sentence with a pronoun construction (e.g. *Joe washes his hands* → **his hands are washed by Joe*), etc. It is therefore necessary, for each sentence already transformed, to check if it is or is not possible to apply the [Passive]→ operation, and if so, to build the corresponding specialized operation.

How many verifications and/or specialized operations would it be then necessary to construct? First of all, let us recall that a given transformation operation can be applied to a single sentence several times: for example the sequence of transformations in Figure 13.7 contains the [Neg]→ operation twice. If we take as a base the thousand elementary transformations that can be described by completing Figure 13.5, it will be necessary to take account of 1,000 sentence structures, that is to say to tie up or construct a thousand specialized operations, just to implement the [Passive]→ operation. If we wish to describe the 1,000 transformations instead of only the [Passive]→ operation, then we will need to tie up or construct potentially 1,000 × 1,000, which is one million specialized operations where any two transformations are involved, a billion specialized operations where three transformations are involved, etc. To analyze sentences that contain up to half a dozen transformations – they are relatively common – it would be necessary to construct $1,000^6 = 10^{18}$ specialized operations.

More generally, the set of elementary transformations can be seen as an alphabet Σ containing 1,000 letters: sequences of transformations therefore can be seen as words built on this alphabet, that is to say Σ* and the equivalence classes between sequences of transformations constitute languages on Σ*. Each equivalence class is a (potentially infinite) language. For example, the simple transformation operation [Pro0]→ is equivalent to an infinite number of sequences of transformations, among which are the following:

[Pro0]→[Neg]→[Neg-inv], [Pro0]→[Neg]→[Neg-inv]→[Neg]→
[Neg-inv], ... , [Pro0]→[Pro0-inv]→[Pro0], [Pro0]→[Pro0-inv]→
[Pro0]→[Pro0-inv]→ [Pro0], ... , [Neg]→[Pro0]→[Neg-inv]→
[Pro0-inv]→[Pro0]→[Neg]→ [Neg-inv], ... [Neg]→[Pro0]→
[Pro0-inv]→[Neg-inv]→[Pro0]→[Neg]→ [Neg-inv], ...

What kind of grammar would be needed to describe such languages? The fact that the number of [Neg]→ should be equal to the number of [Neg-inv]→ in all the sequences equivalent to the transformation [Pro0], with no obvious constraints on the position of these operations[9], indicates that neither regular grammars, nor context-free grammars have the power needed to describe such languages[10].

13.3. Transformational analysis with NooJ

We have seen that applying sequences of elementary transformation operations poses serious theoretical problems. And using only direct transformation operations would not be possible since they would be infinite in number...

Moreover a transformational grammar would have to be massively redundant with the language's generative grammar. In fact, if we compare the grammars in Figures 13.2, 13.3, 13.4 and 13.6, we see that they all share

---

9 Remember that sentences (2a) and (2b) are not equivalent.

10 This is not the case of Dyck languages for which the operations [Neg] and [Neg-inv] would play the role of balanced parentheses: here, the only constraint is that there are just as many [Neg] and [Neg-inv] operations. Moreover, if an [Ext] operation is present in the sequence of transformations, the [Neg] and [Neg-inv] must cancel each other out either before or after the [Ext] operation, but not across.

the same description of sentence structures and noun phrases (the same NP graph). By refining them, for example so they can handle complex verb groups, adverbs, insertions and embedded clauses etc. their redundancy will become more and more intolerable: no one would want to have to describe the same elements NP, VG, CLAUSE, ADV, etc. thousands of times, for each transformation operation. A sequence of transformations, like the one in Figure 13.7 would involve re-parsing the same phrases five times, which seems to me to be pointless.

Note now that all the sentences in the language should already be described in its generative grammar, otherwise it would not even be possible to apply a single transformation to them. We can therefore ask ourselves if it makes sense to construct a "transformational grammar" independently of the generative grammar. I think not: it would be much better to analyze and generate all the sentences of a language by using a single grammar. To do this, NooJ uses its parser and generator in tandem.

13.3.1. *Applying a grammar in "generation" mode*

NooJ carries out transformational analysis and generation automatically, without needing to add transformation operations to the generative grammar. In other words, there is no independent "transformational" level in the formalization of the language: the transformations for each sentence are computed from the generative grammar that recognizes the sentence. The basic idea behind NooJ's approach is to use the generative grammar in both analysis and generation modes. For example if one given grammar recognizes the following sentences:

> *Joe eats an apple. Joe does not eat an apple. An apple is eaten by Joe. It is Joe who eats an apple. It is Joe who does not eat an apple. etc.*

then NooJ should be able both to recognize as well as produce all of them. The equivalence between these sentences therefore exists by the mere fact that a generator can produce all these sentences if it is given any of them. In other words, it is the generative grammar that plays the role of defining transformational equivalency classes.

The following figure shows the *Declaratives* graph that recognizes and produces all the declarative sentences that we saw in Figure 13.1.

Note the features (for example +Cleft0, +NomV, +Pro0, etc.) that are produced by the grammar when NooJ parses or generates sentences. These features actually represent the results of a transformational analysis of the sentence.

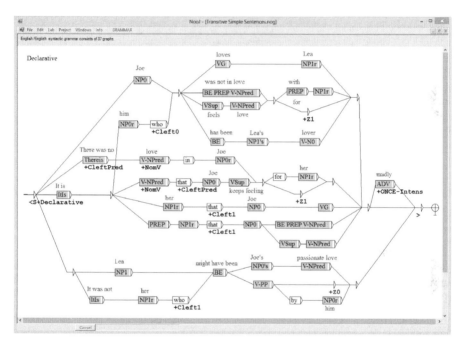

Figure 13.8. *Grammar for declarative transitive sentences*

13.3.2. *The transformation's arguments*

The aim is to build a grammar that can be used both to parse and generate any sentence in the language, not simply the sentence *Joe loves Lea*. The previous grammar has therefore been generalized in order to recognize any direct transitive sentence. But then we must ensure that the sentences generated from one given sentence have the same arguments as the input sentence: if we input the sentence *my cousin eats the cake*, there is no question of producing the sentence *Joe loves Lea*, or even *my cousin is eaten by the cake.* To ensure that the sentences generated by the system have the same arguments as the sentence analyzed, and that these arguments are correctly placed, we use the NooJ global variables[11].

For example, let us say that the subject of the sentence analyzed will be stored in variable @S, the verb in variable @V, and the direct object in variable @O. Now consider the simplified grammar in Figure 13.9.

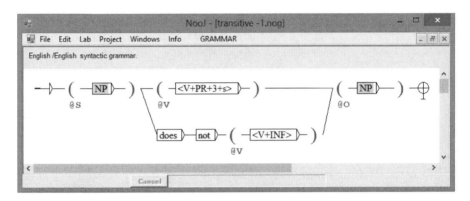

Figure 13.9. *Grammar used in mixed "analysis + generation"mode*

If we apply this grammar to the sentence *my cousin eats the cake*, variable @S will hold the value "my cousin", variable @V will hold the value "eats" and variable @O will hold the value "the cake". When this grammar is used in generation mode[12], NooJ will produce the two sequences:

@S @V @O. @S does not @V @O

Note that the variables take the ALUs as values and not simple word forms. Consequently, @V can correspond to many word forms: *eats, eat, eaten, eating,* as well as *eater* and *eaters* if the corresponding derivation has been formalized with a property +DRV. In the top path on the graph, the

---

11 Global variables (prefixed by the character "@") are variables whose range is global: they are not necessarily defined in the same graph or one of its daughter graphs and their value can be transmitted by the parser to the generator. Global variables enable computations to be carried out that we judged beyond our project framework in section 1.4, such as resolving anaphors and pronoun coreference.

12 In NooJ, run the command GRAMMAR > Transformations.

constraint <V+PR+3+s> is imposed, whereas in the bottom path, the constraint <V+INF> is imposed. The previous sequence then produces the following two sentences:

> *my cousin eats the cake. my cousin does not eat the cake.*

If we apply this grammar to a large number of transitive sentences, such as for example *the FCC changes the definition of broadband*, NooJ will produce the corresponding negative sentence, for example, *the FCC does not change the definition of broadband*, etc.

We not only want sentences to be generated; we also want the generated sentences to be associated with an analysis that represents the transformations that link each sentence to their equivalent elementary sentence. To do this, we add outputs to the grammar, shown in Figure 13.10.

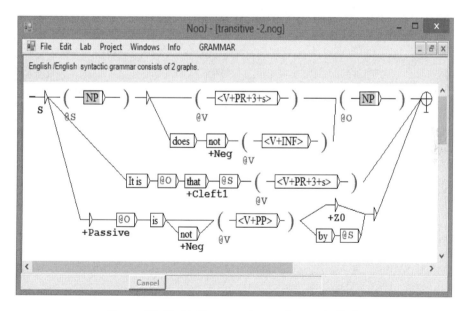

Figure 13.10. *Linking complex sentences to their transformational properties*

For example, if we parse the sentence *Joe does not see my cousin*, the grammar above will produce seven sentences, including the sentence *It is my cousin that Joe sees*, and will associate it with the output +Cleft1 (object extraction). It will also produce the sentence *my cousin is not seen* and associate it with the features +Passive, +Neg and +Z0 (delete subject), as we see in the Figure 13.11.

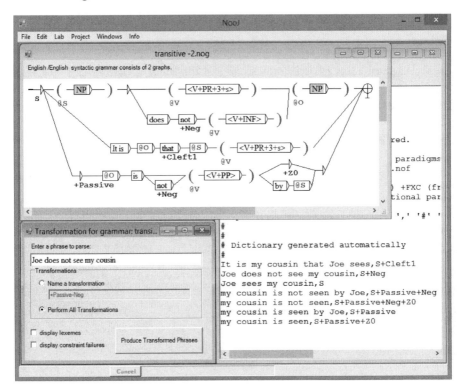

Figure 13.11. *Automatic transformation*

This grammar is of course simplified: the grammar in the English NooJ module[13] handles pronouns (e.g. *Joe sees Lea → He sees her*), agreement between the subject and the verb (e.g. *my cousins have not seen Ida*), potential nominalizations, aspectual and modal verbs, intensifiers, etc. and produces more than 2 million transitive declarative sentences as well as 3 million interrogative sentences.

In conclusion, it is possible to describe a large number of transformations just by constructing the generative grammar that recognizes all the sentences

---

13 There are comparable grammars for French see [SIL 11] and Portugese, see [BAR 08].

that can be transformed into one another; this grammar can be used both to parse and generate a set of equivalent sentences on demand, and to provide a transformational analysis for each matching or generated sentence.

13.4. Question answering

Question answering is an NLP pilot project and was the subject of annual competitions at the TREC conference until 2007[14]. A Question Answering system is typically a software application that processes a query (the question) and manages to find its answer by parsing a potentially huge corpus of texts (such as Wikipedia or even the whole WEB).

A transformational engine such as NooJ's could be used as the basis of a Question Answering software. The basic idea is that a question such as "Where did Obama go?" can be seen as a transformed version of the elementary sentence *"Obama went to India"*. It is then possible to construct an automatic application that finds, for a given question, all its transformed sentences (i.e. its answers) in texts.

The notion of transformation can further be generalized by adding synonyms of terms and expressions to the grammar. For example, we would like the previous question to find the following sentences as well:

... President Obama and the First Lady traveled to India this week...
... the President is the first to have visited India...
(www.whitehouse.gouv, January 2014).

In order to be able to establish this correspondence, we need to link the verb *to go to* to its synonyms *to travel to* and *to visit*[15]. In the same way, we also need to link *President* (as well as other synonyms: Chief of State, Head of State, Commander in Chief, etc.) to the proper name *Barak Obama*.

---

14 See trec.nist.gov. There too, statistical methods were over-represented, see [ITT 07] for a representative example of the methods used.
15 Thesauruses (the dictionary WORDNET among them) can be used to expand the original query.

13.5. Semantic analysis

Semantic analysis consists of producing logical predicates from texts written in natural language. The same exact method employed to produce transformed sentences from a given sentence could also be used to produce logical representations of the sentence's meaning. In addition to sentences such as *Lea is not loved by Joe, It is Joe who loves Lea,* etc. we could just as well produce logical formulae such as NOT(love(Joe,Lea)). We actually saw how to produce these annotations in section 12.2.5 *Dependency trees.*

Semantic representation of sentences, whatever their format (in the form of PROLOG predicates, XML tags, AVM, etc.) has many applications in NLP. It is typically used by expert system software to compute inferences in knowledge databases. For example, [ROU 06] describes an application in epidemiology that computes PROLOG predicates by parsing texts from the Epidemia corpus; these predicates are used to feed a knowledge database: an expert system processes them to automatically locate epidemiological events, consolidate symptoms and compute inferences.

Information Retrieval and Text Mining tools often represent information in the form of XML annotations such as the following:

<BUY   BUYER="Arlington   Value   Capital"   OBJ="IBM" NBSHARES="128000"> *For his part, Allan Mecham, manager and CEO of Arlington Value Capital, bought 120,000 shares of IBM, i.e. 6.9% of his portfolio* </BUY>

These annotations are then used by *Business Intelligence* applications which can compute nets (to display relations between business partners), perform statistical analyses (to bring to light correlations between events), etc.

Automatic generation programs produce texts in natural language[16] from a semantic representation; if we first analyze a text to produce its semantic representation, we can then reformulate this semantic representation

---

16 [DAN 85] introduces a software capable of producing short news dispatches, written in good style, from a form describing an event: the names of a murderer and victim, the weapon used, date, place, etc.

automatically, in order to summarize, or translate the initial text into another language[17].

13.6. Machine translation

Transformation operations can be used to produce a translation of a given text, as also seen in Figure 6.18. By using variables and constraints, it is possible to build more general translation grammars, such as in Figure 13.12.

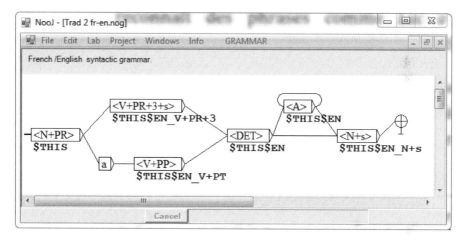

Figure 13.12. *Simple French → English translation*

In this French to English grammar, the variable $THIS takes the current ALU's value. $THIS$EN then takes this ALU's +EN property's value, i.e. its English translation. For example, for the following lexical entries from the French dictionary:

```
le,DET+EN="the"
petit,A+EN="little"
```

---

17 The European project EUROTRA (1978-1992) aimed to build an automatic translation software capable of translating 9 languages into each other. EUROTRA parsed a text in a source language, computing its semantic representation called *Intermediate Representation*, then used this representation to produce the text in the target language. So, EUROTRA could translate any language into any other language, by building 9 parsers and 9 generators, instead of having to construct $2 \times 9 \times 9$ bilingual translation systems.

the variable $THIS$EN will take the respective values *the* and *little*. NooJ carries out morphological operations on variables. For example if $THIS$EN has the value *see*, the operation $THIS$EN_V+PT will compute as *saw*. The previous grammar therefore recognizes French sentences such as *Lea a vu la petite chaise* and produces the corresponding sentence in English: *Lea saw the little chair*.

The previous grammar translates sentences word for word; it should be noted however that, thanks to our definition of multiword units defined in section 3.4.1, it still translates the following sentences correctly:

> *Joe a organisé cette table ronde* → *Joe organized this round table*
> *Lea a mangé la totalité du pain de seigle* → *Lea ate the whole rye bread*
> *Ida a cuit trois pommes de terre* → *Ida cooked three potatoes*

since *table ronde, la totalitéde, pain complet* and *pomme de terre* constitute ALUs and are therefore processed as blocks. Nevertheless, in several cases, word order is different in the two languages. For example the French noun phrase *la belle chaise bleue* should be translated by the English noun phrase *the beautiful blue chair*, i.e. by moving all the adjectives to the left of the noun. The following grammar (Figure 13.13) does exactly that.

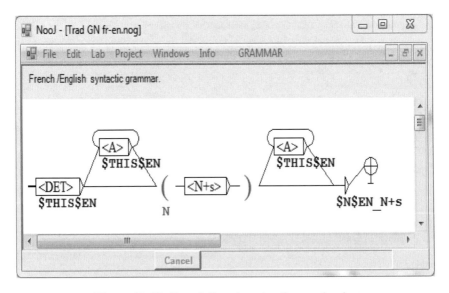

Figure 13.13. *Translation changing the word order*

First, the two sequences of adjectives are translated, then, the translation of the noun is produced right at the end of the sequence.

The following grammar (Figure 13.14) takes account of the noun's number: singular or plural.

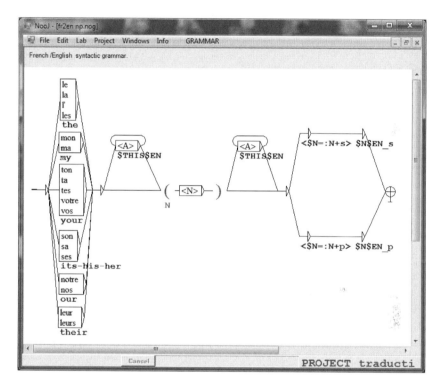

Figure 13.14. *Translation with constraints*

This grammar recognizes French noun phrases made up of a determiner, an optional sequence of adjectives, the noun, then a facultative sequence of adjectives placed after the noun. For example *ma belle voiture rouge*, then produces their English translation[18], *my beautiful red car*.

---

18 The idea of inserting translated words into the grammar of the source language is not new. For example [SAL 99] incorporates the translation of recognized phrases in English in his French grammar.

– the determiner is translated instantly. If the determiner is *son*, *sa* or *ses*, it is not possible to know its English translation without computing its reference[19], therefore it is translated with "it-his-her";

– the adjectives placed before and after the noun are translated right away. For instance, if the current adjective is linked to the following lexical entry:

```
rouge,A+EN="red"
```

the variable $THIS$EN has the value, "red";

– the noun in the noun phrase is stored in variable **$N**. The grammar checks whether it is singular or plural, then it is translated[20]. For example, if **$N** has the value, "crayons", the NEN variable will have the value, "pencil" whereas the compound variable NEN_p will get the value, "pencils".

NooJ has been used to construct a dozen automatic translation prototypes, see for example [BAR 08] for English → Portuguese translation; [FEH 10] for Arabic → French translation of named entities, that includes a morphological system to transliterate Arabic proper names into the Latin alphabet; [BEN 14] for Arabic → English translation of some syntactic constructions; and [WU 10] for French → Chinese translation of some noun phrases. But building a complete set of grammars capable of translating any real-world text would not be simple, and it would first be necessary to construct a full grammar for the source language. The three main difficulties to overcome are then:

– ambiguity in the source language. If analyses of the source text have not been able to resolve all the lexical, syntactic and semantic ambiguities, multiple translations must be produced;

– translating terms that have several possible translations in the target language. For example, the verb *to eat* is translated into German as *essen* or *fressen* depending on whether its subject is human or animal. In Chinese, the adjective *big* is translated differently depending on whether it describes a

---

19 Computing pronoun references outside of the current sentence is not possible within our strictly linguistic project framework, as discussed in section 1.4.

20 This grammar is simplified. In particular, some plural French nouns should be translated in the singular in English (e.g. "informations" → "information"), whereas some singular French nouns should be translated in the plural in English (e.g. "pantalon" → "pants").

person, an abstraction or a thing. To translate a text correctly, it is then necessary to add to the analysis of the source language, analyses specific to the target language;

– there will still be extra-linguistic problems to resolve, for example when we need to compute an English pronoun:

Il mange (Luc) → He eats
Il mange (le rat) → It eats
Il pleut→ It rains

13.7. Conclusion

In this chapter, I have introduced a transformational engine capable of parsing any sentence (simple or complex) described by a grammar, and automatically producing all its corresponding transformed sentences. Each sentence produced is associated with its "transformational analysis" in the form of a sequence of features, which describes the sequence of transformations that links the produced sentence to its corresponding elementary sentence.

Contrary to traditional transformational grammars, the system suggested here does not require building a specific grammar that would be independent of a purely syntactic description of the language. In other words, building the language's generative grammar also allows us to describe its sentences from a transformational point of view.

The applications for a linguistic engine capable of processing transformations are spectacular, and I have introduced just a few: generating paraphrases, question answering, semantic analysis, and automatic translation.

13.8. Exercises

1) Build a transformational grammar that breaks down sentences in which the subjects and/or complements are coordinated, to produce corresponding elementary sentences, for example:

Joe and Paul love Lea → *Joe loves Lea + Paul loves Lea*
Joe loves Lea and Ida → *Joe loves Lea + Joe loves Ida*

2) Modify the previous grammar so that it implements the following semantic analysis.

Joe and Paul love Lea → love (Joe,Lea) AND love (Paul,Lea)
Joe loves Lea and Ida → love (Joe,Lea) AND love (Joe,Ida)

3) Build a French→English grammar capable of translating all the French sentences built from the vocabulary {aime[loves], ces[these], les[the], gâteaux[cakes], Marie, voit[sees]}. Construct a bilingual dictionary that contains the following three lexical entries: {aime, gâteaux, voit}; the grammatical words *ces* and *les* will be translated directly by the grammar, whereas the proper noun *Marie* will simply be recopied.

13.9. Internet links

For a presentation on applications for automatic semantic analysis of texts, see the pages en.wikipedia.org/wiki/Knowledge-based_systems and en.wikipedia.org/wiki/Expert_system.

The Association for Computational Linguistics has a special interest group on automatic translation, see: www.sigmt.org.

For a presentation on the project EUROTRA, see en.wikipedia.org/wiki/Eurotra.

The automatic translation system OpenLogos is now a free and open source, see: logos-os.dfki.de.

Conclusion

This book describes a research project at the heart of linguistics: formalizing five levels of phenomena linked to the use of written language: orthography, vocabulary, morphology, syntax and semantics. This project involves defining the basic elements at each level (letters, ALUs, morphemes, phrases and predicates) as well as a system of rules that enables these elements to be assembled at each linguistic level.

Computers are an ideal tool for this project:

– computers require linguists to digitize linguistic elements, that is to represent them by sequences of bits. We saw in the first part of this work how to represent a language's alphabet and vocabulary. Complex problems emerge during this fundamental step:

    1) the number of elements of vocabulary is in the order of several hundred thousand,

    2) the variety of phenomena to formalize just vocabulary recognition in texts necessitates developing a number of complex procedures and linking them to one another,

    3) many variants and exceptions to most general rules (contraction, elision, capitals, ligatures, inflexion, derivation, etc.) need to be taken into account;

– computers can automatically recognize languages defined by the grammars introduced by Chomsky and Schützenberger. We saw in Part 2 four types of grammar:

1) regular languages can be described mathematically with the help of regular expressions and finite-state graphs,

2) context-free languages can be described by context-free grammars and recursive graphs,

3) context-sensitive languages can be described by context-sensitive grammars,

4) all recursive enumerable languages can be described by unrestricted grammars;

– computers offer linguists the possibility of parsing large quantities of texts. We saw in the third section how to apply formalized linguistic resources (in the form of electronic dictionaries and grammars) in cascade to parse texts from lexical, morphological, syntactic and semantic perspectives, with each intermediary analysis being stored in the text annotation structure (TAS).

Lexical analysis takes care of several problems that can be represented by regular grammars and therefore processed by finite-state graphs. The number of graphs to be built, their size and interactions mean that a full lexical analysis is far from being simple to implement: a complex software program is therefore necessary to identify the atomic linguistic units (ALUs) in texts automatically.

Syntactic analysis as it is traditionally known involves several levels of analyses, using local grammars (which handle small contexts), full generative grammars (which compute sentences' structure) as well as contextual constraints (which verify various types of ALU compatibility within phrases and sentences). The first two kinds of phenomena can be handled by finite-state graphs and by recursive graphs, whereas as agreements are much better handled by context-sensitive grammars.

Formalizing languages requires systematically describing links between elementary sentences and the complex, transformed sentences that actually occur in real-world texts. This description does not require the construction of a specific *transformational grammar*, as generative grammars used to carry out syntactic analyses already enable transformational parsers and generators to be implemented. Having automatic transformational parsers and generators opens the way to implementing great software applications:

linguistic semantic analyzers[1], question-answering applications, Machine Translation, etc.

Building a formalized description of vocabulary (in the form of electronic dictionaries) and grammar (in the form of regular, context-free and context-sensitive grammars) is now within our reach, and the effort devoted to such a project would not be colossal, especially compared to the effort made to build large-size tagged corpora used by statistical NLP applications.

---

1 By linguistic semantic analyzer, I mean an analyzer capable of producing all the units of meaning (predicates with their arguments) that represent the linguistic meaning of a complex sentence within the limits explained in 1.4. In particular, it would not compute co-references (for example to know who "he" refers to) nor inferences (for example to infer the sentence *Joe can vote now* from the sentence *Joe had his 18-year birthday 2 months ago*).

Bibliography

[AHO 03] AHO A., LAM M., SETHI R. *et al.*, *Compilers: Principles, Techniques, and Tools*, 2nd ed., Addison Wesley, 2006.

[ALL 07] ALLAUZEN C., RILEY M., SCHALKWYK J., "Open Fst: a general and efficient weighted finite-state transducer library", *Proceedings of the 12th International Conference on Implementation and Application of Automata (CIAA)*, vol. 4783, pp. 11–23, 2007.

[AME 11] *American Heritage Dictionary of the English Language*, Fifth Edition. Boston: Houghton Mifflin Company, 2011.

[AOU 07] AOUGHLIS F., "A computer science dictionary for NooJ", *Lecture Notes in Computer Science*, Springer-Verlag, vol. 4592, p. 341–351, 2007.

[BAC 59] BACKUS J., "The syntax and semantics of the proposed international algebraic language of the Zurich ACM-GAMM conference", *Proceedings of the International Conference on Information Processing*, UNESCO, pp. 125–132, 1959.

[BAL 02] BALDRIDGE J., Lexically Specified Derivational Control in Combinatory Categorial Grammar, PhD Dissertation. Univ. of Edinburgh, 2002.

[BAR 08] BARREIRO A., "Para MT: a paraphraser for machine translation", *Lecture Notes in Computer Science*, Springer-Verlag, vol. 5190, pp. 202–211, 2008.

[BAR 14] BARREIRO A., BATISTA F., RIBEIRO R. *et al.*, "Open Logos Semantico-Syntactic Knowledge-Rich Bilingual Dictionaries", *Proceedings of the 9th edition of the LREC Conference*, 2014.

[BEN 15] BEN A., FEHRI H., BEN H., "Translating Arabic relative clauses into English using NooJ", *Formalising Natural Languages with NooJ 2014*, Cambridge Scholars Publishing, Newcastle, 2015.

[BEN 10] BEN H., PITON O., FEHRI H., "Recognition and Arabic-French translation of named entities: case of the sport places", *Finite-State Language Engineering with NooJ: Selected Papers from the NooJ 2009 International Conference*, Sfax University Press, Tunisia, 2010.

[BER 60] BERNER R., "A proposal for character code compatibility", *Communications of the ACM*, vol. 3, no. 2, pp. 71–72, 1960.

[BIN 90] BINYONG Y., FELLEY M., *Chinese Romanization: Pronunciation and Orthography*, Sinolingua, Peking, 1990.

[BLA 90] BLAKE B., *Relational Grammar*, Routledge, London, 1990.

[BLO 33] BLOOMFIELD L., *Language*, Henry Holt, New York, 1933.

[BÖG 07] BÖGEL T., BUTT M., HAUTLI A. *et al.*, "Developing a finite-state morphological analyzer for Urdu and Hindi: some issues", *Proceedings of FSMNLP07*, Potsdam, Germany, 2007.

[BRI 92] BRILL E., "A simple rule-based part of speech tagger", *Proceedings of the ANLC'92 3rd Conference on Applied Natural Language Processing*, Association for Computational Linguistics, Stroudsburg, PA, 1992.

[BRU 02] BRUNSTEIN B., "Annotation guidelines for answer types", *Linguistic Data Consortium*, Philadelphia, 2002.

[DON 13] DONNELLY C., STALLMAN R., *GNU Bison-The Yacc-Compatible Parser Generator: Bison Version 2.7*, FSF, p. 201, 2013.

[CHA 97] CHARNIAK E., "Statistical techniques for natural language parsing", *AI Magazine*, vol. 18, no. 4, p. 33, 1997.

[CHO 57] CHOMSKY N., *Syntactic Structures,* Mouton: The Hague, 1957.

[CHR 92] CHRISTIANSEN M., "The (non) necessity of recursion in natural language processing", *Proceedings of the 14th Annual Conference of the Cognitive Science Society*, Cognitive Science Society, Indiana University, pp. 665–670, 1992.

[CHR 99] CHROBOT A., COURTOIS B., HAMMANI-MCCARTHY M. *et al.*, Dictionnaire électronique DELAC anglais: noms composés. Technical Report 59, LADL, Université Paris 7, 1999.

[COU 90a] COURTOIS B., "Un système de dictionnaires électroniques pour les mots simples du français", in COURTOIS B., SILBERZTEIN M. (eds), *Dictionnaires électroniques du français*, Larousse, Paris, pp. 5–10, 1990.

[COU 90b] COURTOIS B., SILBERZTEIN M., *Les dictionnaires électroniques*, Langue française no. 87, Larousse, Paris, 1990.

[CAL 95] DALRYMPLE M., KAPLAN R., MAXWELL J. *et al.*, *Formal Issues in Lexical-Functional Grammar*, CSLI Publications, Stanford, 1995.

[DAN 85] DANLOS L., *Génération automatique de textes en langue naturelle*, Masson, Paris, 1985.

[DON 07] DONABEDIAN B., "La lemmatisation de l'arménien occidental avec NooJ", *Formaliser les langues avec l'ordinateur : De INTEX à NooJ*, Les cahiers de la MSH Ledoux, Presses universitaires de Franche-Comté, pp. 55–75, 2007.

[DON 13] DONNELLY Ch. S. R., The Bison Manual, https://jdcqivvcr.updog.co/amRjcWl2dmNyMTg4MjExNDIzWA.pdf, 2013.

[DUB 97] DUBOIS J., DUBOIS-CHARLIER F., *Les verbes français*, Larousse, Paris, 1997.

[DUB 10] DUBOIS J., DUBOIS-CHARLIER F., "La combinatoire lexico-syntaxique dans le Dictionnaire électronique des mots", *Langages,* vol. 3, pp. 31–56, 2010.

[DUR 14] DURAN M., "Formalising Quechua Verb Inflection", *Formalising Natural Languages with NooJ 2013: Selected Papers from the NooJ 2013 International Conference* (Saarbrucken, Germany), Cambridge Scholars Publishing, Newcastle, 2014.

[EIL 74] EILENBERG S., *Automata, Languages and Machines*, Academic Press, New York, 1974.

[EVE 95] EVERAERT M., VAN DER LINDEN E.-J., SCHENK A. *et al.* (eds), *Idioms: Structural and psychological perspectives*, Erlbaum, Hillsdale, NJ, 1995.

[FEH 10] FEHRI H., HADDAR K., BEN H., "Integration of a transliteration process into an automatic translation system for named entities from Arabic to French", *Proceedings of the NooJ 2009 International Conference and Workshop*, Sfax, University Press, pp. 285–300, 2010.

[FEL 14] FELLBAUM C., "Word Net: an electronic lexical resource for English", in CHIPMAN S. (ed.), *The Oxford Handbook of Cognitive Science*, Oxford University Press, New York, 2014.

[FIL 08] FILLMORE C., "A valency dictionary of English", *International Journal of Lexicography Advance Access*, October 8, 2008.

[FRE 85] FRECKLETON P., Sentence idioms in English, Working Papers in Linguistics 11, University of Melbourne. 1985.

[FRI 03] FRIEDERICI A., KOTZ S., "The brain basis of syntactic processes: functional imaging and lesion studies", *Neuroimage*, vol. 20, no. 1, pp. S8–S17, 2003.

[GAZ 85] GAZDAR G., KLEIN E., PULLUM G. *et al.*, *Generalized Phrase Structure Grammar*, Blackwell and Cambridge, Harvard University Press, Oxford, MA, 1985.

[GAZ 88] GAZDAR G., "Applicability of Indexed Grammars to Natural Languages", in REYLE U., ROHRER C. (eds), *Natural Language Parsing and Linguistic Theories*, Studies in Linguistics and Philosophy 35, D. Reidel Publishing Company, pp. 69–94, 1988.

[GRA 02] GRASS T., MAUREL D., PITON O., "Description of a multilingual database of proper names", *Lecture Notes in Computer Science*, vol. 2389, pp. 31–36, 2002.

[GRE 11] GREENEMEIER L., "Say what? Google works to improve YouTube auto-captions for the deaf", *Scientific American*, 23rd June 2011.

[GRO 68] GROSS M., *Grammaire transformationnelle du français, 1: le verbe*, Larousse, Paris, 1968.

[GRO 75] GROSS M., *Méthodes en syntaxe*, Hermann, Paris, 1975.

[GRO 77] GROSS M., *Grammaire transformationnelle du français, 2: syntaxe du nom*, Larousse, Paris, 1977.

[GRO 86] GROSS M., *Grammaire transformationnelle du français, 3: syntaxe de l'adverbe*, Cantilène, Paris, 1986.

[GRO 94] GROSS M., "Constructing lexicon-grammars", *Computational Approaches to the Lexicon*, Oxford University Press, pp. 213–263, 1994.

[GRO 96] GROSS M., "Lexicon Grammar", in BROWN K., MILLER J. (eds), *Concise Encyclopedia of Syntactic Theories*, Elsevier, New York , pp. 244–258, 1996.

[HAL 94] HALLIDAY M., *Introduction to Functional Grammar*, 2nd edition, Edward Arnold, London, 1994.

[HAR 70] HARRIS Z., *Papers in Structural and Transformational Linguistics*, Springer Science and Business Media, Dodrecht, 1970.

[HAR 02] HARALAMBOUS Y., "Unicode ettypographie: un amour impossible", *Document Numérique*, vol. 6, no. 3, pp. 105–137, 2002.

[HER 04] HERBST T., HEATH D., ROE I. *et al.*, (eds). *A Valency Dictionary of English: A Corpus-Based Analysis of the Complementation Patterns of English Verbs, Nouns and Adjectives*, Mouton de Gruyter Berlin, 2004.

[HO 78] HO S.H., "An analysis of the two Chinese radical systems", *Journal of the Chinese Language Teachers Association*, vol. 13, no. 2, pp. 95–109, 1978.

[HOB 99] HOBBS A., Five-Unit Codes, The North American Data Communications Museum, Sandy Hook, CT, available at: www.nadcomm.com/fiveunit/fiveunits.htm, 1999.

[HOP 79] HOPCROFT J., ULLMAN J., Introduction to Automata Theory, Languages and Computation, Addison-Wesley Publishing, Reading Massachusetts, 1979.

[ITT 07] ITTYCHERIAH A., ROUKOS S., "IBM's statistical question answering system", TREC-11 Proceedings, NIST Special Publication, available at: trec.nist.gov/pubs.html, 2007.

[JOH 74] JOHNSON D., Toward a Theory of Relationally-Based Grammar, Garland Publishing, New York, 1974.

[JOH 12] JOHNSON S.C., Yacc: Yet Another Compile Compiler, AT&T Bell Laboratories Murray Hill, NJ, Nov. 2012.

[JOS 87] JOSHI A., "An introduction to tree adjoining grammars", in MANASTER-RAMER A. (ed.), Mathematics of Language, John Benjamins, Amsterdam, pp. 87–114, 1987.

[JUR 00] JURAFSKY D., MARTIN J., Speech and Language Processing: An Introduction to Natural Language Processing, Computational Linguistics and Speech Recognition, Prentice Hall, New York, 2000.

[KAP 82] KAPLAN R., BRESNAN J., "Lexical-functional grammar: a formal system for grammatical representation", in BRESNAN J. (ed.), The Mental Representation of Grammatical Relations, pp. 173–281, MIT Press, Cambridge, 1982.

[KAR 97] KARTTUNEN L., TAMÁS G., KEMPE A., Xerox finite-state tool, Technical report, Xerox Research Centre Europe, 1997.

[KAR 07] KARLSSON F., "Constraints on multiple center-embedding of clauses", Journal of Linguistics, vol. 43, no. 2, pp. 365–392, 2007.

[KLA 91] KLARSFELDG., HAMMANI-MCCARTHY M., Dictionnaire électronique du LADL pour les mots simples de l'anglais, Technical report, LADL, Université Paris 7, 1991.

[KLE 56] KLEENE S.C., "Representation of events in nerve nets and finite automata", Automata Studies, Annals of Mathematics Studies, vol. 34, pp. 3–41, 1956.

[KÜB 02] KÜBLER N., "Creating a term base to customise an MT system: reusability of resources and tools from the translator's point of view", Proceedings of the 1st International Workshop on Language Resources in Translation Work and Research (LREC), Las Palmas de Gran Canaria, pp. 44–48, 2002.

[KUP 08] KUPŚĆ A., ABEILLÉ A., "Growing tree Lex", Computational Linguistics and Intelligent Text Processing, vol. 4919, pp. 28–39, 2008.

[LEC 98] LECLÈRE C., "Travaux récents en lexique-grammaire", *Travaux de linguistique,* vol. 37, pp. 155–186, 1998.

[LEC 05] LECLÈRE C., "The lexicon-grammar of french verbs: a syntactic database", in KAWAGUCHI Y., ZAIMA S., TAKAGAKI *et al.* (eds.), *Linguistic Informatics – State of the Art and the Future,* pp. 29–45, Benjamins, Amsterdam/Philadelphia, 2005.

[LEE 90] LEEMAN D., MELEUC S., "Verbes en table et adjectifs en *–able*", in COURTOIS B., SILBERZTEIN M. (eds), *Dictionnaires électroniques du français,* Larousse, Paris, pp. 30–51, 1990.

[LEV 93] LEVIN B. English Verb Classes and Alternations. The University of Chicago Press, Chicago, 1993.

[LIN 08] LIN H.C., "Treatment of Chinese orthographical and lexical variants with NooJ", in BLANCO X., SILBERZTEIN M. (eds), *Proceedings of the 2007 International NooJ Conference,* pp. 139–148, Cambridge Scholars Publishing, Cambridge, 2008.

[LIN 10] LINDÉN K., SILFVERBERG M., PIRINEN T., *HFST Tools for Morphology: An Efficient Open-Source Package for Construction of Morphological Analysers,* University of Helsinki, Finland, 2010.

[MCC 03] MCCARTHY, D., KELLER B., CARROLL J.,"Detecting a continuum of compositionality in phrasal verbs", *Proceedings of the ACL 2003 Workshop on Multiword Expressions,* 2003.

[MAC 10] MACHONIS P., "English phrasal verbs: from Lexicon-Grammar to Natural Language Processing", *Southern Journal of Linguistics,* vol. 34, no. 1. pp. 21–48, 2010.

[MAC 12] MACHONIS P., "Sorting NooJ out to take multiword expressions into account", in VUČKOVIĆ K. *et al.* (ed.), *Proceedings of the NooJ 2011 Conference,* pp. 152–165, Cambridge Scholars Publishing, Newcastle, 2012.

[MAC 94] MACLEOD C., GRISHMAN R., MEYERS A., "Creating a Common Syntactic Dictionary of English", *Proceedings of the International Workshop on Shareable Natural Language Resources,* Nara, Japan, August 10–11, 1994.

[MAC 04] MACLEOD C., GRISHMAN R., MEYERS A. *et al.*, "The NomBank Project: an interim report", *HLT-NAACL 2004 Workshop: Frontiers in Corpus Annotations,* 2004.

[MAN 99] MANNING C., SCHÜTZE H., *Foundations of Statistical Natural Language Processing,* MIT Press, Cambridge, 1999.

[MAN 01] MANI I. (ed.), *Automatic Summarization,* John Benjamins Publishing, Amsterdam, Philadelphia, 2001.

[MAR 93] MARCUS M., SANTORINI B., MARCINKIEWICZ M., "Building a large annotated corpus of English: the Penn Treebank", *Computational Linguistics*, vol. 19, no. 2, pp. 313–330, 1993.

[MCI 81] MCILROY D., "Development of a spelling list", *IEEE Transactions on Communications*, vol. 30, no. 1, pp. 91–99, 1981.

[MEL 87] MEL'ČUK I., *Dependency Syntax: Theory and Practice*, Albany State University Press of New York, 1987.

[MES 08a] MESFAR S., Analyse morpho-syntaxique automatique et reconnaissance des entités nommées en arabe standard, Thesis, University of Franche-Comté, 2008.

[MES 08b] MESFAR S., SILBERZTEIN M., "Transducer minimization and information compression for NooJ dictionaries", *Proceedings of the FSMNLP 2008 Conference*, Frontiers in Artificial Intelligence and Applications, IOS Press, The Netherlands, 2008.

[MOG 08] MOGORRON P., MEJRI S., Las construccionesverbo-nominales libres y fijas, available at: halshs.archives-ouvertes.fr/halshs-00410995, 2008.

[MON 14] MONTELEONE M., VIETRI S., "The NooJ English Dictionary", in KOEVA S., MESFAR S., SILBERZTEIN M. (eds.), *Formalising Natural Languages with NooJ 2013: Selected Papers from the NooJ 2013 International Conference*, Cambridge Scholars Publishing, Newcastle, UK, 2014.

[MOO 56] MOORE E., "Gedanken experiments on sequential machines", *Automata studies, Annals of mathematics* studies, vol. 32, pp. 129–153, Princeton University Press, 1956.

[MOO 00] MOORE R.C., "Removing left recursion from context-free grammars", *6th Applied Natural Language Processing Conference / Proceedings of the 1st Meeting of the North American Chapter of the Association for Computational Linguistics Conference*, Association for Computational Linguistics, , pp. 249–255, 2000.

[MOO 97] MOORTGAT M., "Categorial type logics", in VAN BENTHEM J., MEULEN T. (eds), *Handbook of Logic and Language*, Elsevier, pp. 93–178, 1997.

[NUN 94] NUNBERG G., SAG I., WASOW T., "Idioms", *Language*, vol. 70, pp. 491–538, 1994.

[POL 84] POLLARD C., Generalized Phrase Structure Grammars, Head Grammars, and Natural Language, Ph.D. thesis, Stanford University, 1984.

[POL 94] POLLARD C., SAG I., *Head-Driven Phrase Structure Grammar*, University of Chicago Press, Chicago, 1994.

[RAY 06] RAYNER M., HOCKEY B., BOUILLON P., *Putting Linguistics into Speech Recognition: The Regulus Grammar Compiler*, CSLI Publications, Stanford, 2006.

[RHE 88] RHEINGOLD H., *They Have a Word for It: A Lighthearted Lexicon of Untranslatable Words and Phrases*, Jeremy P. Tarcher Inc., Los Angeles, 1988.

[ROC 97] ROCHE E., SCHABES Y. (eds), *Finite-State Language Processing*, MIT Press, Cambridge, MA, 1997.

[ROU 06] ROUX M., EL ZANT M., ROYAUTÉ J., "Projet Epidemia, intervention des transducteurs NooJ", *Actes des 9èmes journées scientifiques INTEX/NooJ*, Belgrade, 1–3 June 2006.

[SAB 13] SABATIER P., LE PESANT D., "Les dictionnaires électroniques de Jean Dubois et Françoise Dubois-Charlier et leur exploitation en TAL", in GALA N., ZOCK M. (eds), *Ressources Lexicales, Linguisticae Investigationes Supplementa 30*, John Benjamins Publishing Company, Amsterdam, 2013.

[SAG 02] SAG I., BALDWIN T., BOND F. *et al.*, "Multiword Expressions: A Pain in the Neck for NLP", in *Proceedings of the Third International Conference on Intelligent Text Processing and Computational Linguistics*, pp. 1–15, Mexico City, 2002.

[SAL 83] SALKOFF M., "Bees are swarming in the garden: a systematic synchronic study of productivity", *Language*, vol. 59, no. 2, 1983.

[SAL 99] SALKOFF M., *A French-English Grammar: A Contrastive Grammar on Translation Principles*, John Benjamins, Amsterdam, 1999.

[SAL 04] SALKOFF M., "Verbs of mental states", in *Lexique, syntaxe et lexique-grammaire. Papers in honour of Maurice Gross*, volume 24 of *Lingvisticæ Investigationes Sup-plementa*, pp. 561–571, Benjamins, Amsterdam/ Philadelphia, 2004.

[SAU 16] SAUSSURE F., *Cours de linguistique générale*, Payot, Paris, 1916.

[SCH 05] SCHMID H., "A programming language for finite-state transducers", *Proceedings of the 5th International Workshop on Finite State Methods in Natural Language Processing (FSMNLP)*, Helsinki, Finland, 2005.

[SIL 87] SILBERZTEIN M., "The lexical analysis of French", *Electronic Dictionaries and Automata in Computational Linguistics*, vol. 377, pp. 93–110, 1987.

[SIL 90] SILBERZTEIN M., "Le dictionnaire électronique des mots composés", in COURTOIS B., SILBERZTEIN M. (eds), *Dictionnaires électroniques du français*, Larousse, Paris, pp. 11–22, 1990.

[SIL 93a] SILBERZTEIN M., *Dictionnaires électroniques et analyse automatique de textes: le système INTEX*, Masson, Paris, 1993.

[SIL 93b] SILBERZTEIN M., "Groupes nominaux libres et noms composés lexicalisés", *Linguisticae Investigationes*, vol. XVII, no. 2, pp. 405–425, 1993.

[SIL 95] SILBERZTEIN M., "Dictionnaires électroniques et comptage des mots", *3es Journées internationales d'analyse statistique des données textuelles (JADT)*, Rome, 1995.

[SIL 03a] SILBERZTEIN M., NooJ Manual, available at: www.nooj4nlp.net, 2003.

[SIL 03b] SILBERZTEIN M., "Finite-State Recognition of the French determiner system", *Journal of French Language Studies*, Cambridge University Press, pp. 221–246, 2003.

[SIL 06] SILBERZTEIN M., "NooJ's linguistic annotation engine", in KOEVA S. *et al.* (ed.), *INTEX/NooJ pour le Traitement automatique des langues*, pp. 9–26, Presses universitaires de Franche-Comté, 2006.

[SIL 07] SILBERZTEIN M., "An alternative approach to tagging", in KEDAD Z. *et al.* (ed.), *Proceedings of NLDB 2007*, pp. 1–11, LNCS series, Springer-Verlag, 2007.

[SIL 08] SILBERZTEIN M., "Complex annotations with NooJ", in BLANCO X., SILBERZTEIN M. (ed.), *Proceedings of the International NooJ Conference*, pp. 214–227, Barcelona, Cambridge Scholars Publishing, Newcastle, 2008.

[SIL 09] SILBERZTEIN M., "Disambiguation tools for NooJ", in SILBERZTEIN M., VÁRADI T. (eds), *Proceedings of the 2008 International NooJ Conference*, pp. 158–171, Cambridge Scholars Publishing, Newcastle, 2009.

[SIL 10] SILBERZTEIN M., "Syntactic parsing with NooJ", in HAMADOU B., SILBERZTEIN M. (eds), *Finite-State Language Engineering: NooJ 2009 International Conference and Workshop*, Centre for University Publication, Tunisia, 2010.

[SIL 11] SILBERZTEIN M., "Automatic transformational analysis and generation", *Proceedings of the 2010 International Conference and Workshop*, pp. 221–231, Greece, 2011.

[SIL 15] SILBERZTEIN M., "The DEM and the LVF dictionaries in NooJ", in MONTELEONE M., MONTI J., PIA DI BUONO M. *et al.* (eds), *Formalizing Natural Languages with NooJ 2014*, Cambridge Scholars Publishing, 2015.

[SLA 07] SLAYDEN G., How to use a Thai dictionary, available at: thai-language.com, 2007.

[SMI 14] SMITH G., *Standard Deviations: Flawed Assumptions, Tortured Data, and Other Ways to Lie with Statistics*, Overlook Hardcover, p. 304, 2014.

[STE 77] STEELE, G. "Debunking the 'Expensive Procedure Call' Myth or 'Procedure Call Implementations Considered Harmful' or, 'LAMDBA: The Ultimate GOTO'", *Massachusetts Institute of Technology*, Cambridge, MA, 1977.

[THO 68] THOMPSON K., "Regular expression search algorithm", *Communications of the ACM*, vol. 11, no. 6, pp. 419–422, 1968.

[TOP 01] TOPPING S., The secret life of Unicode: a peek at Unicode's soft underbelly, available at: www.ibm.com/developerworks/java/library/u-secret.html, 2001.

[TRO 12] TROUILLEUX F., "A new French dictionary for NooJ: le DM", in VUČKOVIC K. *et al.* (ed.), *Selected Papers from the 2011 International NooJ Conference*, Cambridge Scholar Publishing, Newcastle, 2012.

[TRO 13] TROUILLEUX F., "A description of the French nucleus VP using co-occurrence contraints", in DONABÉDIAN A. *et al.* (ed.), *Formalising Natural Languages with NooJ*, Selected Papers from the NooJ 2012 International Conference, Cambridge Scholars Publishing, 2013.

[TUR 37] TURING A., "On Computable Numbers, with an Application to the Entscheidungsproblem", *Proc. London Math. Soc.*, 2nd series, vol. 42, pp. 230–265, 1937.

[VIE 08] VIETRI S., "The formalization of Italian lexicon-grammars tables in a Nooj pair dictionary/grammar", *Proceedings of the International NooJ Conference*, Budapest, Cambridge Scholars Publishing, Newcastle, 8–10 June 2008.

[VIE 10] VIETRI S., "Building structural trees for frozen sentences", *Proceedings of the NooJ 2009 International Conference and Workshop*, pp. 219–230, Sfax, University Publication Center, 2010.

[VIJ 94] VIJAY SHANKER K., WEIR D., "The equivalence of four extensions of context-free grammars", *Mathematical Systems Theory*, vol. 27, no. 6, pp. 511–546, 1994.

[VOL 11] VOLOKH A., NEUMANN G., "Automatic detection and correction of errors in dependency tree-banks", *Proceedings of the 49th Annual Meeting of the Association for Computational Linguistics: Human Language Technologies*, vol. 2, pp. 346–350, 2011.

[WU 10] WU M., "Integrating a dictionary of psychological verbs into a French-Chinese MT system", *Proceedings of the NooJ 2009 International Conference and Workshop*, pp. 315–328, Sfax, University Publication Center, 2010.

Index

Other titles from

in

Cognitive Science and Knowledge Management

2015

LAFOURCADE Mathieu, JOUBERT Alain, LE BRUN Nathalie
Games with a Purpose (GWAPs)

SAAD Inès, ROSENTHAL-SABROUX Camille, GARGOURI Faïez
Information Systems for Knowledge Management

2014

DELPECH Estelle Maryline
Comparable Corpora and Computer-assisted Translation

FARINAS DEL CERRO Luis, INOUE Katsumi
Logical Modeling of Biological Systems

MACHADO Carolina, DAVIM J. Paulo
Transfer and Management of Knowledge

TORRES-MORENO Juan-Manuel
Automatic Text Summarization

2013

TURENNE Nicolas
Knowledge Needs and Information Extraction: Towards an Artificial Consciousness

ZARATÉ Pascale
Tools for Collaborative Decision-Making

2011

DAVID Amos
Competitive Intelligence and Decision Problems

LÉVY Pierre
The Semantic Sphere: Computation, Cognition and Information Economy

LIGOZAT Gérard
Qualitative Spatial and Temporal Reasoning

PELACHAUD Catherine
Emotion-oriented Systems

QUONIAM Luc
Competitive Intelligence 2.0: Organization, Innovation and Territory

2010

ALBALATE Amparo, MINKER Wolfgang
Semi-Supervised and Unsupervised Machine Learning: Novel Strategies

BROSSAUD Claire, REBER Bernard
Digital Cognitive Technologies

2009

BOUYSSOU Denis, DUBOIS Didier, PIRLOT Marc, PRADE Henri
Decision-making Process

MARCHAL Alain
From Speech Physiology to Linguistic Phonetics